Global Instability

Global Instability assesses the state of the world economy as we enter the new millennium. As the 1997–98 financial crises in Asia once again demonstrated, national governments are increasingly at the mercy of global financial markets; yet little has been done to strengthen international economic institutions. Globalisation creates new problems, which require new solutions. New regional and global structures are needed to give us the ability to control our economic environment.

Internationally renowned contributors examine the key problems besetting the world economy in the era of globalisation and outline possible solutions. They reject the current orthodoxy in mainstream economics, challenging the fatalistic belief that the new globalised economy resists any change of course.

The book reviews international economic institutions, the linked crises which recently hit Asian economies and the implications of globalisation, the role of multinational investment, the IMF and the World Bank. *Global Instability* is a disturbing analysis of the contemporary economy, and will be vital reading for anyone in management, business, or economics.

The Editors: Jonathan Michie is Professor of Management at Birkbeck College, University of London. **John Grieve Smith** is a Fellow of Robinson College, University of Cambridge. Recent works which they have co-edited include *Globalization, Growth and Governance*; *Employment and Economic Performance*; *Creating Industrial Capacity*, and *Managing the Global Economy*.

Contemporary political economy series

Edited by Jonathan Michie
Birkbeck College, University of London, UK

This series presents a fresh, broad perspective on the key issues in the modern world economy, drawing in perspectives from management and business, politics and sociology, economic history and law.

Written in a lively and accessible style, it will present focused and comprehensive introductions to key topics, demonstrating the relevance of political economy to the major debates in economics and to an understanding of the contemporary world.

Forthcoming titles:

Reconstructing Political Economy
The great divide in economic thought
William K. Tabb

The Political Economy of Competitiveness
Employment, public policy and corporate performance
Michael Kitson and Jonathan Michie

Global Instability

The political economy of world economic governance

Edited by
Jonathan Michie and
John Grieve Smith

London and New York

First published 1999
by Routledge
11 New Fetter Lane, London EC4P 4EE

Simultaneously published in the USA and Canada
by Routledge
29 West 35th Street, New York, NY 10001

Routledge is an imprint of the Taylor & Francis Group

Typeset in Galliard by
M Rules, London
Printed and bound in Great Britain by
TJ International Ltd, Padstow, Cornwall

British Library Cataloguing in Publication Data
A catalogue record for this book is available from the British Library

Library of Congress Cataloguing in Publication Data
Global instability: the political economy of world economic
governance/[edited by] Jonathan Michie and John Grieve Smith.
p. cm.
Includes bibliographical references and index.
1. International finance. 2. Business cycles. 3. Economic history
– 1990– 4. Investments, Foreign. 5. Competition, International.
I. Michie, Jonathan. II. Grieve Smith, John.
HG3881.G5755 1999
332'.042–dc21   98-42021
                                                        CIP

ISBN 0-415-20222-1 (hbk)
ISBN 0-415-20223-X (pbk)

Contents

PART II
Global instability

PART III
A new structure for international payments

Figures and tables

Contributors

Philip Arestis is Professor of Economics at the University of East London, England.

Elissa Braunstein is in the Department of Economics and the Political Economy Research Institute (PERI), University of Massachusetts at Amherst, USA.

Gerald Epstein is Chair of the Department of Economics and Director of the Political Economy Research Institute (PERI), University of Massachusetts at Amherst, USA.

Ilene Grabel is Assistant Professor of International Finance at the Graduate School of International Studies, University of Denver, USA.

John Grieve Smith is a Fellow of Robinson College, University of Cambridge, England.

Stephany Griffith-Jones is at the Institute of Development Studies, Sussex University, England.

Laurence Harris is Professor of Economics and Pro-Director (Research) at the School of Oriental and African Studies, University of London, England.

Jenny Kimmis is at the Institute of Development Studies, Sussex University, England.

Jonathan Michie is Professor of Management, Birkbeck College, University of London, England.

Avadhoot Nadkarni is at the S.N.D.T. Women's University, Mumbai, India.

Thomas I. Palley is Assistant Director of Public Policy at the AFL-CIO, Washington, DC, USA.

Malcolm Sawyer is Professor of Economics at the University of Leeds, England.

Ajit Singh is Professor of Economics at the University of Cambridge, England.

John Smithin is Professor of Economics, Department of Economics and Schulich School of Business, York University, Canada.

Paz Estrella Tolentino is in the Department of Management, Birkbeck College, University of London, England.

Bernard M. Wolf is in the Department of Economics and Schulich School of Business, York University, Canada.

Preface and acknowledgements

All the following chapters were commissioned specifically for this book and draft versions were discussed at a working conference in May 1998 at Robinson College, Cambridge. We are grateful to the authors for travelling to Cambridge to participate in these discussions and to Robinson College for hosting this event. We are also grateful to the contributors to our earlier books *Unemployment in Europe* (Academic Press, 1994), *Managing the Global Economy* (Oxford University Press, 1995), *Creating Industrial Capacity: Towards Full Employment* (Oxford University Press, 1996), *Employment and Economic Performance* (Oxford University Press, 1997), and *Globalisation, Growth and Governance: Creating an Innovative Economy* (Oxford University Press, 1998) who kindly agreed that their royalty payments would go to the Robinson College Economic Research Fund which met the remainder of the expenses, and to the contributors to this book for similarly donating their royalties to help fund future such events.

We are grateful for their participation to Luisa Affuso, Max Beber, Keith Cowling, Martin Fetherston, Valpy FitzGerald, Andrew Glyn, Paul Hirst, Will Hutton, Carolyn Jones, Andrew Jukes, Michael Kitson, Simon Lee, Frank McHugh, Robin Marris, Roland Muri, Sheila Page, Mića Panić, Ray Petridis, Shay Ramalingam, Brian Reddaway, Andy Robinson, Bob Rowthorn, Sanjiv Sachdev, Grahame Thompson, Ben Turok, Peter Warburton, Ryo Watabe, and Frank Wilkinson.

Our thanks as editors go to all the contributors for the speedy incorporation of points made in May 1998 on their draft chapters; Geoff Harcourt, Jane Humphries, and Kit McMahon for chairing the sessions at the May conference; Alison Kirk and Andreja Zivkovic of Routledge for the speedy turnaround of the manuscript; and Lesley Haird for typing and other help. Our personal thanks as always go respectively to Carolyn, nine-year-old Alex and three-year-old Duncan, and to Jean.

Jonathan Michie
John Grieve Smith

Introduction

Jonathan Michie

Almost five years ago we argued that the demise of the post-war era of full employment had been followed by more than twenty years of global instability (Michie and Grieve Smith, 1995). Sadly, this has now become more than twenty-five years, with inadequate public policy over the past few years having left the underlying problems, if anything, even worse than before.

As the 1997–98 financial crises in Asia once again demonstrated, national governments have become increasingly at the mercy of global financial markets; yet little has been done in response to strengthen international economic institutions. The Bretton Woods structure has in some respects stood up remarkably well to the changing scene over the last fifty years or so. But clearly 'globalisation' has created new problems, which require new solutions. The growth of speculative capital movements and the consequent exchange rate instability has been an obvious and pressing case for some time. But the current re-emergence of private debt and solvency crises on the pre-war pattern has complicated and accentuated the problem. Instead of wringing our hands at the loss of power of national governments, we need to set in place new regional and global structures, which will give us the ability to control our economic environment.

The following chapters examine the problems now besetting the world economy, and outline possible solutions. Although the spirit of the time may seem inimical to cooperative approaches, there are signs that the climate of opinion may be changing in response to recent events. The most widespread problem is the effect of the growth of speculative capital movements on exchange rate instability. Does this mean that we have no alternative to a regime of freely floating rates, apart from regional currency unions such as the European Exchange Rate Mechanism? Or is there a middle-way between fixed, and free floating rates in some form of managed rate system, with automatic or discretionary adjustments? Can speculative movements be offset by new forms of official action, or at least damped down by a Tobin tax or other such financial regulation (for example, of derivative trading)? Will the adoption of the European single currency make international monetary cooperation easier between the major players? These are some of the key questions examined in the chapters that follow.

The liberalisation of their capital markets has made the developing countries particularly vulnerable to variations in the flow of capital. What are the basic causes of the solvency problems in Asian countries? Has deregulation gone too far? Is the supply of productive investment capital to developing countries adequate – in terms of both volume and reliability? Are the World Bank and other international financial institutions playing a satisfactory role? Can fresh international resources be mobilised to finance economic development – for example by levying a Tobin tax, or via an enforced lending requirement on persistent credit countries? Have adequate steps been taken to avoid further international debt crises?

A thorough review is undertaken of existing international economic institutions, their historic role and the needs of today. The authors – who come from both sides of the Atlantic, as well as from India – have all written in these fields before, and share a common desire to establish a new and more effective global financial regime.

Structure of the book

The 1997–1998 Asian crises

Part I of the book analyses the series of linked crises that hit the Asian economies in the course of 1997 and 1998.

In the first of these four chapters, Ajit Singh examines alternative theories of these crises, paying particular attention to the idea that the Asian economic system itself was the main cause of the financial turmoil. In '"Asian capitalism" and the financial crisis' (Chapter 1), Singh also analyses the IMF policy programmes in East Asia. The chapter argues that the fundamental reason for these crises is to be found in too little government control over the financial liberalisation process which the countries concerned had been implementing in the preceding period. In addition, the IMF appeared to have misdiagnosed the crises, and proposed inappropriate policies (such as further financial liberalisation, severe fiscal austerity, and steep rises in interest rates).

These conclusions are supported by the analysis of the following chapter, by Ilene Grabel. In 'Rejecting exceptionalism: reinterpreting the Asian financial crises' (Chapter 2), Grabel argues that the conventional, 'exceptionalist' explanation of these crises suggested that each was the outcome of political corruption, unsustainable economic policies, or some other such exceptional factor. The chapter demonstrates, against such conventional wisdom, that the crises of 1997 and 1998 were due instead to the private sector's excessive reliance on hard currency-denominated foreign loans, along with the failure on the part of government to control portfolio investment flows. By relying on these two types of private capital flows – in the absence of sufficient foreign exchange reserves – the economies involved in the crises of 1997 and 1998 were rendered vulnerable to the risks of currency and investor exit. Once these risks were realised, governments found their ability to manoeuvre limited. Grabel goes on to argue that the policies advocated by the IMF and pursued by various of the governments have rendered these economies more – rather than less – vulnerable to the recurrence of such crises in the future.

In Chapter 3, 'Stabilizing capital flows to developing countries', Stephany Griffith-Jones and Jenny Kimmis argue that large surges of short-term and potentially reversible capital flows to developing countries can have very negative effects. First, these surges can destabilise exchange rates and asset prices. And second, such flows pose the risk of sharp reversals, which can result in serious losses of output, investment and employment, bringing increased poverty. In the case of the Asian crises, such reversals were truly dramatic.

Finally, on the Asian crises, Thomas Palley argues (Chapter 4, 'International finance and global deflation: there is an alternative') that these crises, and the IMF's initial response, revealed two important things. First, the new international economic order is unstable and susceptible to financial crashes that carry the risk of global deflation. Second, the IMF is deeply imbued with an economic philosophy that impedes achieving international financial stability and widely shared economic prosperity. He argues that the IMF philosophy has given rise to an economic outlook that recommends fiscal austerity, financial liberalisation, and export-led growth irrespective of circumstances. Over time, Palley suggests, such a policy configuration is likely to aggravate the problem of financial instability, and increase the risk of global deflation being triggered. Instead of this, two things are required: first, to remedy the underlying structural weaknesses that afflict the international financial system; and second, to reform the IMF.

Global instability

Part II of the book, on 'Global instability', analyses the continued drive towards an ever more *laissez-faire* and deregulated world economy, and discusses what can and should be done to develop a more rational and humane alternative. Increased transnational investment, world trade liberalisation, and the explosion of short-term capital flows are dealt with in Chapters 5–7 respectively.

Part II opens with an analysis of 'globalisation' – the widening and deepening of international economic interactions. Braunstein and Epstein argue that it is a mistake to see globalisation as synonymous with marketisation and economic liberalisation (Chapter 5, 'Creating international credit rules and the Multilateral Agreement on Investment: what are the alternatives?'). Economic liberalisation is simply the form that such globalisation is currently taking, given the global neo-liberal regime. Thus, many of the problems which appear to stem from globalisation are due to the neo-liberal regime of deregulation and *laissez-faire* within which these developments are occurring. The chapter analyses these processes and problems with particular emphasis on multinational corporations and foreign direct investment, and the Multilateral Agreement on Investment (MAI). Braunstein and Epstein argue that the MAI and similar initiatives not only create new international relations but also fundamentally change national relations and governance. And within the present context, these national changes – just as the international ones – are on very much free market lines. It is thus a mistake to see such developments as simply restructuring international economic relations. They therefore conclude that for both international and domestic reasons it is necessary to work on two levels – strengthening national controls over capital flows while at the same time working towards an alternative set of international structures.

In Chapter 6 ('World trade liberalisation: national autonomy and global regulation'), Avadhoot Nadkarni pursues this dual analysis. He discusses on the one hand the way in which new global structures and agreements undermine national autonomy and, on the other hand, considers to what kind of global structures power is being transferred. Chapter 6 focuses on world trade liberalisation and the new multilateral trading system under the aegis of the World Trade Organisation. Nadkarni argues that the new structures of global governance need to take more cognisance of broader policies than is the case at present, including global redistribution policies. These would need to be quite different from the current multilateral trading system.

Part II concludes with an analysis of foreign exchange dealings and the related capital flows. Specifically, Arestis and Sawyer discuss the contribution which a tax on foreign exchange dealings might make to better world economic governance (Chapter 7, 'What role for the Tobin tax in world economic governance?'). They argue that the introduction of such a transactions tax would enhance the capability of national governments to pursue economic policies which stimulate a higher level of demand, hence allowing higher output and living standards, and lower unemployment. In addition, the aggregate demand effects of the tax itself might give a further boost through its redistributory effects, which would most likely be towards those with a higher propensity to spend. Finally, they warn that such matters are far from purely technical: two political obstacles would need to be overcome. First, to achieve the degree of international co-ordination that would be required. And second, to overcome the political power of the financial sector which would most likely resist any restriction or tax on their activities.

A new structure for international payments

This conclusion, on the need for institutional reform to the international financial institutions, leads onto the third and final part of the book, on 'A new structure for international payments'. The first three chapters of this final part consider the role of, respectively, international institutional arrangements and agreements on multinational investment, the IMF, and the World Bank.

In Chapter 8, 'Transnational rules for transnational corporations: what next?', Paz Estrella Tolentino charts the course of the various attempts from Bretton Woods onwards to regulate the operation of transnational corporations and the associated foreign direct investments. This relates back to the discussion of the Multinational Agreement on Investment in Chapter 5. The current agreement is being negotiated very much by and for the industrialised economies and the transnational corporations based in these countries. Both the process and content of the agreement will need to be broadened if it is to receive the degree of legitimacy necessary to be sustainable.

In Chapter 9 Laurence Harris asks 'Will the real IMF please stand up: what does the fund do and what should it do?' Harris suggests that the IMF has become very different from the institution that Keynes and White had envisaged at the time of Bretton Woods, and that it is now attempting to do a range of quite different tasks. He argues that several of its current roles have arisen from the absence of other, more appropriate, institutions. Hence in the context of a millennium version of Bretton Woods, other institutions would have to be considered.

In Chapter 10, 'A world central bank?', John Smithin and Bernard Wolf argue that it is important to retain as much scope as possible for independent national policy-making in the current global economic environment, and in contemporary political circumstances. The first reason for retaining a degree of national policy-making is the issue of democratic accountability. The second is the potential deflationary bias of international bureaucracies in practice. The problem, they argue, is that contemporary economic and political orthodoxy is such that the international bureaucrats who administer global economic and financial institutions do so in a manner informed by neo-conservative economic theory, as well as by neo-conservative political ideology.

Finally, in Chapter 11, 'A new Bretton Woods: reforming the global financial system', John Grieve Smith provides an overview of many of the central themes running throughout the book, and draws out the key policy implications. First, on the economic issues, he cites Keynes's argument that without controls on capital movements, 'Loose funds may sweep round the world disorganising all steady business' (Keynes, 1941). Certainly, short-term borrowing in foreign currencies was a major factor in the Asian crises of 1997 and 1998. The chapters in Part I show that the main factors behind these crises were recurring ones. As Grieve Smith argues, unless these are tackled soon, they are likely to lead to further, and possibly greater, upsets. The chapter goes into some detail on the sort of policy measures required, at the heart of which would lie a combined attack on exchange rate instability and speculative capital movements through a system of managed exchange rates. It also argues that any discussion of more effective international structures cannot be separated from the question of what objectives and general approach to economic policy those in charge of any new organisations will adopt. Improving the machinery of international economic governance must go hand in hand with a revolution in the approach to economic policy that guides international organisations. Restoring world economic governance to the political agenda depends on a rejection of the monetarist-inspired orthodoxy of the 1980s and 1990s.

Conclusion

The problems witnessed in today's global economy are not just technical, economic ones. They are also political. Devising new structures of World Economic Governance requires, as a starting point, that this be recognised. This means that to be successful, any alternative needs to not only spell out appropriate policy and institutional developments, it also needs to win sufficient political support to force through the necessary change of course.

In this context, ideological issues also play a role. It is thus necessary to expose the current complacent orthodoxy in mainstream economics, and challenge the fatalistic belief that the new globalised economy rules out any change of course. As many of the chapters that follow demonstrate, the fact that the economy is becoming increasingly internationalised does not dictate the form that this process is taking. The free market, *laissez-faire* agenda is one being pursued by those who benefit from such a deregulated, winner-take-all environment. It is not the only choice. And for the majority of the world's population, it is an inappropriate one.

References

Keynes, J.M. (1941), 'The Post-War Currency Policy', (8 September 1941), *Keynes Papers Volume XXV*, Basingstoke: Macmillan.

Michie, J. and Grieve Smith, J. (eds) (1995), *Managing the Global Economy*, Oxford: Oxford University Press.

Part I

The 1997–1998 Asian crises

1 'Asian capitalism' and the financial crisis

Ajit Singh

I Introduction

With the economic crisis in East Asia and a continuing boom in the US, American triumphalism is in the air. The latter is perhaps not unexpected and probably does no harm. But what is more questionable is the view held in the highest circles in the US Government and international financial organisations in Washington which causally links the so-called Asian model of capitalism to the economic and financial crisis which is currently engulfing the hitherto highly successful economies of East and South East Asia.

Thus, Mr Greenspan, the respected chairman of the US Federal Reserve, in his testimony before the Senate Foreign Relations Committee suggested that, in the last decade or so, the world has observed 'a consensus towards, for want of a better term, the Western form of free-market capitalism as the model which should govern how each individual country should run its economy . . . We saw the breakdown of the Berlin wall in 1989 and the massive shift away from central planning towards free market capitalist types of structures. Concurrent to that was the really quite dramatic, very strong growth in what appeared to be a competing capitalist-type system in Asia. And as a consequence of that, you had developments of types of structures which I believe at the end of the day were faulty, but you could not demonstrate that so long as growth was going at 10 per cent a year.'[1] Mr Larry Summers, the US Treasury Under Secretary, puts the matter in slightly different terms. The *Financial Times* (20 February 1998) reports him as arguing that the roots of the Asian financial crisis lie not in bad policy management but in the nature of the economies themselves. Summers states: '[this crisis] is profoundly different because it has its roots not in improvidence but in economic structures. The problems that must be fixed are much more microeconomic than macroeconomic, and involve the private sector more and the public sector less.' Similar views have been expressed perhaps in more measured terms by the Managing Director of the IMF, Mr Michel Camdessus.[2]

A central aim of this chapter[3] is to systematically assess the validity of this influential and important thesis, i.e., the chapter will explore to what extent, if any, the so-called 'Asian model' is responsible for the present crisis in countries like Thailand, Indonesia, Malaysia and Korea. This question is also important in part because in economic terms until very recently this model seems to have been exceptionally successful. It is no exaggeration to say that the industrialisation and economic development of the Asian newly industrialising countries (NICs), as well as Japan in the post-World War II period, has been the most successful example of fast economic growth in history. Moreover, the 'Asian model', in addition to its economic merits, has also had a number of attractive qualities from a social point of view, e.g. poverty reduction, lifetime employment in large corporations and relatively equal income distribution. In contrast, the alternative Western or American model has acquired some unappealing social characteristics as it is increasingly based on the doctrine of promoting labour market flexibility. Social protection which hitherto workers enjoyed is being greatly diminished and a growing number of jobs are being 'informalised'.[4]

In view of the economic and social merits of the Asian model, it is important to ask whether the model also entailed some long-run hidden costs. Was it for example likely to lead to the kind of crisis which descended suddenly and almost simultaneously on several of the hitherto highly successful economies. Such an analysis will obviously involve, *inter alia*, an assessment of other factors which may have been responsible for the crisis.

From the practical policy perspective, the central issues for the affected East Asian countries are the appropriateness and the effectiveness of the IMF remedies. Will these measures enable these economies to adjust quickly so that they can go back to their long-term trend growth path? Or will the world witness another 'lost decade' of the kind experienced by Latin America in the 1980s under IMF tutelage following the debt crisis.

The chapter is organised as follows. Section II reports on the economic and social achievements of the leading East Asian NICs and of the Asian model over the last three to four decades. As we shall see, Joseph Stiglitz, former Chairman of the US Council of Economic Advisers and now Chief Economist at the World Bank, and an eminent but dissident member of the Washington Establishment, is quite right to observe that 'no other economic model has delivered so much, to so many, in so short a span of time'. Section III outlines the essential characteristics of the Asian model. These have been the subject of an intense debate in the past, but as will be shown below, current events appear to be leading to a consensus on the broad contours of the system. Section IV examines alternative theories of the current financial crisis, paying particular attention to the idea that the Asian economic system itself is the main cause of the financial turmoil. Section V reviews the evidence bearing on these issues. Section VI analyses the IMF policy programmes in East Asia including, *inter alia*, the extent, if any, to which these may have contributed to the crisis. Section VII sums up the analytical conclusions of the chapter and comments on their policy implications.

II   Industrialisation and catch-up in Asia, 1955–1995

The Asian model of 'guided' capitalist development originated in and is epitomised by the post-World War II experience of Japan, especially in the high growth period between 1950 and 1973. In the early 1950s, after the economy had recovered from the war and at the end of the period of US occupation, the Japanese economic situation was not much different from that of a developing country. The total value of Japanese exports in 1952 was less than that of India's (Krueger, 1995); exports consisted mainly of textiles and other labour intensive products. In 1955, Japan produced only 5 million tons of steel and 30,000 automobiles. US production at that time was 90 million tons of steel and nearly 7 million cars. Japan possessed few natural resources for producing steel or other heavy industrial products, and indeed the Japanese costs of producing steel were at that time considerably greater than the prevailing world prices. Nevertheless, disregarding short term comparative advantage and against almost all economic advice, the Ministry of International Trade and Industry (MITI) deliberately encouraged and orchestrated the development of heavy industry in Japan. The rest is history. By the mid-1960s, Japan emerged as the lowest cost steel producer in the world and was outselling the US steel industry in the US itself. By early 1970, it was producing as much steel as the US. By 1975, Japan had overtaken Germany as the largest exporter of automobiles in the world. By 1980, Japan produced more automobiles than the US. Looking back on this phenomenal growth, this incredible catch-up occurred over the relatively short space of 30 years.

One might argue that Japan was a special case because it had been undergoing industrialisation since the Meiji Restoration in 1870. However, Korea, which consciously followed the Japanese economic strategy was unequivocally backward in industrial development in the 1950s. In 1955 Korea's per capita manufacturing output was only $US 8 compared with $US 7 in India and $US 60 in Mexico.[5] Less than four decades later, Korea has become an industrially developed economy. It competes with advanced economies in a wide range of industrial products. Next to the US, it is the second most important country in the world in electronic memory chip technology (DRAM). By the year 2000, Korea was expected to become the fourth largest producer of automobiles in the world.

The Japanese and Korean development models have been followed to varying degrees in Taiwan and Singapore but, more significantly, also in Malaysia, Indonesia, and Thailand. There are important differences in aspects of industrial strategy followed by these five countries compared with that of Japan and Korea. The second group of countries have, for example, relied much more on FDI compared with the first group. Nevertheless, all these countries have followed the basic model of guided capitalist development rather than relying on free competitive markets.

The outstanding economic success of this group of East and South East Asian countries, together with Hong Kong, is widely acknowledged. These countries have been able to industrialise quickly and grow very fast over the last three decades (see Tables 1.1 and 1.2). Indeed, since 1980, this part of the world has emerged as the most dynamic region in the world economy (Table 1.1). Between 1980 and 1995, developing East Asia was growing at three times the rate of growth of the world economy.

Table 1.1 Trends in GDP growth: selected developing regions and industrial countries, 1965–1996 (average annual % growth)

	1965–1980	*1980–1989*	*1990–1996*
Low-income economies (excluding China and India)	4.8	2.9	1.4
China	6.8	10.2	12.9
India	3.6	5.8	3.8
Middle income economies	6.3	2.2	0.2
Latin America	6.0	1.7	3.6
Sub-Saharan Africa	4.2	1.7	0.9
South Asia	3.6	5.7	3.9
East Asia and Pacific	7.3	7.9	9.4
All low and middle income economies	5.9	3.1	1.9
High income economies	3.8	3.2	1.7
US	2.7	3.0	2.5
Japan	6.6	4.1	1.2
Germany	3.3	2.2	1.1
World	4.1	3.1	1.8

Sources: World Bank (1992, 1996); IMF (1996).

Note: The World Bank defines income groups according to GNP per capita in 1994 as follows:
(1) low income $725 or less;
(2) middle income $8,955 or less;
(3) high income $8,956 or more.

Table 1.2 GDP growth: East and South East Asian NICs, 1970–1996 (average annual % growth)

	1970–1979	*1980–1989*	*1990–1996*
Hong Kong	9.2	7.5	5.0
Singapore	9.4	7.2	8.3
Taiwan	10.2	8.1	6.3
South Korea	9.3	8.0	7.7
Malaysia	8.0	5.7	8.8
Thailand	7.3	7.2	8.6
Indonesia	7.8	5.7	7.2
China	7.5	9.3	10.1

Source: *The Economist*, 1 March 1997.

Significantly, fast growth was accompanied by low inflation as is indicated by the data for the affected Asian countries in Table 1.3. Moreover, World Bank (1993) notes 'For the eight HPAEs [high performing Asian economies], rapid growth and declining inequality [in income distribution] have been shared virtues,' as comparisons over time of equality and growth using Gini coefficients illustrate.'[6] In addition, as Stiglitz rightly emphasises, one of the most important achievements of Asian countries during this period was an enormous reduction in poverty. Stiglitz (1998a) observes: 'In 1975, 6 out of 10 Asians lived on less than $1 a day. In Indonesia, the absolute poverty rate was even higher. Today, 2 out of 10 East

Asians are living in absolute poverty. Korea, Thailand and Malaysia have eliminated poverty and Indonesia is within striking distance of that goal. The USA and other western countries, which have also seen solid growth over the last 20 years but with little reduction in their poverty rates, could well learn from the East Asian experience.'[7] Indonesia's success in reducing poverty is particularly remarkable. In

Table 1.3 Key indicators for Asian crisis economies: Malaysia, Indonesia, Thailand and Korea (% of GDP unless otherwise noted)

	1975–1982 (average)	1983–1989 (average)	1990–1996 (average)	1995	1996	1997[g]
Malaysia						
Real GDP growth[a]	7.1	5.4	8.8	9.5	8.6	7.0
Inflation[b]	5.3	2.0	3.5	3.4	3.5	3.7
Domestic saving	21.6	29.4	32.1	33.5	36.7	37.0
Fixed capital formation	29.4	28.5	38.3	43.0	42.2	42.7
Current account	−2.0	−0.7	−6.0	−10.0	−4.9	−5.8
Fiscal balance	−6.3	−4.0	0.0	3.8	4.2	1.6
External debt service	3.8	9.0	6.0	6.6	5.4	8.4
Indonesia						
Real GDP growth[a]	6.2	5.5	8.0	8.2	8.0	5.0
Inflation[b]	15.0	8.1	8.6	9.4	7.9	8.3
Domestic saving	19.3	23.2	28.9	29.0	28.8	27.3
Fixed capital formation	19.8	24.3	27.4	28.4	28.1	26.5
Current account	−1.2	−3.5	−2.6	−3.3	−3.3	−2.9
Fiscal balance	−2.6	−1.3	0.3[d]	0.8	1.4	2.0
External debt service	3.5	6.8	8.6	8.5	9.0	10.5
Thailand						
Real GDP growth[a]	7.0	8.1	8.6	8.7	6.4	0.6
Inflation[b]	9.0	3.1	5.1	5.8	5.9	6.0
Domestic saving	19.6	25.4	34.2	34.3	33.1	31.8
Fixed capital formation	23.6	27.7	40.4	41.8	40.8	35.8
Current account	−5.6	−3.2	−6.9	−8.0	−7.9	−3.9
Fiscal balance	−5.8	−3.0	2.8	2.6	1.6	−0.4
External debt service	3.8	5.8	4.5	5.0	5.4	7.1
Korea						
Real GDP growth[a]	7.0	9.6	7.7	8.9	7.1	6.0
Inflation[b]	17.6	3.8	6.4	4.5	4.9	4.3
Domestic saving	25.7	32.7	35.0	35.1	33.3	32.9
Fixed capital formation	29.4	29.4	36.7	36.6	36.8	36.6
Current account	−4.6	2.5	−1.9	−2.0	−4.9	−2.9
Fiscal balance	−2.7	−0.3	−1.0	0.0	0.0	0.0
Import cover[c]	n.a.	1.4[e]	2.2[f]	n.a.	n.a.	n.a.

Sources: IMF, 1997, *World Economic Outlook: Interim Assessment*, December; World Bank.

Notes
a Percentage per annum.
b Average annual % change of consumer price index.
c Gross international reserves in months of import cover.
d 1991 and 1994 data unavailable.
e 1980–1990.
f 1995 figure.
g IMF estimate.

Table 1.4 Selected ASEAN countries: social indicators of development, 1970–1994

	1970	1980	1994
Infant mortality rate (per thousand births)			
Indonesia	119	90	53
Malaysia	46	30	12
Philippines	67	52	40
Thailand	75	48	35
Life expectancy (in years)			
Indonesia	48	56	64
Malaysia	61	68	71
Philippines	57	62	65
Thailand	60	65	69
Adult illiteracy rate (% of population, above 15 years)			
Indonesia	43	33	16
Malaysia	42	26	17
Philippines	17	17	5
Thailand	21	12	6

Source: *IMF Survey*, vol. 26, no. 16, 18 August 1997, p. 263.

1970, 60 per cent of the population was living below the official poverty line. By 1996, the proportion had fallen to 12 per cent, while during this period the population had increased from 117 to 200 million (*IMF Survey* 16 August 1997). Table 1.4 shows changes in social indicators of development for selected ASEAN countries between 1970 and 1994.

There is still further evidence which suggests that these high performing economies, most of which were working under some version of the Asian model, not only achieved fast growth for the last three decades, but that this growth was widely shared. Between 1980 and 1992, real wages in the fast growing Asian NICs rose at a rate of 5 per cent a year, whilst at the same time employment in manufacturing increased by 6 per cent a year. Some of these hitherto labour surplus economies began to experience a labour shortage and imported labour from neighbouring countries. Overall, in South East and East Asia, there was a vast improvement in the standards of living of literally hundreds of millions of people, especially if China is also included in this group of countries.[8]

The above highly positive East Asian record stands in striking contrast to that of large parts of the developing world in the recent period. In relation to Latin America, for example, ILO (1995) reports that during the 1980s and the early 1990s there was a steady fall in modern sector employment, with paid employment falling at a rate of 0.1 per cent a year. This reversed the trend of the previous three decades, when steady economic growth had led to a significant expansion of modern-sector employment. Tokman (1997) reports that there has been a huge 'informalization' of the labour force in Latin America since the debt crisis of the early 1980s, that is, four out of five new jobs that have been created during the last fifteen years are low quality, informal jobs paying low wages. The average real wage in Latin American manufacturing in 1995 was still below its pre-debt crisis level.

III The East Asian model

Before any causal connection can be established between the Asian model of capitalism and the current financial crisis in the South East and the East Asian countries, it is important to be clear about the precise nature of this model of development. In this connection it is interesting to observe that, in the 1990s, the international financial institutions' (IFIs) theses – specifically the World Bank's – concerning (a) the basic characteristics and (b) the effectiveness of the Asian model have undergone a number of distinct changes.

At the first stage, in a seminal contribution,[9] World Bank (1991) claimed the East Asian countries were successful because they followed a 'market-friendly' strategy of development and integrated their economies closely with that of the world economy. In order for the term not to be a mere tautology, the Bank's economists to their credit defined 'market-friendly' in a fairly precise way as follows:

1   'intervene reluctantly', i.e. the government should intervene in economic activity only if the private sector is unable to do the tasks required
2   interventions should be subject to checks and balances
3   interventions should be transparent. This characterisation essentially suggested a 'night watchman' state, the main task of which was to provide the legal framework and the infrastructure necessary for private enterprise to flourish.

These propositions concerning the East Asian economies could not however be sustained as they were greatly at variance with facts. Critics pointed out that all the evidence suggested that the governments in countries like Japan and Korea did not 'intervene reluctantly'. Rather, they pursued a vigorous industrial policy, the basic purpose of which was to change the matrix of prices and incentives facing private enterprise in the direction preferred by the planners. Similarly students of the subject pointed out that neither Japan nor Korea for instance closely integrated their economies with the rest of the world. Although both countries were export-oriented, both of them made extensive use of selected import controls to protect specific industries.[10] Moreover, both countries discouraged rather than promoted inward foreign investment.

At the second stage, in response to these criticisms, in another seminal publication in 1993 (*The East Asian Miracle*), World Bank economists significantly changed their characterisation of the East Asian model. The fact of enormous government interventions in these economies was now fully acknowledged. The World Bank (1993) stated:

Policy interventions took many forms – targeted and subsidised credit to selected industries, low deposit rates and ceilings on borrowing rates to

increase profits and retained earnings, protection of domestic import industries, the establishment and financial support of government banks, public
investment in applied research, firm- and industry-specific export targets,
development of export marketing institutions, and wide sharing of information between public and private sectors. Some industries were promoted
while others were not.

Nevertheless, the Bank argued that, although the government intervened heavily,
these interventions were neither necessary nor sufficient for the extraordinary success of the East Asian countries. The World Bank (1993) concludes:

> What are the main factors that contributed to the HPAE's superior allocation
> of physical and human capital to high yielding investments and their ability to
> catch up technologically? Mainly, the answer lies in fundamentally sound,
> market-oriented policies. Labour markets were allowed to work. Financial
> markets . . . generally had low distortions and limited subsidies compared
> with other developing economies. Import substitution was . . . quickly
> accompanied by the promotion of exports . . . the result was limited differ-
> ences between international relative prices and domestic relative prices in
> the HPAE's. Market forces and competitive pressures guided resources into
> activities that were consistent with comparative advantage . . .

In other words it was suggested that, notwithstanding the facts of heavy government intervention in East Asian economies, the Bank's traditional policy
conclusions – that countries should seek their comparative advantage, get the
prices right, have free markets as far as possible – are still valid.

Now, in the wake of the current financial crisis in South East Asia, the IMF in
particular is suggesting that important characteristics of the East Asian model are
dysfunctional.[11] Especially singled out for criticism are: (a) the close relationship
between government and business, and (b) various distortions to competitive
markets. The relationships under (a) are regarded as creating crony-capitalism,
leading to corruption and a myriad inefficiencies in resource allocation. The infer-
ence is that these countries should go back to the World Bank (1991) prescription
of a 'night watchman' state and an economy which is closely integrated with the
world economy.

The Bank's critics vigorously dispute its theses on the lack of effectiveness of
interventions in the East Asian economies.[12] There is, however, now much greater
agreement between the two sides on the broad description of the model as outlined in the first of the two quotations from World Bank (1993) above. Based on
my own previous research and that of other scholars, there would be more or less
agreement on the following important characteristics of the East Asian model in
its 'ideal form':[13]

1   The close relationship between the government and business where the
    government does not do anything without consulting business and vice versa.

2   Many interventions are carried out through a system of 'administrative guid-ance' rather than through formal legislation.

3   The relationship between the corporation and the financial system in coun-tries like Japan and Korea has also been very different from that of the US and the UK. The former countries have followed, for example, the so-called main bank system which involves long-term relationships between the corporations and the main banks. This enables Japanese or Korean managers to take a long-term view in their investment decisions. The managers are not con-strained by the threat of hostile take-overs on stock markets as is the case in the Anglo-Saxon countries.

4   There are differences in the internal organisation of East Asian corporations compared with those of the US and the UK. The former involve co-operative relationships between management and labour, epitomised by the system of lifetime employment. This implies considerable imperfections in the labour market.

5   As for the competition in product markets, such competition is not regarded by the East Asian authorities as an unalloyed good. Unlike in countries like the US, economic philosophy in the East Asian countries does not accept the dictum that 'the more competition the better'. The governments in these countries have taken the view that, from the perspective of promoting invest-ment and technical change, the optimal degree of competition is not perfect or maximum competition. The governments have therefore purposefully managed and guided competition: it has been encouraged but also restricted in a number of ways.[14]

6   Following this basic economic philosophy outlined above, the East Asian governments have sought not 'close' but what might be called 'strategic' inte-gration with the world economy, i.e. they have integrated up to the point where it has been useful for them to do so. Thus during their high-growth, developmental phases, Japan (between 1950 and 1973) and Korea (1970s and 1980s) integrated with the world economy in relation to exports but not imports; with respect to science and technology but not finance and multi-national investment.

As noted above, this is a characterisation of the East Asian model as an ideal type. Not all countries, or even Japan and Korea, have followed the model exactly at all times in the post-war period. As far as the government–business relationships are concerned there is a continuum with the closest relationship to be found in Korea, and the least close in Thailand. Malaysia and Indonesia fall in between. Similarly, the main bank system worked differently in Korea compared with Japan. Unlike Japan, where the 'main banks' were by and large private entities, in Korea for much of the period these were directly state-controlled. Only in the recent period have they been privatised. Nevertheless, there is considerable truth in the view that the Asian way of doing business and the institutional structures it has generated are considerably different from those of countries like the US and the UK.

IV Causes of the crisis

Table 1.5 outlines the salient financial facts concerning the crisis in the East and South East Asian countries (July 1997–February 1998). In the worst affected country, Indonesia, the stock market had fallen by more than 80 per cent and the exchange rate of the rupiah against the dollar by almost 75 per cent. This implies that a foreign investor who invested $100 in a company quoted on the Indonesian stock market would have seen the value of the investment fall by 96 per cent during the half year. By the same token, it also means that if a foreign corporation had to pay $100 to acquire an Indonesian company in July 1997, it could in principle purchase it now for only $4. This is of course not just a theoretical possibility, but as Krugman (1998) notes, there is evidence of a 'fire sale' of East Asian assets currently in progress in the wake of the financial crisis.[15] The twin crises of the stock and currency markets have also resulted in corporate and financial sector bankruptcies with huge losses of production and jobs.

Those who attribute the crisis to the failings of the Asian model suggest that, while there may have been various immediate triggers – a property price bubble, macroeconomic mistakes (for example, supporting for far too long a nominally fixed exchange rate), a fall in the rate of growth of exports, or a regional contagion effect – the underlying causes were structural and an integral part of the Asian model of capitalism. The crisis manifested itself in the form of 'overinvestment' (see further below), misallocation of foreign capital inflows, and severe problems in the financial sector. The financial structure of the corporations and the banks, as well as other deficiencies of the state-guided or state-directed financial systems in Asian countries, made these economies very fragile. IMF (1997, p. 14) points to the following specific structural weaknesses of the most affected economies:

- In Korea, the industrial structure has been heavily influenced by government intervention, including, as well as directed credits, regulations and explicit or implicit subsidies. The resulting lack of market discipline has contributed to the problem of unproductive or excessive investment that has played a role in the build-up of the recent crisis.

Table 1.5 South East Asian and Asian countries (% movements in equity markets and exchange rates), 1 July 1997–18 February 1998

Country	Equity markets	Exchange rate (against US$)
Indonesia	−81.2	−73.5
South Korea	−32.3	−48.1
Thailand	−47.9	−43.2
Malaysia	−59.0	−33.3
Singapore	−45.0	−13.2
Hong Kong	−36.6	Pegged to US$

Source: *Financial Times*, 20 February 1998.

- In Indonesia, trade restrictions, import monopolies, and regulations have impeded economic efficiency and competitiveness, and reduced the quality and productivity of investment.

- In Thailand, political disarray at various times during 1996–97, including in the wake of the November 1996 general election, delayed the implementation of necessary policy measures. In these and other cases, the power of special interests has often appeared to have had considerable influence on the allocation of budgetary resources and other public policy actions.

- In a number of countries, uncertainty has been increased and confidence adversely affected by inadequate disclosure of information and data deficiencies, particularly with regard to extra-budgetary fiscal transactions, the quasi-fiscal activities of the central bank, directed lending, the problem loans of financial institutions, official foreign exchange reserves and their management (including reserve-related liabilities), and private sector short-term debt. There has also often been a lack of transparency in policy implementation, such as with the decisions regarding public infrastructure projects and ad hoc tax exemptions.

The failure of the Asian model thesis has powerful proponents including Mr Greenspan, Mr Summers and the IFIs. But it is by no means the only significant available theory with respect to the financial crisis. Many Asian political leaders have put forward an entirely different perspective. They are prone to blame the whole of the crisis on the activities of foreign speculators and reject the view that the crisis was essentially 'home grown' (to use the phrase of the IMF Deputy Managing Director, Mr Stanley Fischer).

A more sophisticated version of this 'external factors' view is contained in the academic literature spawned by the Mexican crisis of 1994.[16] These contributions, based on careful theoretical and empirical analyses, show that it is entirely possible for a financial crisis to occur even when a country's fundamentals are totally sound. It may arise because of changes in investor sentiment or perceptions which may be triggered off entirely by external events such as changes in interest rates or equity prices in advanced countries. Some of these theories suggest that such crises of confidence can be self-fulfilling prophecies. Other models use the analogy of the classic panic-induced run on the banks to describe the present financial crisis in East Asian countries.

A third important theory ascribes the crisis to liberalisation of the global financial markets, and particularly to the deregulation of the capital account which many Asian countries had undertaken in the preceding period. It is suggested that the latter was the main cause of the crisis rather than any structural factors connected with the Asian development model. Indeed, it is argued that if these countries had continued to follow the Asian model of state-guided investment and state direction of the financial system, there would not have been a crisis at all in the first place. The crisis occurred directly as a result of deregulation and liberalisation when the governments relinquished controls over the financial sector as well as corporate investment activities. This led to misallocation (towards, for example, the property sector) of investment as well as overinvestment.

As these theories are central in determining the choice of remedies for the crisis, it is clearly important to know which of them is more congruous with the facts. The events are too close to be able to provide anywhere near a definitive explanation of the crisis, but the following section will review the evidence.

V   Evidence on the theories concerning the crisis

The survey below of available evidence bearing on the alternative theories of the present financial crisis in South East and East Asian countries is organised around the following themes:

1   the role of fundamentals;
2   the proximate cause of the crisis – the capital supply shock;
3   the role of structural factors; and
4   financial liberalisation.

V.1   Fundamentals

The most important point to note here is that all the affected countries prior to the crisis had for a long time enjoyed strong 'fundamentals'. This is evident from our earlier discussion in section II and from the more detailed data presented in Tables 1.1–1.3. Thailand, Indonesia, Malaysia, and Korea had all recorded extraordinarily strong economic growth for many years; their inflation rates were usually in single figures and much below the developing country average. These countries also had high domestic savings rates, indeed considerably greater than those of other developing countries including Brazil, Mexico, and India (the three countries for which data is provided in Table 1.6 for comparative purposes).

Moreover, the crisis countries had healthy fiscal positions. The public sector finances were either in surplus or had small sustainable deficits. The fiscal position of these countries compared very favourably with the average of developing countries as well as with that of Brazil, Mexico, and India.

A potentially significant blemish on this generally positive pre-crisis long-term economic record was the position of the current account balance in some of the affected countries. Thailand and Malaysia have experienced huge current account deficits, which in the 1990s amounted to nearly 6.9 per cent of GDP in the case of Thailand, and 6 per cent of GDP for Malaysia. In 1996 the Thai current account deficit was almost 8 per cent of GDP while that of Malaysia had fallen to 4.9 per cent. Nevertheless, it is also the case that both those countries had a relatively low debt service to exports ratios throughout the 1990s: 4.5 per cent for Thailand, and 6 per cent for Malaysia. Furthermore, in the case of Malaysia, as Table 1.7 on external capital flows indicates, the high current account deficit was to a considerable extent financed by a strong net inflow of foreign direct investment.

Table 1.6 Key indicators of comparator countries: Brazil, Mexico and India (% of GDP unless otherwise noted)

	1970–1980 (average)	1980–1990 (average)	1990–1994 (average)	1995
Brazil				
GDP growth[a]	8.6	2.3	1.0	3.0
Inflation[b]	36.6	557.8	1,840.5	84.5
Savings[c]	19.2	18.1	18.7	19.9
Investment[d]	21.8	20.9	20.4	21.9
Current account	–4.4	–1.9	–0.1	–2.6
Fiscal balance	0.0	–8.1	–3.3	n.a.
External debt	21.9	37.0	30.1	23.1
Import cover[e]	n.a.	2.8	5.9	7.9
Mexico				
GDP growth[a]	6.7	2.4	1.4	–7.2
Inflation[b]	16.8	65.2	16.3	35.5
Savings[c]	17.8	n.a.	n.a.	15.0
Investment[d]	20.7	20.2	19.7	15.7
Current account	n.a.	–1.2	–5.9	–0.3
Fiscal balance	–3.5	–9.0	n.a.	n.a.
External debt	23.7	52.8	37.6	66.3
Import cover[e]	n.a.	2.1	2.3	2.1
India				
GDP growth[a]	3.3	5.9	4.3	6.1
Inflation[b]	8.2	9.1	10.2	10.1
Savings[c]	19.4	20.7	21.7	22.7
Investment[d]	16.8	20.8	22.4	23.7
Current account	–0.4	–2.3	–1.5	–1.8
Fiscal balance	–4.6	–7.5	–6.7	–5.4
External debt	14.0	19.3	33.9	28.9
Import cover[e]	n.a.	4.9	4.1	5.2

Source: World Bank.

Notes
a Constant prices, percentage per annum.
b Average annual percentage growth of consumer price index.
c Gross national savings as percentage of GDP.
d Gross domestic fixed investment as percentage of GDP.
e Gross international reserves in months of import cover.

The Korean current account deficit in 1996 was 4.9 per cent of GDP, an unusually high figure for Korea. Korea was not, however, a persistent offender: its average deficit during the 1990s was less than 2 per cent of GDP. The larger 1996 deficit was caused by special circumstances, notably the collapse of prices of semi-conductors of which Korea was a major exporter. However, this sharp increase in the current account deficit was a temporary phenomenon, as one would expect from a highly diversified export-oriented economy. Indeed, in the last quarter of 1997 the Korean economy recorded a huge current account surplus of $3 billion. Indonesia's current account deficit during the 1990s averaged 2.6 per cent of GDP; in 1996 it was 3.3 per cent, an entirely sustainable figure on the

Table 1.7 Capital flows to Asian crisis economies: Malaysia, Indonesia, Thailand and Korea (% of GDP)[a]

	1983–1988[b]	1989–1995[b]	1992	1993	1994	1995	1996	1997[c]
Malaysia								
Net private capital flows[d]	3.1	8.8	15.1	17.4	1.5	8.8	9.6	4.7
Net direct investment	2.3	6.5	8.9	7.8	5.7	4.8	5.1	5.3
Net portfolio investment	n.a.	n.a.	n.a.	n.a.	n.a.	n.a.	n.a.	n.a.
Other net investment	0.8	2.3	6.2	9.7	−4.2	4.1	4.5	−0.6
Net official flows	0.3	0.0	−0.1	−0.6	0.2	−0.1	−0.1	−0.1
Change in reserves[e]	−1.8	−4.7	−11.3	−17.7	4.3	2.0	−2.5	3.6
Indonesia								
Net private capital flows[d]	1.5	4.2	2.5	3.1	3.9	6.2	6.3	1.6
Net direct investment	0.4	1.3	1.2	1.2	1.4	2.3	2.8	2.0
Net portfolio investment	0.1	0.4	0.0	1.1	0.6	0.7	0.8	−0.4
Other net investment	1.0	2.6	1.4	0.7	1.9	3.1	2.7	0.1
Net official flows	2.4	0.8	1.1	0.9	0.1	−0.2	−0.7	1.0
Change in reserves[e]	0.0	−1.4	−3.0	−1.3	0.4	−0.7	−2.3	1.8
Thailand								
Net private capital flows[d]	3.1	10.2	8.7	8.4	8.6	12.7	9.3	−10.9
Net direct investment	0.8	1.5	1.4	1.1	0.7	0.7	0.9	1.3
Net portfolio investment	0.7	1.3	0.5	3.2	0.9	1.9	0.6	0.4
Other net investment	1.5	7.4	6.8	4.1	7.0	10.0	7.7	−12.6
Net official flows	0.7	0.0	0.1	0.2	0.1	0.7	0.7	4.9
Change in reserves[e]	−1.4	−4.1	−2.8	−3.2	−3.0	−4.4	−1.2	9.7
Korea								
Net private capital flows[d]	−1.1	2.1	2.4	1.6	3.1	3.9	4.9	2.8
Net direct investment	0.2	−0.1	−0.2	−0.2	−0.3	−0.4	−0.4	−0.2
Net portfolio investment	0.3	1.4	1.9	3.2	1.8	1.9	2.3	−0.3
Other net investment	−1.6	0.8	0.7	−1.5	1.7	2.5	3.0	3.4
Net official flows	0.0	−0.3	−0.2	−0.6	−0.1	−0.1	−0.1	−0.1
Change in reserves[e]	−0.9	−0.8	−1.1	−0.9	−1.4	−1.5	0.3	−1.1

Source: IMF, 1997, *World Economic Outlook, Interim Assessment*, December.

Notes
a Net capital flows comprise net direct investment, net portfolio investment, and other long- and short-term net investment flows, including official and private borrowing.
b Annual averages.
c IMF estimates.
d Because of data limitations, other net investment may include some official flows.
e A minus sign indicates an increase.

past record of the economy. The only country where the current account deficit could be regarded as a real problem was Thailand. This is mainly because the deficit was being financed by bank borrowings (see Table 1.7).

It is also relevant to observe that, as late as September 1997, the Korean debt had a high rating from western rating agencies. Similarly, until almost the eve of the financial crisis in August 1997, the IMF was praising the Indonesian government for its successful management of the economy as well as for its achievements in reducing poverty.[17]

To sum up, all the affected Asian countries had strong 'fundamentals' in the sense of a proven record of being able to sustain fast economic growth. In view of their export orientation, they also had the ability to service their debts in the long term. They did, however, suffer to varying degrees from short term imbalances such as overvalued exchange rates, as well as short term liabilities of the financial sector which exceeded the value of the central bank's reserves. This required some macroeconomic adjustments and restructuring of debts. In other words, these countries had problems of liquidity rather than solvency. In this context Wolf's (1998b) observations concerning Indonesia are pertinent:

> Dwell for a moment, on Indonesia: its current account deficit was less than 4 per cent of GDP throughout the 1990's; its budget was in balance; inflation was below 10 per cent; at the end of 1996 the real exchange rate (as estimated by J.P. Morgan) was just 4 per cent higher than at the end of 1994; and the ratio to GDP of domestic bank credit to the private sector had risen merely from 50 per cent in 1990 to 55 per cent in 1996. True, the banking system had mountains of bad debt, but foreign lending to Indonesian companies had largely bypassed it. Is anyone prepared to assert that this is a country whose exchange rate one might expect to depreciate by about 75 per cent? Some exchange-rate adjustment was certainly necessary; what happened beggars belief.

V.2 The capital supply shock

It is generally agreed that the proximate cause of the crisis in all the four affected countries was the capital supply shock – the sudden interruption and reversal of normal capital inflows into these economies. Table 1.8, which provides aggregate financing figures for these countries plus the Philippines, indicates that their net external capital inflows more than doubled between 1994 and 1996 – from a little over $40 billion to more than $90 billion. The latter figure greatly exceeded the combined current account deficits of these countries, allowing them to build sizeable reserves. In 1997, however, there was a huge capital supply shock: the net inflow of $93 billion in 1996 turned into a net outflow of $12 billion in 1997, a turnaround of $105 billion. The latter figure is equivalent to 10 per cent of the pre-crisis GDP of these countries (Wolf, 1998a). The decomposition of the capital inflows in Table 1.8 suggests that the most volatile item was commercial bank lending which turned from a positive figure of over $50 billion in 1996 to a negative figure of $21 billion in 1997.

What the above evidence on the 'fundamentals', as well as the analysis of section II on the long-term supply-side capabilities of these economies suggests is that, whatever the trigger for the crisis (whether external macroeconomic imbalances or the liabilities of the financial institutions) the foreign commercial banks grossly over-reacted, giving rise to a classic panic-induced bank-run, with the difference that it is the external creditors who were withdrawing their funds (from, say, Thailand) before the country defaulted. Such behaviour on the part of the banks makes default or a major IMF bailout a self-fulfilling prophecy.

Table 1.8 Five Asian economies, external financing (US $ billions)[a]

	1994	1995	1996	1997[b]	1998[c]
Current account balance	–24.6	–41.3	–54.9	–26.0	17.6
External financing (net)	47.4	80.9	92.8	15.2	15.2
Private flows (net)	40.5	77.4	93.0	–12.1	–9.4
Equity investment	12.2	15.5	19.1	–4.5	7.9
Direct equity	4.7	4.9	7.0	7.3	9.8
Portfolio equity	7.6	10.6	12.1	–11.6	–1.9
Private creditors	28.2	61.8	74.0	–7.6	–17.3
Commercial banks	24.0	49.5	55.5	–21.3	–14.1
Non-bank private creditors	4.2	12.4	18.4	13.7	–3.2
Official flows (net)	7.0	3.6	–0.2	27.2	24.6
International financial institutions	–0.4	–0.6	–1.0	23.0	18.5
Bilateral creditors	7.4	4.2	0.7	4.3	6.1
Resident lending/other (net)[d]	–17.5	–25.9	–19.6	–11.9	–5.7
Reserves excluding gold	–5.4	–13.7	–18.3	22.7	–27.1

Source: *IMF Survey*, vol. 27, no. 3, 9 February 1998, p. 35.

Notes
a The countries are: Malaysia, Indonesia, Thailand, Korea and the Philippines.
b Estimate.
c Forecast.
d Including resident net lending, monetary gold and omissions.

V.3 Structural factors

Turning to the 'structural factors' connected with the Asian model, which the IMF and others implicate in the crisis, we first consider the issue of 'transparency'. It is suggested that, because of the nature of the Asian corporations (involving extensive cross-subsidisation of subsidiaries) and their close, non-arm's-length relationship with banks, and similar relationships between banks and governments, the markets did not have enough information about the true financial status of the corporations and the banks. This is regarded as being one important reason for the overreaction by the markets.[18]

However, in relation to this proposition, the following observations are relevant. First, as Stiglitz (1998a) notes, following financial liberalisation there have been similar banking crises in the early 1990s even in the Scandinavian countries. These countries would be regarded by many as being at the top of any international transparency league: the availability of reliable information was evidently not adequate by itself to prevent financial panics. Second, it is specifically claimed that international banks did not have accurate and timely information on the shortening maturity of bank claims on Asian countries. This complaint is also controversial. As Professor Alexandre Lamfalussy, the former chief economist at the Bank of International Settlements noted in a recent letter to the *Financial Times* (13 February 1998):

> the Bank for International Settlement is encouraged to speed up the publication of its statistics on international bank lending . . . The suggested improvement will surely do no harm but it will not do much good either as long as market participants and other concerned parties fail to read publicly available information or to draw practical conclusions from it.
>
> In the summer of 1996 the BIS reported in its half yearly statistics that by end-1995 the total of consolidated bank claims on South Korea, Thailand, Indonesia, and Malaysia reached $201.6bn. It reported in January 1997 that by mid-1996 the figure rose to $226.5bn and six months later, that by end-1996 it reached $247.8bn – an increase of 23 per cent in one year. For each of these dates the maturity breakdown was available. It was therefore known by mid-summer 1996 that bank claims maturing within one year made up 70 per cent of the total for South Korea, 69.4 per cent for Thailand, 61.9 per cent for Indonesia, but 'only' 47.2 per cent for Malaysia.

Professor Lamfalussy goes on to add:

> Moreover, in its Annual Report published on June 10 1996, the BIS did not hesitate to use strong words describing developments that had taken place already in 1995: 'By year end, Thailand had become the largest bank debtor in the developing world'.

Third, in relation to this argument about transparency and information, it is also pertinent to note that international banks lent huge sums of money to merchant banks in South Korea. Most of the latter did not have a long enough track record, being less than two years old (Chang, 1998). Many would regard such lending practices to be highly imprudent, if not reckless.

Turning to other structural features of the Asian model which it has become customary to blame for the crisis, we consider first the questions of overinvestment and misallocation of investment in countries like Thailand to the non-productive property sector. Here the IMF's critics are quite right to say that, if in the process of financial liberalisation, the governments of countries like Korea and Thailand had not eschewed control over their financial sector and corporate investment activity, such overinvestment and misallocation would not have occurred. Indeed, until financial liberalisation, the Thai government had regulated investment going into the property sector. It was therefore not the Asian model but the abandonment of one of its essential features which was directly responsible for the observed weaknesses that came to the fore.

Another structural characteristic of the Asian model which is the subject of much adverse comment in orthodox analysis of the current crisis pertains to corporate finance. As is well known, the typical corporation particularly in Japan,

Korea, or Thailand is heavily geared, i.e. has a high ratio of debt to equity capital of the shareholders. The Korean *chaebol* enterprises which spear-headed that country's extraordinarily successful industrialisation drive and the continuous technological upgrading of its exports over the last three decades are typically family owned. They are however very big – 11 South Korean companies are included in *Fortune* magazine's top 500 in the world. To put this figure into perspective, it may be useful to note that Switzerland, a far more developed economy, also has only 11 companies in the world's top 500.[19] In order for the families to be able to own such huge corporations, the equity component of the total invested corporate capital tends to be small relative to debt. Table 1.9 shows the debt–equity ratios of leading Korean corporations. Table 1.10 provides a comparative analysis of the debt–equity ratios of the largest quoted companies in nine emerging markets in the 1980s and 1990s. It clearly indicates that the Korean companies are relatively very heavily geared with a median value of 4.3 between 1980 and 1994. However, the bottom two parts of the table indicate that between the early 1980s and the early 1990s, this ratio fell from 5.48 to 3.96. The table also reveals that the Asian corporations, including those from India, have considerably higher debt–equity ratios than those of the Latin American corporations.

However, the important point to note is that such corporate financial arrangements have been functional within the traditional Asian economic system. This is in part due to the continuous monitoring of the corporations by 'main banks' with

Table 1.9 Debt–equity ratios of Korean *chaebol*

Company	Total assets (billion won)	Debt (billion won)	Debt–equity ratio
Samsung	50,856.4	37,043.6	268.2
Hyundai	53,183.7	43,319.3	439.1
Daewoo	34,205.6	26,383.2	337.3
Lucky-Goldstar	37,068.4	28,765.6	346.5
Hanjin	13,904.5	11,787.7	556.9
Kia	14,161.9	11,890.9	523.6
Ssangyong	15,807.2	12,701.4	409.0
Sunkyong	22,726.6	18,040.3	385.0
Hanwha	10,967.7	9,718.8	778.2
Daelim	5,793.3	4,586.5	380.1
Kumho	7,398.0	6,117.9	477.9
Doosan	6,402.0	5,594.0	692.3
Halla	6,626.5	6,320.8	2,067.6
Sammi	2,515.4	2,593.3	3,329.0
Hyosung	4,124.4	3,252.8	373.2
Hanil	2,628.1	2,231.8	563.2
Dong-Ah Construction	6,287.9	4,905.8	355.0
Kohap	3,653.6	3,123.6	589.4
Jinro	3,940.5	3,895.2	8,598.7
Dongkuk Steel	3,697.5	2,536.4	218.4

Source: *Financial Times*, 8 August 1997.

Table 1.10 Top listed manufacturing corporations, nine developing countries, distribution of their average gearing ratios

Gearing	Argentina	India	Jordan	Korea	Malaysia	Mexico	Peru	Thailand	Zimbabwe
Whole period	1991–95	1980–92	1980–94	1980–94	1983–94	1984–94	1991–95	1987–94	1980–95
Mean	0.70	3.24	1.04	5.22	1.03	0.60	0.67	1.23	3.86
Standard deviation	0.66	10.90	1.08	4.98	1.96	1.61	0.60	0.98	57.35
Minimum	0.02	0.31	0.05	0.42	0.03	−1.94	0.04	0.00	0.07
First quartile	0.29	1.50	0.43	2.53	0.32	0.16	0.30	0.60	0.47
Median	0.53	2.28	0.67	4.30	0.64	0.32	0.51	1.00	0.68
Third quartile	0.84	3.16	1.16	6.39	1.11	0.61	0.79	1.52	1.04
Maximum	4.70	259.41	7.49	61.97	29.12	24.49	4.24	6.78	1,090.44
Range	4.68	259.10	7.44	61.55	29.10	26.43	4.21	6.78	1,090.37
Early period		1980–83	1980–83	1980–83	1983–86	1984–87		1987–90	1980–83
Mean		3.44	1.13	6.90	1.04	0.95		1.27	0.87
Standard deviation		14.46	1.26	5.84	2.14	2.04		1.00	0.55
Minimum		0.31	0.05	1.47	0.03	0.04		0.03	0.07
First quartile		1.47	0.43	4.30	0.31	0.32		0.62	0.52
Median		2.37	0.74	5.48	0.62	0.52		1.03	0.78
Third quartile		3.13	1.24	7.81	1.12	0.84		1.62	1.14
Maximum		259.41	7.49	61.97	29.12	24.49		6.78	4.95
Range		259.10	7.44	60.51	29.10	24.45		6.76	4.88
Late period		1989–92	1991–94	1991–94	1991–94	1991–94		1991–94	1992–95
Mean		3.06	0.98	3.38	1.02	0.13		1.18	6.97
Standard deviation		6.03	0.92	2.87	1.74	0.35		0.95	81.91
Minimum		0.50	0.13	0.42	0.06	−1.94		0.00	0.08
First quartile		1.53	0.45	1.81	0.33	0.03		0.59	0.45
Median		2.21	0.62	2.62	0.68	0.16		0.97	0.63
Third quartile		3.19	1.13	3.96	1.09	0.27		1.41	0.92
Maximum		83.38	4.17	27.56	22.42	1.53		6.56	1,090.44
Range		82.88	4.04	27.14	22.36	3.47		6.55	1,090.35

Source: Glen, Singh and Matthias (forthcoming).

Note: Gearing is the ratio of total liabilities divided by shareholders' equity.

whom they have long term relationships, as well as to the close oversight by the government over the banks. These arrangements were particularly useful during Korea's industrialisation drive, as the corporations were induced by the government to enter into new technological areas involving huge risks. Left to themselves, the corporations may not have been able to undertake such risks, but with the government becoming in effect a co-partner through the banking system, such technological risks were 'socialised'. Following the work of Williamson (1976), Lee (1992) has characterised this system as essentially constituting an internal capital market. In view of the well known weaknesses of free capital markets (e.g., a tendency towards short termism and quick profits) such an internal capital market may in fact be more efficient than the former.[20]

However, such a corporate system became dysfunctional when, for example, in Korea the government undertook during the last few years a process of financial liberalisation (under pressure from the US government and the IFIs, but see the discussion in section VII). Korea resisted allowing non-residents to buy majority stakes in its corporations. However, its mistake was to implement other components of capital account liberalisation by permitting Korean companies and banks to raise money abroad without the traditional supervision and control. So, in that sense, it was again financial de-regulation (i.e. the dismantling of a fundamental aspect of the previous system) which rendered the system dysfunctional and fragile.

It is interesting in the above context to consider the case of India. As Table 1.10 indicates, the Indian corporations are also very highly geared. Moreover India's fundamentals, as Tables 1.3 and 1.4 (discussed earlier) indicate, were much weaker than those of the East Asian countries. Nevertheless, India has not had a financial crisis. At a time of deep turbulence in the currency markets of its South East and East Asian neighbours, the Indian currency market has been a model of stability. Why? Most observers would agree that the main reason for this is that India has extremely limited capital account liberalisation. It does not allow its corporations or banks to borrow or lend capital abroad without government approval. It has carried out some liberalisation by allowing non-residents to purchase shares directly on the Indian stock markets, but they cannot become majority shareholders. This limited, cautious openness, the relatively small size of foreign portfolio inflows as well as that of the stock market itself have been helpful to the Indian economy. The Indian currency is consequently much less vulnerable to changes in investor sentiment or speculative attacks from outside.

VI   The IMF policy programme and the East Asian crisis

As the financial crisis deepened in East Asia and more and more countries became involved, the IMF assembled large financial packages to bail out the affected countries. However, this aid was available only in return for draconian conditionality. Apart from their usual policies of demand restraint (cuts in money supply, high interest rates, fiscal retrenchment, etc.) the IMF went further. It demanded far-reaching changes in the economic and social systems of these countries. These changes included still more liberalisation of the financial sector (including permitting hostile take-overs of domestic firms by non-residents); changes in the system of corporate governance, in labour laws, in government business relations, and in competition policy. Such measures were insisted on because it was believed (erroneously as we have seen above) that the root cause of the crisis was the 'dirigiste' institutional structures and policies of these countries.

The IMF policy programmes for the affected Asian countries may be faulted for a number of important reasons.[21]

1   The IMF's traditional policy programme of demand restraint etc. is typically designed to deal with countries with persistent current account disequilibria, fiscal deficits, and over-heated economies. For the Asian economies, however, except perhaps to some extent for Thailand, the problem has been one of capital account disequilibrium rather than that of current account imbalances. Moreover, as we have seen earlier, the public sector finances in these countries have been by and large in equilibrium and it is the private sector which is in severe disequilibrium. In these circumstances, the large fiscal austerity demanded by the IMF's original programmes for these countries would have made matters worse rather than better, pushing the countries deeper into recession, and thereby exacerbating the private sector financial disequilibria.

2   The high real interest rates entailed by the IMF programmes would have similarly deleterious effects on the private sector's viability. Such rates will lead to the bankruptcy of a large part of the sector, deepening the depression of the real economy. In response to this criticism, the IMF has argued that higher interest rates are required for restoring international confidence in the countries' policies. Stiglitz's (1988a,b) counter-argument is that there is little empirical evidence to support the view that high interest rates improve confidence. He goes on to add that one could perhaps make a case for an increase in interest rates for a brief spell, but countries like Indonesia and Thailand have had real interest rates of 20 per cent or more now for nearly nine months.

There is some truth in both these contentions. Evidence from the financial crisis in the various parts of the world suggests that higher interest rates help before a crisis has occurred (i.e. they may forestall the crisis), but once the crisis has taken place, increasing interest rates is regarded by the market as a sign of weakness and is therefore counter-productive.

3   The IMF is quite right to stress the importance of prudential regulation and supervision of the financial sector. Certainly, financial liberalisation by the affected countries without such regulations was a serious mistake. However, to forestall the crisis, the IMF should have discouraged financial liberalisation by these countries until the appropriate regulatory regime was in place. This the institution did not do, presumably because of its own strong commitment to external account liberalisation. Further, it is a moot point whether under a regime of free capital flows, prudential regulation of the domestic financial sector, without that of international banks as well, would have been enough

to prevent a financial crisis (Akyuz, 1997; Stiglitz, 1998b).

4   The misdiagnosis of the crisis by the IMF (that it has been due to the *dirigiste* model of the Asian capitalism rather than being caused by internal and external financial liberalisation) has had serious adverse short as well as long term consequences for the affected countries. It is certainly arguable that the Fund's emphasis on what it perceived to be the fundamental structural difficulties of the Asian model (crony capitalism, corruption etc.), panicked foreign investors still further, and thereby worsened the crisis (Feldstein, 1998a, 1998b).

5   As the evidence outlined earlier (the strong fundamentals, the large inflows of private capital from abroad and IMF's own seal of approval for economic management of these countries until the eve of the crisis), suggests the East Asian crisis was originally one of liquidity rather than solvency. In these circumstances, it would have been preferable for the Fund to have acted as an intermediary to help bridge the gap between lenders and borrowers over the mismatch of maturities. Instead, the institution raised huge sums of money for bailouts and imposed far-reaching conditionalities on the crisis countries which could be interpreted as signalling a deeper solvency rather than a mere liquidity crisis.

6   Professor Feldstein (1998a, 1998b) makes an important point of political economy concerning the IMF programmes which deserves serious consideration by the international community. He notes that the IMF is an international agency whose purpose ought to be to provide technical advice and, as appropriate, the financial assistance necessary to help countries overcome a balance of payments crisis with as little loss of output and employment as possible. It may also wish to ensure that the country continues to follow the right economic policies so that, as far as possible, the situation does not recur. However, he suggests that the IMF 'should not use the opportunity to impose other economic changes that, however helpful they may be, are not necessary to deal with the balance-of-payments problem and are the proper responsibility of the country's own political system'.

Professor Feldstein proposes the following three-point test for the structural aspects of the IMF conditionalities:

> In deciding whether to insist on any particular reform, the IMF should ask three questions: Is this reform really needed to restore the country's access to international capital markets? Is this a technical matter that does not interfere unnecessarily with the proper jurisdiction of a sovereign government? If the policies to be changed are also practised in the major industrial countries of Europe, would the IMF think it appropriate to force similar changes in those countries if they were subject to a fund program? The IMF is justified in requiring a change in a client country's national policy only if the answer to all three questions is yes.
>
> (Feldstein, 1998b)

Unfortunately, the answers to none of the three questions above for Korea, for example, is in the affirmative. The structural reforms the IMF has asked for include labour regulations, corporate governance, the relationship between government and business. These clearly involve deeply political matters. Apart from the questions of morality and national sovereignty, even in practical terms insisting on such far-reaching conditionalities would not appear to be a good idea at all for resolving a financial crisis. Few governments can deliver such reforms in a short space of time and this unnerves the markets, making the resolution of the crisis more difficult.

VII Analytical conclusions and policy implications

VII.1 Analytical conclusions

The main analytical arguments of this chapter may be summarised as follows. First, the current widely held and highly influential thesis that the root cause of the present financial crisis in South East and East Asian countries lies in the *dirigiste* model of Asian capitalism pursued by these countries is seriously mistaken. The analysis of the chapter suggests that the fundamental reason for the crisis is to be found not in too much, but rather in too little government control over the financial liberalisation process which these countries implemented in the recent period.

Second, in view of the rather different circumstances of the Asian countries (compared with the kinds of countries that usually face financial difficulties), the IMF staff appear to have misdiagnosed the crisis. They have therefore proposed inappropriate remedies (for example, further financial liberalisation, large fiscal austerity, a steep rise in real interest rates) which are likely to deepen the crisis. Moreover, market confidence, which was of critical importance in the evolution of the crisis, is unlikely to have been helped by the IMF's emphasis on the ostensible fundamental structural weaknesses of these countries and requirement that they should implement far-reaching reforms in their economic and social systems. All these factors contributed to turning what was essentially a liquidity problem into one of solvency.

Third, as explained in the previous sections, the governments of the affected countries made serious errors by not controlling the financial liberalisation process. Although it is true that the IMF as well as the US government have been urging capital account liberalisation for these countries, it is also the case that a growing domestic constituency also supported such liberalisation. Thus, for example, prior to the crisis, Thailand and Malaysia were vying with one another as well as with Hong Kong and Singapore to assume the role of regional financial centre. This necessarily entailed considerable financial liberalisation. In the euphoria accompanying the large inflows of capital during the 1980s and 1990s, the benefits of becoming a regional financial centre were readily seen (the development of the financial services industry, skilled employment etc.). However, the governments seemed oblivious to the potential costs.[22]

In addition to the pursuit of financial liberalisation without proper institutional controls, the governments of some of the crisis countries (particularly Thailand) might also have made some macroeconomic mistakes, for example, not adjusting the exchange rate, relying on short-term capital to finance a large current account deficit. Nevertheless, a central argument of this chapter is that, although these government policy errors may have initiated the crisis, this was compounded by other factors: the lack of co-ordination between banks and the desire of each bank not to renew its short-term loans following the crisis of confidence; the herd behaviour of international investors which was partly responsible for the 'contagion' throughout the region; and, as suggested above, the inappropriate policy response from the IMF to the confidence crisis. Thus a liquidity problem has been transformed into a far more serious solvency problem.

VII.2 Policy implications

What are the policy implications of these conclusions? The basic policy issues which are closely interlinked are as follows:

1   how to restore investor confidence so that normal capital flows in the region are resumed;
2   how to ensure that long-term growth in the real economy is restored as quickly as possible; and
3   how to provide immediate assistance to the millions of people who are likely to become unemployed or pushed back into poverty once again.

The importance of the last issue cannot be exaggerated. This is not just for humanitarian reasons but it is also necessary for maintaining social peace (see further Singh, 1998a). To provide such assistance effectively and on an adequate scale will require not only considerable imagination but also a large expansion in government activity and often direct intervention in the market processes. Such emergency safety net programmes may include wider subsidies, food-for-work schemes and public works projects, including the kind of labour intensive infrastructural projects which the ILO has pioneered in countries like Indonesia. How to pay for these measures within the limits of fiscal prudence, let alone within the IMF fiscal austerity programmes, will be a major issue of political economy for these countries.

Turning to the first policy issue, the most important requirement for achieving a resumption of normal capital flows to the affected countries are economic policies which are credible and have wide domestic political support. Such credibility is much more likely to be achieved if there is political unity in the country and if there is close co-operation not only between government and business but also labour and civil society organisations in a national programme to resolve the economic situation. This would inevitably mean that the burden of adjustment would need to be equitably shared by all sections of society. Thus, the traditional Asian model of capitalism essentially based on corporatism becomes all the more essential if the present acute economic crisis is to be overcome.

The first best approach to resolving the present crisis of confidence is for the IMF and the affected countries to co-operate closely on the essential and immediate narrow task of restoring their access to the international capital markets. For this purpose, the IMF should act as an intermediary between the international banks and other major creditors on the one side and the private sector debtors on the other, in order to achieve a rapid restructuring of the debt. In this role, the institution needs to reiterate to investors and creditors the healthy fundamentals of these countries, their proven strong supply-side potential, their export orientation and therefore their ability in the medium to long term to service their debts. It is significant and most encouraging that in response to the criticism of its policy programmes, the IMF has already made some important changes such as softening the strong demand restraint measures required of Thailand and Korea. Although somewhat late in the day (rather than before the crisis began) the Fund has also been participating in discussions to facilitate the re-scheduling of the debts. However, the institution needs to go a great deal further in the direction of its critics. For the long term, the IMF should seriously re-examine its whole project of promoting capital account liberalisation in developing countries.[23]

Notes

1 Quoted in the *International Herald Tribune*, 13 February 1998.
2 See, for example, Mr Camdessus's speech to Transparency International reported in the *IMF Survey*, 9 February 1998.
3 This chapter is an abbreviated and updated version of Singh, 1998a. The author and the editors are grateful to the ILO, Geneva for permission to reproduce material.
4 This is not to deny that some East Asian countries have denied trade union rights and thus repressed their labour force for certain periods. Nevertheless, East Asian workers have enjoyed a far higher growth of real wages than workers anywhere else.
5 The source of these figures is Maizels (1963), quoted in Amsden and Hikino (1993).
6 The World Bank's conclusion of declining income inequality in East Asian economies is, however, subject to important qualifications. See further, Singh (1995a, 1997a) and UNCTAD (1997).
7 'Restoring the Asian Miracle', *Wall Street Journal*, Europe (3 February 1998, p. 4).
8 Although China has a different political system, there is evidence that during the last two decades of the relative liberalisation and marketisation of the economy, the country has attempted to emulate the East Asian model. See further, Nolan (1995) and Singh (1996a).
9 The significance of this contribution is discussed in Singh (1995a).
10 As late as 1978, long after Japan had become a member of the OECD and had greatly reduced or abolished most formal import restrictions of the earlier era, its manufactured imports were only 2 per cent of GDP. The comparable figures for countries like France, Germany and Britain were at that time five to six times as large. See Singh (1994).
11 As indicated earlier, the World Bank's Chief Economist, Professor Stiglitz, takes a rather different view of the crisis than that of the Fund. However, as Wade and Veneroso (1998) suggest the position is closer to that of the IMF than to Professor Stiglitz.

12 For comprehensive critical analyses of the World Bank (1993) theses, see the contributions in Amsden (1994); see also Singh (1995a).
13 See Singh (1995a, 1997a, 1997b, 1998b); see also Okimoto (1989), Tsuru (1993), Amsden (1989), Wade (1990) and Amsden and Singh (1994).
14 For a fuller discussion, see Amsden and Singh (1994).
15 Krugman reports that in the case of South Korea, the price of its corporations to foreign buyers essentially fell by 70 per cent during 1997. Thus, the stock market value of Korean Air Lines with a fleet of more than 100 aircraft at the end of 1997 was only $240 million. This is approximately the price of two Boeing 747s. However, any acquirer would also have to take on the Korean Air Lines debt of $5 billion.
16 See for example Calvo and Mendoza (1996), Sachs, Tornell and Velasco (1996), Cole and Kehoe (1996), Krugman (1998).
17 See *IMF Survey*, vol. 26, no. 16, 18 August 1997.
18 Thus Mr Camdessus (1998): 'In Korea, for example, opacity had become systemic. The lack of transparency about government, corporate and financial sector operations concealed the extent of Korea's problems – so much so that corrective action came too late and ultimately could not prevent the collapse of market confidence, with the IMF finally being authorised to intervene just days before potential bankruptcy.'
19 See further Singh (1995b).
20 There is a large literature on these issues. For a fuller discussion, see further Singh (1996b); Singh and Weisse (1998).
21 See also Sachs (1997); Stiglitz (1998a, 1998b); Feldstein (1998a, 1998b); Wade and Veneroso (1998); Amsden and Euh (1997); Akyuz (1997).
22 Chang (1998) notes that a major ambition of the previous South Korean government was for the country to become an OECD member during its own term of office. In pursuit of that ambition the government was willing to forsake important parts of the Asian model, particularly control over investment activity and the financial transactions of large firms and banks.
23 For a fuller discussion of the issues concerning capital account liberalisation see further Singh (1997b), Singh and Weiss (1998).

References

Akyuz, Y. 1997. 'The East Asian Financial Crisis: Back to the Future?', unpublished paper. Geneva: UNCTAD.
Amsden, A. (ed.). 1994. 'Reviews of World Bank, 1993', *World Development*, vol. 22, no. 4.
Amsden, A. 1989. *Asia's Next Giant: South Korea and Late Industrialization*. Oxford: Oxford University Press.
Amsden, A. and Euh, Y.-D. 1997. 'Behind Korea's Plunge', *New York Times*, 27 November.
Amsden, A. and Hikino, T. 1993. 'Innovating or Borrowing Technology: Explorations in Paths to Industrial Development', in R. Thompson (ed.), *Learning and Technological Change*. London: Macmillan.
Amsden, A. and Singh, A. 1994. 'The Optimal Degree of Competition and Dynamic Efficiency in Japan and Korea', *European Economic Review*, vol. 28, pp. 941–951.
Aoki, M. and Patrick, H. (eds). 1994. *The Japanese Main Bank System: Its Relevance for Developing and Transforming Economies*. Oxford: Clarendon Press.
Calvo, G. and Mendoza, E. 1996. 'Mexico's Balance of Payments Crisis: A Chronicle of a Death Foretold', *Journal of International Economics*, vol. 41, nos 3/4, November, pp. 235–264.
Camdessus, M. 1998. 'Good Governance Has Become Essential in Promoting Growth and Stability', address to Transparency International, *IMF Survey*, vol. 27, no. 3, 9 February.

Chang, H.-J. 1998. 'Reform for the Long Term in South Korea', *International Herald Tribune*, 13 February.

Cole and Kehoe. 1996. 'A Self-fulfilling Model of Mexico's 1994–1995 Debt Crisis', *Journal of International Economics*, vol. 41, nos 3/4, November, pp. 309–330.

Feldstein, M. 1998a. 'Trying to Do Too Much', *Financial Times*, 3 March.

Feldstein, M. 1998b. 'Refocusing the IMF', *Foreign Affairs*, March/April 1998.

Glen, J., Singh, A. and Matthias, R. 1999. 'How Intensive is Competition in Emerging Markets? An Analysis of Corporate Rates of Return in Nine Emerging Markets', IMF Working Paper. Washington, DC: IMF (forthcoming).

ILO. 1995. *World Employment Report*. Geneva: ILO.

IMF. 1997. *World Economic Outlook: Interim Assessment*. Washington, DC: IMF (December).

Krueger, A. 1995. 'East Asian Experience and Endogenous Growth Theory', in T. Ito and A. Krueger (eds), *Growth Theories in Light of the East Asian Experience*. Chicago: University of Chicago Press.

Krugman, P. 1998. 'What Happened to Asia?' (unpublished).

Lee, C.H. 1992. 'The Government, Financial System and Large Private Enterprises in Economic Development in South Korea', *World Development*, vol. 20, no. 2, pp. 187–197.

Maizels, A. 1963. *Industrial Growth and World Trade*. Cambridge: Cambridge University Press.

Nolan, P. 1995. 'Large Firms and Industrial Reform in Former Planned Economies: The Case of China', DAE Working Papers, Amalgamated Series no. 9516. University of Cambridge, Department of Applied Economics.

Okimoto, D.I. 1989. *Between MITI and the Market*. Palo Alto, California: Stanford University Press.

Ros, J. 1997. 'Employment, Structural Adjustment and Sustainable Growth in Mexico', Employment and Training Papers 6. Geneva: ILO.

Sachs, J. 1997. 'IMF Orthodoxy Isn't What Southeast Asia Needs', *International Herald Tribune*, 4 November.

Sachs, J., Tornell, A. and Velasco, A. 1996. 'Financial Crises in Emerging Markets: The Lessons from 1995', *Brookings Papers on Economic Activity*, no. 1, pp. 147–215.

Singh, A. 1998a. *Financial Crisis in East Asia: "The End of the Asian Model?"*, Issues in Development, Discussion Paper 24. Geneva: ILO.

Singh, A. 1998b. 'Savings, Investment and the Corporation in the East Asian Miracle', Study 9, *The Journal of Development Studies*, vol. 34, no. 6, August, pp. 112–37.

Singh, A. 1997a. 'Catching up with the West: A Perspective on Asian Economic Development and Lessons for Latin America', in L. Emmerij (ed.), *Economic and Social Development into the XXI Century*. Washington, DC: Inter-American Development Bank.

Singh, A. 1997b. 'Financial Liberalisation, Stockmarkets and Economic Development', *Economic Journal*, vol. 107, no. 442, pp. 771–782.

Singh, A. 1996a. 'The Plan, the Market and Evolutionary Economic Reform in China', in A. Abdullah and A.R. Khan (eds), *State, Market and Development: Essays in Honour of Rehman Sobhan*. New Delhi: Oxford University Press.

Singh, A. 1995a. 'The Causes of Fast Economic Growth in East Asia', *UNCTAD Review*.

Singh, A. 1995b. *Corporate Financial Patterns in Industrializing Economies: A Comparative International Study*, Technical Paper no. 2. Washington, DC: IFC.

Singh, A. 1994. 'Openness and the Market Friendly Approach to Development: Learning the Right Lessons from Development Experience', *World Development*, vol. 22, no. 12, pp. 1811–1823.

Singh, A. and Weisse, B. 1998. 'Emerging Stock Markets, Portfolio Capital Flows and Long-Term Economic Growth: Micro- and Macroeconomic Perspectives', *World Development*, vol. 26, no. 4, pp. 607–622.

Stiglitz, J. 1998a. 'Restoring the Asian Miracle', *The Wall Street Journal*, 3 February.

Stiglitz, J. 1998b. 'More Instruments and Broader Goals: Moving toward the Post-Washington Consensus', WIDER Annual Lecture, 7 January. Helsinki, Finland: WIDER.

Tokman, V. 1997. 'Jobs and Solidarity: Challenges for Post-Adjustment in Latin America', in L. Emmerij (ed.), *Economic and Social Development into the XXI Century*. Washington, DC: Inter-American Development Bank.

Tsuru, S. 1993. *Japan's Capitalism: Creative Defeat and Beyond*. Cambridge: Cambridge University Press.

UNCTAD. 1997. *Trade and Development Report*. Geneva: UNCTAD.

Wade, R. 1990. *Governing the Market: Economic Theory and the Role of Government in East Asian Industrialization*. Princeton, NJ: Princeton University Press.

Wade, R. and Veneroso, F. 1998. 'The Asian Financial Crisis: The High Debt Model and the Unrecognized Risk of the IMF Strategy', Working Paper no. 128. New York: Russell Sage Foundation.

Williamson, O.E. 1975. *Markets and Hierarchies: Analysis and Antitrust Implications*. New York: The Free Press.

Wolf. 1998a. 'Caging the Bankers', *Financial Times*, 20 January.

Wolf, 1998b. 'Flows and Blows', *Financial Times*, 3 March.

World Bank. 1997. *World Economic Outlook: Interim Assessment*. Washington, DC: IMF (December).

World Bank. 1993. *The East Asian Miracle: Economic Growth and Public Policy*. New York: Oxford University Press for the World Bank.

World Bank. 1991. *World Development Report: The Challenge of Development*. New York: Oxford University Press for the World Bank.

2 Rejecting exceptionalism
Reinterpreting the Asian financial crises

Ilene Grabel[1]

Introduction

The biggest financial news story of 1997 and 1998 was the series of crises that hit the stock, currency and banking markets in "emerging economies." The "crisis of 1997–8" began in Thailand in May 1997, and through the summer and fall swept through some of the most important and stable economies of Southeast Asia – Malaysia, Indonesia, the Philippines, and Singapore. In late October, the crisis reached Brazil and Russia, and by early December it reached South Korea. In January 1998, a new round of instability shook the South Korean and Indonesian financial markets. In its scope and depth, the crisis of 1997–8 proved to be far more disruptive and less tractable than its December 1994 Mexican predecessor.

The crisis of 1997–8 was notable for a number of reasons.

Since the first of these crises emerged in Thailand in May 1997, the year was marked by a growing contagion. These crises, especially in the Southeast Asian "miracle economies," took officials in multilateral institutions and investors by surprise. Until the summer of 1997, IMF–World Bank reports and business press accounts on the Southeast Asian, Russian and Brazilian markets were uniformly bullish. As the data on net private capital flows in Table 2.1 show, private investors and lenders were quite optimistic about prospects in these countries until their difficulties emerged.

Indeed, as of year-end 1996, four of the countries headed for crisis were among the world's top six recipients of private foreign capital inflows. During 1996, Indonesia received the world's third largest share of private foreign capital inflows ($17.9b), Malaysia the fourth largest share ($16b), Brazil the fifth largest share ($14.7b), and Thailand the sixth largest share ($13.3b) (WSJ, 11/7/97).

A second notable feature of the crisis of 1997–8 was the volume of the IMF bailouts that were negotiated. The December 1997 South Korean bailout of $57b dwarfed what was formerly the world's largest bailout of Mexico in February 1995 (valued at $50b). The other bailouts associated with the crisis were also not small in magnitude: the Thai bailout of August 1997 was valued at $17b, the Indonesian bailout of November 1997 was valued at $43b, and the Philippine bailout of July 1997 was valued at $4b.

Table 2.1 Countries involved in the crisis of 1997–1998: net private capital flows (US $ billions) and annual % change in the stock market index, 1980–1996

Country		1980	1989	1991	1993	1995	1996
Indonesia	PI	0	0.2	0	2.5	4.8	3.0
	DFI	0.2	0.7	1.5	2.0	4.3	8.0
	Loans	1.6	3.0	5.2	−1.0	3.4	6.1
	STK	—	31.0	−40.8	114.6	9.4	24.0
Malaysia	PI	0	0.2	0	3.7	2.3	4.4
	DFI	0.9	1.7	4.0	5.0	4.1	4.5
	Loans	1.1	−1.3	0.4	2.2	4.0	2.5
	STK	—	58.2	9.9	98.0	2.5	24.4
Philippines	PI	0	0.3	0	1.4	2.0	1.9
	DFI	−0.1	0.6	0.5	1.2	1.5	1.4
	Loans	1.3	0.6	0.7	1.5	0.5	1.5
	STK	—	31.2	76.7	154.4	−6.9	22.2
Singapore	PI	−0.1	−0.4	−0.6	−7.9	−7.5	—
	DFI	1.2	2.9	4.9	4.7	7.0	—
	Loans	—	—	—	—	—	—
	STK	—	—	—	—	—	—
South Korea	PI	—	−0.06	0.4	0.2	0.3	—
	DFI	6.0	1.1	1.2	0.6	1.8	—
	Loans	—	—	—	—	—	—
	STK	—	0.3	−12.2	27.7	−14.0	−26.2
Thailand	PI	0	1.4	0.04	3.1	2.2	1.6
	DFI	0.2	1.8	2.0	1.8	2.0	2.3
	Loans	1.8	1.7	3.0	3.2	6.3	10.2
	STK	—	127.3	16.0	88.4	−5.8	−35.0
Brazil	PI	0	0	0.8	5.5	4.4	4.0
	DFI	1.9	1.3	1.1	1.3	4.9	9.9
	Loans	4.6	−3.5	0.6	8.4	8.9	14.0
	STK	—	1,762.5	2,316.0	5,437.2	−1.3	63.8
Russia	PI	—	0	0	0	0.1	5.0
	DFI	—	0	0	0	2.0	2.5
	Loans	—	4.6	4.3	2.9	−0.8	3.2
	STK	—	—	—	—	—	190.6

Sources: PI, DFI and LOAN data are from *Global Development Finance*, 1998, vol. 1, World Bank, Washington, DC, 1998; stock index data are from the *Emerging Stock Markets Factbook*, 1997, International Finance Corporation, Washington, DC, 1997.

Notes: PI = net portfolio equity flows; DFI = net foreign direct investment; Loans = net flow of long-term debt (excluding, IMF loans).
STK = annual % change in local stock market price indexes (1996 data are preliminary); STK Indonesia = JSE Composite (10 Aug 1982 = 100); STK Malaysia = KLSE Composite (Jan. 1977 = 100); STK Philippines = PSE Composite (2 Jan. 1985 = 100); STK South Korea = KSE Composite (Jan. 1980 = 100); STK Thailand = SET (30 April 1975 = 100); STK Brazil = IBOVESPA (1968 = 0.000000001); STK Russia = ASP General 100 (20 June 1994 = 100); data on Hong Kong are not available.

Perhaps most notable about the crisis of 1997–8 was that it occurred *after* the IMF had implemented what was heralded as an important new set of safeguards embodied in the "Special Information Dissemination Standard." The Standard was adopted in April 1996 following the Mexican financial crisis. This new information system involves the development of a Dissemination Standards Bulletin Board in which accurate information on the conditions in a wide range of countries is available to investors worldwide (Fischer, 1997).

This chapter is motivated by the parallels in the conventional wisdom on the causes and consequences of the crisis of 1997–8 and the Mexican crisis of 1994–5. In the Mexican case, what I elsewhere termed the "Mexican exceptionalism thesis" contends that the Mexican experience was largely an aberration stemming from the country's "peculiarities" (Grabel, 1996). Thus, rather than examine the Mexican crisis for evidence of general problems related to financial openness in emerging economies, the experience was dismissed as a unique event (World Bank, 1995).

An interesting feature of the *general* crisis of 1997–8 was the ubiquitous claim of *exceptionalism* that was again invoked to explain these events. Especially in the Southeast Asian cases, much was made of the seemingly newly discovered – yet deeply rooted – patterns of corruption, unsustainable real estate speculation, wasteful government spending, and misguided government policies (IMF Survey, 2/9/98; Safire, 1998). In the Russian case, exceptionalist explanations focused on the problems of corruption, tax evasion and governmental mismanagement (WSJ, 11/3/97; DP, 12/6/97). In the Brazilian case, exceptionalist explanations centered on investors' fears that the government would be unable to withstand political pressure to repudiate the neoliberal program it was pursuing (NYT, 11/11/97).

This chapter will present arguments against the exceptionalist explanations of the crisis of 1997–8. I argue that the crisis of 1997–8 was principally the result of two factors: the private sector's excessive reliance on hard currency-denominated foreign loans, and the government's failure to control portfolio investment flows. By relying on these two types of private capital flows – in the absence of sufficient foreign exchange reserves – the economies involved in the crisis of 1997–8 were rendered vulnerable to the self-reinforcing cycle of investor exit, currency depreciation and financial crisis. I will refer to the vulnerability to exit and currency risk as the "problem of increased risk potential." Once this increased risk potential was realized and the crisis emerged, governments found their ability to maneuver to be quite limited. In efforts to stem the crisis, governments were compelled (either on their own account or as a precondition for IMF assistance) to pursue the very macroeconomic policies that exacerbated their risk potential. I call this the problem of "constrained policy autonomy." The chapter rejects the measures that governments put in place in efforts to resolve the crisis, and proposes that emerging economies instead manage financial flows.

This chapter briefly outlines the stylized facts of the Mexican crisis and presents a general theoretical explanation of the causes of that crisis. Then it turns to the crisis of 1997–8 and argues that the structural dynamics of that crisis are markedly similar – though not identical – to those of the Mexican crisis. In this connection, it will also argue that the resolutions to the crisis of 1997–8 and the Mexican crisis were misguided insofar as they introduced problems of greater risk potential, constrained policy autonomy and recessionary tendencies to these economies. Finally, it offers some thoughts on the types of preventative measures that policymakers in emerging economies should consider lest history repeat itself (again).

The Mexican crisis of 1994–5: exceptionalism emerges

In less than a decade after Mexico's threatened default on its international loans, private investors (though largely not private lenders) returned to Mexico (see Table 2.2).[2] As early as 1989, Mexico was being marketed as the site of one of the world's most dynamic, emerging markets. Investor interest in Mexico was fueled by the government's gestures toward political democratization and economic liberalization, measures which received wide attention in the US. The signing of NAFTA also created new opportunities for investors, and offered them an implicit US guarantee on their investments.

The high returns offered on short-term Mexican government bonds were also extremely attractive to individual and institutional investors. Both the dollar-indexed and the peso-denominated short-term bonds (the *tesobono* and the *cete*, respectively) offered returns that far exceeded returns available elsewhere, especially in the US where lower interest rates during 1993 encouraged investors to look abroad. Attracted by these high returns, portfolio investment began in 1990 to flood Mexico's debt and equity markets (see Table 2.2). Partly as a consequence, the stock market index gained value every year after 1989 (except for 1994; see Table 2.2). During this period of increased private capital inflows, the peso was fixed at a progressively overvalued rate (in nominal and real terms) by the government.

Table 2.2 Mexico: data on net private capital flows (US $ billions) and annual % change in the stock market index, 1980–1996

	1980	1989	1991	1993	1994	1995	1996
PI	0	0	4.4	14.3	4.5	0.5	3.9
DFI	2.2	3.0	4.8	4.4	11.0	9.5	7.6
Loans	6.8	−1.5	4.2	2.5	4.6	16.3	4.3
STK	—	98.0	127.7	47.9	−8.7	16.7	21.0

Sources: PI, DFI and LOAN data are from *Global Development Finance*, 1998, vol. 1, World Bank, Washington, DC, 1998; stock index data are from the *Emerging Stock Markets Factbook*, 1997, International Finance Corporation, Washington, DC, 1997.

Notes: PI = net portfolio equity flows; DFI = Net foreign direct investment; Loans = net flow of long-term debt (excluding IMF loans); STK = annual % change in Mexican stock market price index (1996 data are preliminary); STK Mexico = BMV general (Oct. 1978 = 0.7816).

The emergence of the crisis

A tightening of US monetary policy beginning in February 1994 began to diminish the appeal of Mexican portfolio investment. By April 1994 the Mexican bubble began to lose steam, completely collapsing in December of that year. During 1994 the stock market lost 30 per cent of its value and there were several speculative attacks on the peso. In efforts to stabilize the peso, the government drew down $10 billion dollars of foreign exchange reserves (Dornbusch and Werner, 1994). The conjunction of this financial instability, the Chiapas revolt, and the assassination of the leading Presidential candidate led President Ernesto Zedillo to devalue the peso by 40 per cent on December 20, 1994, and to float the peso just two days later. Rather than stabilize Mexican financial markets, however, the depreciation triggered a cycle of portfolio investor exit and peso depreciation – the combined effect of which was financial crisis. Within the first month of 1995 alone the Mexican government drew down almost 50 per cent of its foreign exchange reserves in efforts to stabilize the peso (*Economist*, 2/4/95).

With the peso and Mexican markets entering a free fall, the dismal state of Mexican financial markets triggered fears of global financial contagion. This contagion scenario involved what was seen as the Mexican government's near certain default on short-term bonds – the *cetes* and especially the *tesebonos*. In Ponzi fashion the Mexican government had been deficit financing its expenditures and obligations with short-term debt, rendering the government vulnerable to a shock from financial markets. The Mexican economy's vulnerability to a financial crisis was exacerbated by the fact that the government's foreign exchange reserves totaled $6b at the end of 1994 and that *tesebonos* worth $29b were due to mature in 1995 (*Finance and Development*, 1997).

The Clinton administration and financial industry analysts argued aggressively that default on Mexican government bonds would trigger a general flight from Mexican financial markets and a further collapse of the peso. Not only did this conjure visions of disaster within Mexico, but it was also seen as the harbinger of significant problems within the US, given its deepening integration with Mexico. The Mexican crisis also led to predictions of systemic financial crisis in other emerging markets, as investors turned bearish on these markets. When this flight did indeed occur, it was termed the "tequila effect."

The Clinton administration responded to the crisis in February 1995 by pressing for a bailout. In exchange for a $20 billion US bailout and $28 billion in international loans, the Mexican government committed to further the 1980s reform agenda of privatization, stabilization, and liberalization. It also agreed to implement restrictive monetary policy, to reduce budget and current account deficits, and to increase the value-added tax and the prices of goods produced by the state. More controversial than the Mexican government's renewed commitment to neoliberalism were the requirements that the majority of the bailout funds be used to cover bond obligations, that the government be able to draw on a $10 billion portion of the bailout earmarked as an emergency fund only at the discretion of the US, that the government get permission from the US for major economic policy decisions, and that the receipts of Mexico's state-owned oil company, Pemex, be used as collateral for the US loans and guarantees.

Though Mexico suffered a severe recession from the fourth quarter of 1994 to the third quarter of 1995 (involving a collapse in output and employment and large increases in inflation, loan defaults, and bank distress), the Mexican economy was seen to have been rehabilitated by 1997 (Lopez, 1997). The Mexican government repaid its bailout loans (with interest) ahead of schedule, economic growth improved impressively in 1996–7, and portfolio and direct foreign investment returned to the country (see Table 2.2). However, the return of private foreign capital was largely driven by foreign investors' purchases of Mexican assets and firms at vastly deflated prices. Thus, while increased openness stimulated the private capital inflows that boosted the economy in 1996–7, these same inflows also reintroduced the possibility that the economy could be destabilized by a new cycle of investor exit and currency depreciation. Moreover, the country's very success in attracting new private capital inflows caused the peso to appreciate. Because of the economy's increased growth in 1996–7 and because of the appreciation of the peso (as well as the decline in world oil prices in 1997), Mexico ran a current account deficit in 1997 (and a larger deficit was projected for 1998). Should the deterioration in the current account reignite investors' fears, the increased openness of the economy makes it more likely that the country could experience a new crisis.

Increased risk potential and constrained autonomy in the Mexican crisis

I now turn to a brief theoretical examination of the causes and consequence of the Mexican crisis. My principal argument is that the structural roots of the crisis were not based in the country's peculiar combination of political corruption, social-political instability and economic mismanagement. Rather, the crisis in Mexico was principally a result of the government's failure to control portfolio investment flows.

Constrained policy autonomy

Prior to the crisis, an "ex-ante" constraint on policy autonomy was apparent in Mexico. The attraction of large inflows of portfolio investment after 1989 resulted from the neoliberal reforms proscribed by the Brady Plan. The need to attract high levels of portfolio investment inflows – given the low levels of foreign lending and aid and the low domestic savings rate – meant that it was necessary for the Mexican government to orient macroeconomic policy toward the objectives of portfolio investors.

When the crisis occurred in 1994, an "ex-post" constraint on policy autonomy obtained. In this context, the government was compelled to try to stem the investor exit and stabilize the peso by tightening monetary policy and expending foreign exchange reserves. This strategy further destabilized financial markets as investors recognized that the government's resources were inadequate to meet bond obligations and to protect the value of the peso. Furthermore, the pursuit of contractionary monetary policy induced a serious recession and aggravated social dislocation in Mexico. The depletion of foreign exchange reserves also impaired the government's ability to ease the dislocation following the crisis and its aftermath.

The stringent bailout provisions were another instance of an ex-post constraint on policy autonomy. The influence of the US and the IMF over Mexican policy was increased by the bailout, and the entire import of policy in the post-crisis period has been aimed at restoring investor confidence via contractionary monetary and fiscal policies.

Increased risk potential

Increased risk potential, too, was in evidence. The portfolio investment inflows following 1989 provided the government and the private sector with resources to which they might not have otherwise had access. But the liquidity of this investment in the context of financial openness, meant that the December 1994 devaluation and the tightening of US monetary policy could further destabilize markets and trigger additional outflows and peso depreciations. Thus, the financial openness that is a precondition of portfolio inflows makes the threat of an investor stampede more apparent. In order to try to contain the crisis, the bailout provisions introduced greater foreign influence in economic decision making. By further opening the economy to capital inflows as the neoliberal tenor of the bailout required, the vulnerability of the Mexican economy to future crises was exacerbated, possibly necessitating future bailouts and introducing further foreign intervention in the economy.

The crisis of 1997–8: exceptionalism redux

The "Asian miracle" economies earned this designation because of their rapid industrialization and high rates of GDP and export growth in the 1980s and 1990s. Given what seemed like the remarkable success of these economies, they were collectively taken by analysts – across the political spectrum – to represent a model that offered valuable lessons to countries seeking to overcome the challenges of late development.[3] Up until the first wave of crisis emerged in Thailand in May 1997, investment analysts remained optimistic on Southeast Asia, and more strikingly, the IMF–WB remained sanguine on the region's prospects. Indeed, as recently as a few months before the IMF bailouts of Thailand and South Korea, the Fund issued reports praising both countries for proper "macroeconomic management" (NYT, 1/4/98).

The rapid evolution of the Southeast Asian economies was the outcome of numerous factors, including a favorable world economic climate, the region's geopolitical significance during the Cold War which gave it access to much foreign aid, and the presence of highly effective illiberal "developmental states."

Currencies were heavily managed by the state; in most cases the currency was pegged to the US dollar (and either fixed completely or allowed to fluctuate within a narrow band). The currency peg (along with the state's general integration with the financial sector) contributed to the stability of Southeast Asian economies during the years of high growth. The currency peg was critical in two other respects as well. The general depreciation of the US dollar relative to the yen that followed the September 1985 Plaza Accord significantly enhanced the global competitiveness of Southeast Asian exports. At the same time, the general appreciation of the yen relative to the US dollar encouraged inward Japanese direct foreign investment.

As can be seen on Table 2.1, the volume of inward portfolio investment to the Southeast Asian (and other emerging) economies began to increase dramatically in the late 1980s. These portfolio investment inflows helped fuel the boom in speculative activities across the region by providing firms with capital and governments with a means to finance their current account deficits. During this time, individual and especially institutional investors sought to capitalize on the high returns available in these booming economies. These economies became even more attractive to investors as they began to embark on programs of internal and external financial liberalization in the late 1980s and early 1990s. Moreover, investors were drawn to Southeast Asian markets as conventional wisdom on investment prospects in the US soured in the face of its loss of industrial leadership in the late 1980s and following the stock market crash of 1987.

Private lending to and within Southeast Asia also grew dramatically during the boom years of the late 1980s and 1990s. This high degree of leveraging was made possible by a number of circumstances. Rampant real estate speculation throughout the region resulted in property value inflation, and hence induced a general inflation in the value of loan collateral. In the context of rising collateral values, domestic and international lenders were eager to make available low-cost loans to the private sector. A January 29, 1998, study by the Institute for International Finance reports that "foreign banks fell over themselves to lend [the region] more money year after year" (NYT, 1/30/98). The total private sector debt held by Southeast Asian borrowers rose to dramatic heights through the mid-1990s. According to the Bank for International Settlements (BIS), the total private sector debt held by Southeast Asian borrowers (excluding Singapore and Hong Kong) was $307b in December 1995, $367b in December 1996, and $389b in June 1997 (NYT, 1/28/98). The same BIS study reports that the largest proportion of the $389b in foreign loans made to the region (again excluding Singapore and Hong Kong) by June 1997 was made by Japanese lenders (32 per cent of the loans), followed by German and French lenders (respectively, 12 per cent and 10 per cent of the loans), and US and UK lenders (each accounting for 8 per cent of the loans) (NYT, 1/28/98).

In many cases, the ability of domestic banks to extend credit was enhanced by direct and indirect governmental support for lending to targeted sectors and firms. The lending base of domestic banks was substantially enhanced by international financial integration which gave domestic banks and borrowers access to low-cost yen- and US dollar-denominated loans. When both US and Japanese interest rates were relatively low, banks in these countries lent vast sums in dollars and yen directly to Southeast Asian firms, while also extending dollar- and yen-denominated loans to banks in the region (which, in turn, lent these funds to domestic firms). As Table 2.3 shows, Southeast Asian borrowers held a large percentage of hard-currency denominated loans during the late 1980s and 1990s. As the boom in Southeast Asian economies unfolded in the mid-1990s a regional division of labor emerged. Wage costs in the "older tigers" like South Korea started rising; these cost pressures led to production shifts to new low-wage centers in the region. In this context, the "younger tiger" economies of the Philippines, Thailand and Indonesia began to experience rapid growth along with many other aspects of the earlier Southeast Asian boom.

Table 2.3 Currency composition of long-term debt (%), 1980–1996

Country		1980	1989	1991	1993	1995	1996
Indonesia	DM	7.8	5.2	4.9	4.1	4.9	4.8
	Yen	20.0	34.4	35.7	37.6	35.3	34.5
	US $	43.5	24.6	19.4	19.9	21.5	24.3
Malaysia	DM	3.3	11.2	4.6	3.0	—	0.8
	Yen	19.0	33.9	36.1	37.5	—	28.0
	US $	36.7	32.6	29.8	29.4	—	55.7
Philippines	DM	2.0	1.6	1.6	1.4	1.5	1.6
	Yen	21.9	30.6	34.3	38.3	36.9	35.3
	US $	51.6	40.6	32.9	30.4	31.5	33.8
South Korea	DM	3.7	3.9	5.2	4.2	—	—
	Yen	16.6	27.1	31.4	32.0	—	—
	US $	53.5	35.3	39.3	45.7	—	—
Thailand	DM	4.7	3.1	3.7	2.3	—	2.1
	Yen	25.3	41.4	45.6	50.1	—	45.4
	US $	41.0	22.9	19.1	22.6	—	32.1
Brazil	DM	8.1	7.9	9.3	5.8	4.8	4.3
	Yen	8.5	5.6	7.5	6.4	6.3	5.8
	US $	67.8	64.1	59.4	63.0	67.4	69.2
Russia	DM	—	28.9	38.6	24.4	24.8	22.4
	Yen	—	3.8	2.7	1.7	1.9	1.6
	US $	—	33.6	34.3	62.5	62.1	65.5
Mexico	DM	4.3	4.2	3.9	3.7	3.0	3.5
	Yen	1.4	10.6	7.2	8.8	7.5	7.7
	US $	78.7	58.9	61.8	60.6	66.1	67.8

Sources: Data on currency composition of debt are from *Global Development Finance*, 1998, vol. 1, World Bank, Washington, DC, 1998.

Notes: DM (%) = % of long-term debt owed in Deutschmarks; Yen (%) = % of long-term debt owed in yen; US $ (%) = % of long-term debt owed in US dollars; data on Hong Kong and Singapore are not available.

Crises in the Asian "miracle economies"

However, by mid-1996 the region began to encounter a number of difficulties. The real estate boom began to lose steam. The decline in property and hence collateral values was highly problematic for the domestic banking industry, given that it was so heavily involved in real estate. Moreover, as the Japanese economy itself began to experience serious problems, Japanese foreign direct investment to Southeast Asia began to slow. Lending from US banks to the region also began to slow during the first six months of 1997. At the same time as US banks were beginning to exit the region, a recent BIS study reports that some Japanese, German, French and British banks – faced with slow growth and sluggish profits at home – began to capitalize on the growing demand for loans by Asian borrowers and began to increase their lending to the region (NYT, 1/28/98). However, by the fall of 1997 even these banks began a dramatic curtailment of lending to the region (NYT, 1/28/98; NYT 1/30/98).

By late 1996 the region was also beginning to confront other difficulties as well. The cost advantages of low-wage production in Southeast Asia were not sufficient to counter the decline in export competitiveness brought about by the appreciation of the US dollar following the 1995 US–Japanese agreement to appreciate the dollar and depreciate the yen. The dollar's appreciation after 1995 also made it more expensive for Southeast Asian borrowers to repay their dollar-denominated loans. Finally, as investors once again became bullish on the US economy in the context of the US stock markets' ascent and rising levels of economic growth, portfolio investors turned their attentions away from emerging economies in general (and Southeast Asia, in particular) and towards the booming US economy. And once the first signs of trouble emerged in Thailand on May 7, 1997, investor skittishness on the region only intensified. It is to these events that we now turn.

Thailand

The Thai economy had been experiencing a speculative boom since the early 1990s. Increases in share and real estate prices and commercial construction activity were particularly important components of the boom. As elsewhere in the region, the stock market's performance was fed by inflows of foreign portfolio investment (see Table 2.1). Foreign portfolio investors were very much attracted to the high returns available on Thai markets following the deregulation that began in 1990. Real estate and commercial construction activity were fueled by the abundance of relatively low-cost short-term loans made available by Japanese and US lenders and by Thai banks (themselves relying on short-term loans from foreign lenders). Foreign lenders were eager to extend these loans because of the perceived strong growth prospects of the economy and the region. These expectations of continued growth were maintained even though Thailand had $60b in foreign debt and only $40b in foreign exchange reserves (NYT, 8/1/97).

News of problems in the Thai economy emerged on May 7, 1997. On that day, the Thai currency – the baht – began to come under pressure by speculators who began selling off their holdings of the currency. This sell-off followed the release of adverse economic news about the Thai economy (that suggested that the boom was ending) and predictions that the Japanese central bank was poised to raise interest rates (*Finance and Development*, 1997). The predicted rise in Japanese interest rates was problematic for Thailand's highly-leveraged private sector which was highly dependent on both yen- (and dollar-) denominated loans (see Table 2.3). In the context of these (feared) adverse developments, investors began to predict that the Thai government would be unable to maintain the baht's fixity, and hence would be forced to devalue the currency. Throughout May 1997 investors exited baht and baht-denominated investments (the latter circumstance caused precipitous declines in Thai share prices).

The government tried in May 1997 to stem speculation against the baht by increasing interest rates (and hence raising the cost of borrowing funds to purchase baht), implementing selective capital controls aimed at making it prohibitively expensive for foreigners to purchase baht offshore, and buying baht with its own foreign currency reserves (NYT, 10/24/97). Investors were not calmed by these measures however. Indeed, as Thai interest rates rose, stock and land prices fell because borrowing became more costly (WSJ, 11/26/97). As the sell-off of baht and baht-denominated investments continued through the spring and early summer of 1997, investors in other emerging markets (such as Malaysia, Indonesia, and the Philippines) began a general exit from these markets as well. This contagion effect (termed the "Asian flu") paralleled the events that followed the investor exit from Mexico.

Rather than devalue the baht, the Thai central bank on July 2, 1997, ended its efforts to defend the currency's fixity, and announced that the baht would henceforth float with market forces. The currency immediately fell by 20 per cent. Fearing further sales of baht and baht-denominated assets, the central bank and the government took action to try to stem speculation by raising the discount rate by 2 per cent to 12.5 per cent and restricting sales by foreigners of Thai stocks (*Economist*, 7/12/97). Following pressure from the government, private banks refused to provide short-term credit to speculators (*Finance and Development*, 1997). Given the intense demand for funds to borrow baht and given the government's efforts to curb such borrowing, offshore interest rates rose to 1,300 per cent per annum. The rise in Thai and foreign interest rates and the collapse in property values led to loan defaults and losses for Thai banks. The bhat's depreciation compounded debt and bank distress as Thai borrowers faced dramatic increases in the domestic currency value of their hard-currency repayment obligations.

Discussions of a Thai bailout began in the summer of 1997. Following the US rejection of Japan's offer to finance a regional assistance fund, an IMF bailout of $17 billion was finalized on August 11, 1997 (NYT, 10/24/97). The bailout stipulated that the Thai government was to reduce public spending, to end public and quasi-public support for failing firms and banks (the government suspended operations of 42 firms and 58 of the country's 91 finance companies) (FT, 10/8/97), to raise taxes (the VAT was raised to 10 per cent from 7 per cent), and to remove the capital controls imposed in May 1997 (*Economist*, 7/12/97; NYT, 8/12/97). Thai interest rates also continued to rise as the central bank attempted to stem portfolio investment outflows and attract new inflows.

Following the crisis and the bailout, living conditions in Thailand worsened as unemployment, prices, and interest rates rose (as numerous banks and factories closed, while still others consolidated operations). Bank lending fell (stalling production) and loan arrears and bankruptcies rose (NYT, 9/21/97). Social protest against the government and political instability emerged as well: on October 21, 1997, 2,000 business and office workers protested in the streets of Bangkok (NYT, 10/2/97); and the Thai government witnessed numerous personnel changes (NYT, 10/24/97).

In searching for answers as to what went wrong in Thailand, the conventional wisdom that quickly emerged among analysts was that they were misled by a corrupt Thai government and by cronyist Thai banks. The government, it was asserted, misled investors by failing to reveal that nearly all of its $40 billion in official reserves were committed to supporting the baht's fixity (NYT, 12/14/97; *Economist*, 8/9/97). Similarly, it was asserted that foreign lenders were simultaneously unaware of the extent of banks' and borrowers' involvement in real estate speculation, of the poor performance of Thai banks (although as early as 1996 13 per cent of all loans were non-performing) (FT, 10/8/97), of the links between Thai banks and failing firms, of the extent of the country's foreign indebtedness (valued at $60 billion) and its large current account deficit (equal to 8 per cent of GDP in 1996) (NYT, 8/1/97; *Economist*, 7/12/97).

Malaysia

In a region marked by high levels of real estate and construction activity, Malaysia's commercial building boom was notable. Prior to the crisis, Malaysia was embarked on plans to build airports and dams, to add to its already impressive landscape of skyscrapers, and to situate itself as a regional center for high technology development. Like Thailand, Malaysia's rapid growth was highly attractive to portfolio and direct foreign investors and to foreign lenders until the crisis emerged (see Table 2.1). Following the exit of these same investors and lenders, analysts devoted much attention to the role of pervasive corruption in bringing about the economy's collapse (BW, 9/22/97).

Pressure against the Malaysian currency, the ringgit, began almost immediately following the floating (and concomitant depreciation) of the Thai baht on July 2, 1997 (*Finance and Development*, 1997). Following the fall in the value of the ringgit, investors exited ringgit-denominated investment (triggering a fall in stock prices) and the banking system began to experience serious difficulties as foreign credit became both expensive and scarce and as deteriorating real estate market conditions undermined the value of collateral (NYT, 9/22/97).

In efforts to reverse the outflow of portfolio investment and to discourage further speculation against the ringgit, the Central Bank and the government of Prime Minister Mohamad Mahathir in July 1997 introduced a number of measures. Overnight, interest rates were increased to 50 per cent on July 10 in order to slow the pace of borrowing by domestic and foreign investors seeking to hedge and/or speculate on the ringgit's further decline (*Economist*, 7/12/97). As in Thailand, the central bank introduced targeted, informal capital controls (which mandated that local banks not provide funds to foreign speculators) in efforts to stem foreign speculation against the currency. The government also ordered restrictions on stock transactions that rewarded investors for declines in stock prices ("short trades") and moved to prop up stock prices for domestic investors. These actions, in conjunction with the growing crisis in Thailand and Indonesia, triggered further portfolio investor flight from Malaysia. The Prime Minister's widely publicized denouncement of foreign currency traders (giving special mention to trader George Soros) at the annual meeting of the IMF–WB on September 21, 1997, exacerbated the flight from the Malaysian stock market as well (NYT, 9/22/97).

In the face of the fall 1997 round of portfolio investor flight, currency depreciation and stock market decline, the Prime Minister ultimately ceded to pressure to reverse the controls implemented in July of that year. Though Malaysia's banking system was not on as shaky a footing as was that of Thailand,[4] the government responded to the crisis by closing 50 finance companies (FT, 10/8/97). Moody's predicted that 5 of the country's 15 commercial banks would be allowed to fail by the end of 1998 (FT, 10/8/97). Note that Malaysia was one of the few countries in the region not to have requested an international bailout.

Indonesia

During the 1990s, international portfolio and direct foreign investors and foreign lenders alike were quite taken with the rapidly growing economy of Indonesia (see Table 2.1). Its currency, the rupiah, was pegged to the dollar (and allowed to fluctuate relative to the dollar within a 12 per cent band) (WJS, 8/15/97).[5] And as elsewhere, following the crisis, analysts focused much attention on the wasteful and corrupt diversion of resources to the expensive "show projects" with which Indonesian President Suharto and his family were very much preoccupied (WSJ, 10/13/97). Local banks – which were significantly controlled by the government – were heavily leveraged as key participants in these show projects and in real estate speculation. As early as 1996, the Indonesian banking sector was experiencing difficulties (bad loans/total loans were 9 per cent) (FT, 10/8/97), but it was not until the crisis emerged that widespread bank failures began to occur. As elsewhere in the region, the Indonesian private sector accumulated a large percentage of dollar- and yen-denominated loans throughout the 1990s (see Table 2.3) – indeed as of February 1998, the Indonesian private sector had $65b in dollar-denominated debt (NYT, 1/27/98).

Following the difficulties that emerged in Thailand on July 2, 1997, investors began exiting Malaysian, Philippine and Indonesian currency and stockholdings because of the view that all of these economies confronted similar problems. In contradistinction to the Malaysian and the Thai cases, the government did not respond to these pressures by attempting to restrict market transactions. Rather, the Indonesian central bank responded to pressure against its currency by widening the rupiah's trading range on July 11, 1997, and by spending about $500m to maintain the wider band (WSJ, 8/15/97). When the currency continued to come under speculative pressure (falling to the bottom of its new band on July 21, 1997), the central bank on August 14, 1997, revoked the trading band entirely. The decision to float the currency triggered a new round of investor exit from the currency and stock markets.

In the context of these developments, the Indonesian government in late October 1997 approached the IMF and the US for assistance. By November 5, 1997, agreement was reached on a $40b bailout package. In exchange for the bailout, the Indonesian government was required to implement a comprehensive program of reform involving privatization, reductions in government subsidies and spending, financial liberalization and the closure of distressed financial institutions (on November 2, 1997, 16 distressed banks were closed) (NYT, 11/2/97; WSJ, 11/3/97). These measures had the same immediate political, economic and social effects as had similar plans throughout the region.

Circumstances took a second negative turn early in January 1998. On January 8, the rupiah plunged after President Suharto unveiled large new spending projects, and hence seemed to be repudiating the spirit of the austerity mandated by the November 1997 bailout. The IMF responded to these events by threatening to terminate the $40b bailout package. Predictably, investors immediately exited the country, causing the currency and share prices to decline further. By January 15, President Suharto announced a new comprehensive reform program involving liberalization of the economy, an end to the special privileges granted to politically favored projects and the rehabilitation of the banking sector (IMF Survey, 2/9/98). The banking reforms include measures to guarantee deposits, to end curbs on foreign ownership of banks, and to create a special agency that would rehabilitate failing banks (NYT, 1/27/98). This new commitment to austerity and reform calmed investors and led to a stabilization of the currency. In this context, the IMF renewed its support package on January 26, 1998 (IMF Survey, 2/9/98).

Indonesia continued to face severe economic and political instability following Suharto's January 1998 recommitment to reform and austerity. On January 29, 1998, the government initiated a "temporary pause" in payments on billions of dollars in private debt to overseas lenders (NYT, 1/28/98). Throughout February 1998 and again in May of that year, the country was wracked by riots, looting and violence over price increases. These developments took a particularly ugly racial turn, as the violence and looting focused on ethnic Chinese merchants (NYT, 2/15/98). The government also continued to spar with the IMF over monetary reform – indeed on February 15, 1998, the government announced that it was planning to implement a currency board, a plan which was soundly rejected by the IMF (NYT, 2/15/98; NYT, 2/10/98). Following (successful) efforts at ousting President Suharto, the new Indonesian administration in May 1998 committed to accelerate the pace of reform.

The Philippines

As was the case in Malaysia and Indonesia, the outward signs of difficulty in the Philippine economy emerged almost immediately following the decision to float the Thai baht on July 2, 1997 (NYT, 8/12/97). Within a few days after the Thai decision, investors began to exit the Philippine peso and liquidate Philippine portfolio investments (as well as Indonesian and Malaysian investments). Overnight interest rates rose to 30 per cent in efforts to protect the currency and to stem further outflows. These efforts were ultimately futile, however. The pace of investor exit accelerated further on July 7, 1997, following the release of a press report that indicated that the Philippine Finance Minister was considering devaluing the peso[6] (*Economist*, 7/12/97). Faced with this unfolding crisis, the Philippine Central Bank followed the route of its neighbors and allowed the peso to float beginning on July 11, 1997.

Investor exit and the depreciation of the peso had similar social, economic, and political consequences as elsewhere in the region. One important consequence of the depreciation was its effect on borrower and bank distress. Insofar as 25 per cent of all foreign loans held by Philippine banks in 1997 were dollar-denominated (down from 30.4 per cent in 1993; see Table 2.3), the depreciation introduced significant repayment difficulties (WSJ, 10/6/97). These difficulties exacerbated those introduced by the higher cost of peso-denominated loans.

In mid-July 1997, the Philippine government also approached the IMF for assistance. On July 18, the IMF agreed (with similar conditions and consequences as elsewhere) to provide the government with a $4b assistance package (NYT, 8/12/97). In contrast to elsewhere in the region, bank closures were not a part of the Philippine bailout plan. This is because high loan loss rates had not been as significant a problem in the Philippines as elsewhere in Southeast Asia (in 1996 the ratio of bad loans to total loans was only 3 per cent) (FT, 10/8/97). However, banking distress began to emerge in mid-1998 as the peso's depreciation increased the cost of foreign loan obligations.

South Korea

The most startling development in Southeast Asia was the collapse of the region's prototypical "miracle economy," South Korea. The conventional wisdom on the collapse was that the regional crisis exposed the failure of an economy whose strength was based on the corrupt and opaque business practices of family-owned financial–industrial conglomerates (the *chaebols*).[7] Analysts also devoted much attention to exposing the duplicity of the Korean government which, it claimed, misled foreign investors and multilateral institutions by secretly bailing out banks with large portfolios of failed loans that stemmed from domestic and international misadventures (NYT, 11/21/97).

In the spate of "post-mortems" on the South Korean economy, relatively little attention was paid to the obvious problems engendered by the dependence of Korean industry and banks (both inside and outside of the *chaebol*) on direct foreign investment from Japan and on portfolio investment inflows and loans from foreign banks.[8] While the South Korean economy was growing rapidly, US, Japanese and European lenders were eager to extend short-term low-cost dollar- and yen-denominated loans directly to South Korea's highly leveraged industrial and financial firms (the latter, in turn, then extended loans to local industry) (see Table 2.3). As of February 1998, South Korean banks owed foreign banks $153b ($23.4b of which was short term until the January 1998 restructuring of some foreign debt) (NYT, 2/10/98). As Chang (1998a) noted, the 30 new South Korean merchant banks were among the most aggressive borrowers of short-term funds on foreign markets, accounting for $20b of the $153b owed to foreign lenders.[9] Domestic indebtedness was also startlingly high: as of February 1998, South Korean firms had $300b in outstanding short-term obligations to local banks (with 50–75 per cent of this debt coming due in three to six months) (NYT, 2/10/98). As of February 1998, at least 20 per cent ($60–$65b) of domestic loans were in default (NYT, 2/10/98).

Once the decline in the South Korean won began (itself triggered by the flight of portfolio investors, foreign lenders and Japanese direct foreign investors, as well as the regional crisis), the currency and the Seoul stock market steadily began to lose value during November 1997–January 1998. When the sell-off of the won began in early November 1997, the government initially vowed that it would not let the won fall below the rate of 1,000 won to one US dollar (IMF Survey, 2/9/98). As the exit from the won intensified, the government tried to calm investors by expanding the won's daily band of flexibility to 10 per cent (up from its daily band of 2¼ per cent) and by spending $10b (which amounted to over one-third) of its foreign exchange reserves in efforts to protect the currency (DP, 12/16/97). But as elsewhere in the region, the government's gesture toward greater currency flexibility only heightened investors' fears about an eventual devaluation of the won. When even this wider band proved untenable, the government on November 17, 1997, let the won float. As investor exit and the won's depreciation continued through November 1997, it became increasingly difficult for Korean banks and industry to meet their foreign currency-denominated loan obligations (DP, 12/16/97).

Following ten consecutive days of declining prices on the Seoul stock market and a 24 per cent loss in value of the won against the US dollar (since late October 1997), the government and the IMF on December 3, 1997, reached agreement on a record $57b bailout. The bailout funds were primarily intended to supplement the foreign currency reserves of the Korean Central Bank (Bank of Korea). These reserves were to be used to aid Korean industry's efforts to re-finance their foreign loans (DP, 12/4/97).

The bailout required South Korea to liquidate and/or restructure its banking system, to open its economy immediately to foreign products, to open its economy to foreign investment by raising the limit on foreign ownership of stock in South Korean companies to 55 per cent, to reduce drastically government spending, and to raise taxes (DP, 12/4/97). In order to draw foreign investment back to Korea, the government announced on December 16, 1997, that it would abolish all remaining controls on its currency, that it would issue $10b of state bonds overseas, and that it was willing to allow foreigners to purchase domestic commercial banks (DP, 12/16/97).

After signing the bailout, the South Korean economy continued to decline. By December 21, 1997, it became clear that large-scale defaults on the private sector's $100–$110b in obligations (in hard currency) to foreign creditors were imminent.[10] On December 23, the South Korean government began negotiating with foreign banks to defer the private sector's loan payments. In order to preclude these defaults, the World Bank and the Asian Development Bank immediately announced that they had respectively extended to South Korea emergency loans of $3b and $2b. That same week, the Clinton administration announced that it would join with other industrial countries in supplying the country with additional emergency aid of $10b (DP, 12/24/97). A group of the world's major commercial and investment banks announced on December 29 that they would rollover $15b in South Korean obligations until the end of January 1998. Following these announcements – and the passage by Korea's National Assembly on December 29 of a financial reform program involving further liberalization and opening of financial sector – the IMF on December 30, 1997, approved an early disbursement of a $2b portion of the bailout funds to the government (IMF Survey, 1/12/98). When in January 1998, it became apparent that it would be difficult – if not impossible – for South Korean firms to meet their foreign repayment obligations, a coalition of thirteen international banks agreed on January 29 to restructure $24b of the short-term debt scheduled to come due during 1998 (IMF Survey, 2/9/98). The restructuring involved swapping these short-term loans for new debt that would come due in one to three years.

As elsewhere in the region, the economic restructuring necessitated by the bailout was associated with serious economic, social, and political dislocation. As the availability of credit diminished and its cost rose, corporate bankruptcies and unemployment increased. The February 1998 changes in laws governing the country's lifetime employment policies resulted in further increases in unemployment.

Singapore and Hong Kong: the Southeast Asian crises that never were

It is notable that the economies of Singapore and Hong Kong were ultimately not destabilized by the events that affected their neighbors. In general, these economies were distinguished from those of their neighbors by their low levels of hard-currency foreign indebtedness and by the fact that their monetary authorities had very large holdings of hard currency reserves. For these reasons, the initial investor exit from Singapore and Hong Kong (in August 1997 and September–October 1997, respectively) never escalated into a fully fledged panic because investors had little reason to fear loan defaults and/or significant currency depreciations.

SINGAPORE

In the context of the unfolding regional crisis, investors began to exit investments in Singapore's stock market and began to sell their holdings of the Singapore dollar late in the summer of 1997. Since the Singapore dollar was among the region's only freely floating currency, the wave of investor exit that began on August 12, 1997, induced a dramatic depreciation of the currency. Indeed, the currency fell to a three-year low against the US dollar during August 1997. The Singapore Monetary Authority did not make any effort to intervene in currency markets in order to stabilize the currency. However, it did take steps to stem portfolio investment outflow and reverse the wave of currency sales by raising interest rates and by letting it be known that it had hard currency reserves sufficient to finance up to six months of imports (BW, 8/11/97). These measures were successful and the flight ended shortly after it began.

HONG KONG

Investor flight from the Hong Kong stock market (the *Hang Seng*) began on September 2, 1997 (NYT, 9/2/97). Investor exit continued through the fall of 1997 and accelerated rapidly following a wave of speculation against the Hong Kong dollar in early and mid-October 1997. By October 23–24, 1997, investors were betting heavily that the Hong Kong government would be forced to devalue the currency (which has been pegged at 7.75 Hong Kong dollars to the US dollar since 1984) (NYT, 10/24/97). This investor exit resulted in the single largest one-day drop in the Hong Kong stock market since the Tiananamen Square events of 1989 (when stocks fell by 10.4 per cent on October 24, 1997) (NYT, 10/24/97). Faced with these circumstances the Hong Kong government vowed to defend the fixed value of the currency. To do so, the government raised interest rates quite dramatically – overnight interest rates were raised to 300 per cent – and spent about $1 billion of its $88b in foreign exchange reserves defending the currency's value (WSJ, 11/26/97; NYT, 10/24/97). The government's actions, however, did not have the intended effect of calming investors. This was because Hong Kong stock prices and property values (both of which are at the heart of the economy) fell in response to the dramatic increase in interest rates (NYT, 10/24/97). Stock prices continued to drop throughout October 1997 following further sales by investors. Just a few days after the government tried to stabilize markets, stocks again fell by another 6 per cent (on October 28, 1997) (NYT, 10/28/97).

The investor exit finally ended once it became clear to investors that the Hong Kong government would not renounce the peg and that it was prepared to use its $88b of foreign currency reserves to maintain it. Although the investor exit from Hong Kong ended, clearly the country's high interest rates proved damaging to the economy as stock and property market activity and consumer spending contracted in 1998 (NYT, 2/2/98).

Crises elsewhere in 1997–8

Brazil

In the last few years, the rapidly growing economy of Brazil was an important site of foreign direct and portfolio investment (see Table 2.1). Foreign investors were attracted to the economy because of the opportunities presented by privatization and by the attractive returns available on government bonds. These private capital inflows were made available to the country despite the fact that they served as a principal source of finance for the country's large fiscal and current account deficits (respectively, 5 per cent of GDP and 4.4 per cent of GDP), despite the widely perceived overvaluation of the currency (the real), and despite the potential for social unrest created by the country's notable levels of income and wealth inequality (WSJ 11/7/97; NYT, 10/24/97).

In the fall of 1997, signs of the "Asian flu" appeared in Brazil. As investors began exiting the Hong Kong market, a similar exit from Brazilian markets and the currency began on October 23. On that day, the Brazilian stock market index fell by 8 per cent, only to be followed by another dramatic drop five days later. In all, in the three weeks that followed portfolio investor flight from Hong Kong, the Brazilian stock market lost 40 per cent of its value (in US dollar terms) (BW, 12/29/97). The Brazilian Central Bank tried to stem portfolio investment outflows by quickly doubling the official interest rate to 40 per cent (on October 30, 1997) and by expending approximately $8 billion in foreign currency reserves in efforts to protect the value of the real (NYT, 11/11/97).

In the context of the unfolding Asian and domestic crisis, the President, Fernando Henrique Cardoso, announced on November 11, 1997, a severe austerity program that was designed to boost foreign investors' confidence in the economy (and in the currency) by cutting the budget deficit and raising $15b in revenue (NYT, 2/8/98). The program involved the usual measures of fiscal austerity (coupled with the existing monetary austerity). The program aimed to reduce the budget deficit (to 2–3 per cent of GDP) by raising personal taxes by 10 per cent, increasing taxes on air travel, gasoline and liquor, and reducing government spending on social security, pensions and public employment (NYT, 2/8/98). Since the local stock market index rose after the plan was implemented, it seemed that fiscal and monetary austerity had the intended effect on investor confidence despite (or because of) the economic slowdown these measures induced.

Russia

In the two years leading up to October 1997, the Russian stock market was deemed by investment analysts to be one of the "hottest" emerging markets in the world (BW, 3/24/97). A number of the largest emerging market mutual funds were investing from 2–7 per cent of their assets in the Russian market (BW, 3/24/97). Led by portfolio investor interest in petroleum, telephone and utility stocks, the Russian stock index tripled during the eighteen months prior to October 1997 (NYT, 10/29/97). As in Brazil, portfolio investment continued to flow into Russia despite its well-publicized economic and political problems (e.g., severe tax collection difficulties, payroll arrears involving government employees, business corruption and organized crime).

By late October 1997 an investor flight from Russia emerged (as it was occurring in Brazil, Hong Kong and elsewhere in Southeast Asia). The stock market index fell sharply through late October to early December 1997. Following a particularly dramatic market decline on October 29, the government of President Boris Yeltsin halted trading for several hours and purchased rubles on the open market in efforts to stabilize its value (NYT, 10/29/97). The government also increased interest rates on government bonds to 28 per cent in efforts to prevent further portfolio investment flight and to attract new inflows (DP, 12/6/97). These high interest rates placed increased pressure on the already strained resources of the Russian government.

In view of these circumstances, the Russian government approached the IMF for additional assistance. The IMF agreed to provide Russia with $1.7 billion in exchange for a commitment by the government that it would improve tax collection and lower its spending. However, on November 2, 1997, the IMF decided to suspend the quarterly disbursement of $700m on its loan to Russia because of continued dissatisfaction with the government's tax collection (only about 46 per cent of taxes due were being collected) and the large volume of wages in arrears to government employees (arrears payments of $9.3b) (DP, 12/6/97). Faced with these continuing difficulties and continued investor exit, the Russian government raised interest rates on government bonds to 42 per cent on February 2, 1998 (NYT, 2/2/98). The interest rate increase introduced additional burdens to the economy as interest costs on government debt rose.[11]

Rejecting exceptionalism

In the aftermath of the crisis of 1997–8, something of an "Asian (or Russian or Brazilian) exceptionalism" – that paralleled the earlier "Mexican exceptionalism" – emerged among policy analysts. Like Mexican exceptionalism (Grabel, 1996), the new exceptionalism thesis was also without merit.

Proponents of Asian exceptionalism asserted that the crisis was an outcome of deeply rooted corruption and of the over-regulation of the economy throughout the region (e.g., Rubin's speech at Georgetown University, *Treasury News*, 1/21/98; Safire, 1998). Proponents of the corruption thesis did not explain how the corrupt ties that bound firms and governments throughout Southeast Asia led to crisis in 1997–8 while having led to high growth up until that time. That is, why did corruption become catastrophic only in 1997? And moreover, if corruption was indeed widespread – as was asserted – why then were foreign investors and lenders willing to commit vast resources to these economies for so long?

Some advocates of the corruption thesis argued that it was not the mere presence of corruption that caused the collapse, but rather it was the *intensifica-tion* of corruption that triggered the collapse. Granting this point, however, overlooks the structural circumstances that allowed corruption and risk taking to intensify prior to the crisis in some countries. In work on South Korea, Chang (1997, 1998a, 1998b) showed that corruption in fact did intensify because of the government's decision to curtail dramatically its *regulation* of the economy (by terminating longstanding programs of investment coordination and managed competition and by promoting financial liberalization). Thus, according to Chang, to the extent that corruption and risk•taking intensified in South Korea it was an outcome of the government's decision to under- (and not over-) regulate the economy.

Chang's argument regarding South Korea is also more generally applicable to the region. In the case of the region's economies, there were moves toward external and internal financial liberalization. Internal financial liberalization allowed domestic banks to become heavily involved in foreign operations and allowed them to participate in riskier domestic lending activities (themselves made possible by liberalization). The promotion of stock markets along with external financial liberalization contributed to the creation of an attractive investment climate for international portfolio investors. And in the broader context of the speculative booms that liberalization touched off in the region, higher rates of leveraging by the private sector became the norm. Thus, to the extent that risk taking and corruption may have intensified throughout the region, its intensification had its roots in changes in government policies and regulatory patterns that created space for these practices to flourish.

Turning to Russia, exceptionalism (regarding corruption, tax evasion, and crime) was similarly problematic as an explanation of the investor exit from that country. Given that these problems were apparent since the collapse of Communism one cannot invoke their discovery in 1997–8 to account for a sudden investor exit from the stock and the government bond market. It was far more reasonable to attribute the exit from Russia and indeed Brazil to general investor skittishness on emerging markets following the collapse of conventional wisdom on Southeast Asia. Thus, Brazil and Russia fell victim to an emerging market contagion made possible by financial openness.

Increased risk potential and constrained autonomy in the crisis of 1997–8 and the Mexican crisis

In what follows I consider the manner in which the general theoretical arguments regarding the problems associated with emerging economies' dependence on private capital flows are applicable to the crisis of 1997–8. I argue that the crisis was principally caused by the failure of the government to control portfolio investment flows and by the private sectors' excessive reliance on hard currency-denominated private loans. In pursuing this mistaken path, the countries involved in the current crisis were exposed to the problems of increased risk potential and constrained policy autonomy. Though these problems are generally applicable to a range of countries, they emerged with varying force due to different initial conditions.

Constrained autonomy

The ex-ante constraint on policy autonomy did not pertain to the countries of Southeast Asia in the years prior to the current crisis, given their recent histories of rapid economic growth. In the context of the sanguine conventional wisdom on Southeast Asia prior to the crisis, lenders and investors were willing to overlook and even *reinterpret* (per the World Bank's *Asian Miracle Report*) the distinctly non-neoliberal strategies associated with the Asian development model.

In sharp contrast to Southeast Asia, governments and central banks in Brazil and Russia (and Mexico prior to its crisis) had to overcome portfolio and direct foreign investors' perceptions that these economies were risky.[12] In the case of Brazil and Mexico, investors had to be convinced that the economies had been rehabilitated. Rehabilitation was necessary in the Latin American cases because of the region's difficulties during the debt crisis of the 1980s, and because of the history of high inflation, exchange rate volatility, low growth, and the proclivity of "heterodox" governments to nationalize foreign investment. In the Russian case, the government, too, had to overcome investors' fears of high inflation and the country's poor record on tax collection, crime and political stability. In view of these perceived problems, it was necessary that economic and social policy in Brazil, Mexico and Russia be strongly neoliberal as a precondition for the maintenance of investor confidence, and hence in order to attract high levels of private investment. Governments had to pursue privatization and financial and economic liberalization in order to signal private investors and bondholders that it was safe to invest. In Brazil, in particular, the strong profile of President Cardoso's commitment to neoliberal policy at all costs has been critical to the maintenance of private (foreign and domestic) investor confidence.

Thus, in countries such as Russia, Brazil and Mexico, where investor pessimism or disinterest had to be overcome, the credibility of the government's commitment to neoliberal policy was critical to the attraction of private capital flows. For this reason, we can say that the range of macroeconomic and social policies available to these governments was constrained by the overriding objective of attracting private capital flows. By contrast, given the status of the Southeast Asian economies, these governments did not risk repelling private capital by pursuing non-neoliberal strategies.

The evidence on constrained policy autonomy following the crisis (i.e., the ex-post constraint) is strong in the cases of all the countries involved in the crisis of 1997–8 (and Mexico after its crisis). Following the emergence of the crisis in each country, governments and central banks were compelled to take steps to stem the portfolio investment outflow and to prevent the currency from depreciating. These measures principally involved increasing interest rates in order to slow or reverse the investor flight and expending vast quantities of foreign exchange reserves in efforts to stabilize currency and stock prices. These interest rate increases introduced the possibility of defaults on domestic variable rate loans, bank distress, slowdowns in economic activity, rising unemployment, social dislocation and political instability. The depletion of foreign exchange reserves also impaired the government's ability to finance ameliorative policies aimed at easing the dislocation associated with the crisis and its aftermath. Given the problems caused by investor flight and currency depreciation, governments and central banks found it necessary to implement (or intensify in the case of Brazil) macroeconomic policies that would aggravate the consequences of the crisis for the majority of the population and could slow economic activity.

In those countries where a bailout followed the crisis (viz., Indonesia, Thailand, the Philippines, South Korea, and Mexico), all of the bailouts stipulated that governments introduce or intensify neoliberal reform and increase the openness of the economy. The influence of the IMF (and the US in the Mexican case) over macroeconomic and social policy in countries that accepted bailouts was substantially increased. Indeed, the entire direction and import of policy in the post-crisis period was principally aimed at restoring investor confidence and promoting an "Americanization" of these economies via radical neoliberal reform and greater openness to foreign direct and portfolio investment. And in those countries where an IMF bailout was not requested (Malaysia, Brazil, Hong Kong, Singapore) domestic policymakers nevertheless pursued contractionary policies that were markedly similar to those mandated under bailouts elsewhere.

Increased risk potential

The arguments regarding increased risk potential, too, are highly germane to the crisis of 1997–8. To be sure, the expansion of portfolio investment inflows and relatively inexpensive hard currency-denominated loans provided governments and the private sector with resources to which they might not have otherwise had access. These portfolio investment inflows – and the initial rise in stock prices generated by the inflows – no doubt played an important role in stimulating the booms that each of the economies involved in the crisis of 1997–8 experienced. However, the liquidity of this portfolio investment ensured that markets could be destabilized quickly once currencies and stock prices started to come under pressure following investor exit. Such an initial destabilization could – and did – trigger a mutually reinforcing exit of portfolio and currency investors.

A dependence on foreign loans (especially short-term loans) on the part of the private sector in Southeast Asia and foreign bond sales on the part of the public sector in Brazil, Russia and Mexico also introduced increased risk potential to these economies. These economies were rendered vulnerable to the costs of currency depreciations and lender/bondholder herding. When lenders/bondholders began to turn bearish on these economies, currency depreciations of course meant that borrowers faced an increase in the cost of their repayment obligations.

Economic openness also introduced increased risk into the economies involved in the crisis of 1997–8. When US interest rates rose in February 1995, investors began to exit Mexico during that country's crisis. The same dynamic obtained in the current crisis when economic circumstances changed in the US and Japan in 1996–7. Insofar as the bailouts stipulate greater openness on the part of afflicted economies, these economies are rendered more vulnerable to the risk of experiencing the cycle of investor and lender flight followed by currency depreciation and financial crisis.

Financial openness also introduces the possibility of a cross-border contagion. Once one nation realizes the increased risk potential of liquid private capital flows and currency depreciation, it becomes likely that crisis will spread across borders. The likelihood that investors and lenders will see emerging economies in an undifferentiated fashion – the "guilt by association" of the tequila effect or the Asian flu – makes the possibility of cross-border contagion more likely in the case of emerging economies.

The interaction of increased risk potential and constrained autonomy are also relevant to understanding the crisis of 1997–8 and the earlier Mexican crisis. In order to try to contain the crisis of 1997–8 and the earlier Mexican crisis, the bailouts introduced a great deal of external influence in economic decision making. But by further opening the economy to capital inflows (as the neoliberal tenor of the bailouts required), the vulnerability of these economies to future crises may be exacerbated, necessitating future bailouts and increased foreign intervention in the economy. This argument also pertains to those countries that did not receive bailouts (namely, Brazil and Malaysia) since the national governments in these cases initiated reforms that were analogous to those mandated under the bailouts.

Preventing a repeat of the crisis of 1997–8

The measures implemented to address the crisis of 1997–8 are unlikely to prevent their recurrence. Indeed, the increased external orientation and neoliberal reform induced by the crisis render these economies vulnerable to recession and to a repeat of recent history. If there was a silver lining to the crisis of 1997–8 it was that it created some space for policymakers to consider measures that would prevent the recurrence of financial crisis in emerging economies.

This rethinking of the conventional wisdom came from a number of unlikely sources. Malaysian Prime Minister Muhathir's nationalist attacks on international currency speculators (though self-serving) helped indirectly to focus attention on the costs of uncontrolled financial openness in emerging economies. There also seemed to be some signs of a change in thinking on the part of prominent mainstream economists. For example, Stanley Fischer, the IMF's First Deputy Managing Director, made a number of well-publicized speeches in which he expressed doubts about the wisdom of premature capital account liberalization in light of developments in Southeast Asia (NYT, 2/3/98; Fischer, 1997). In Fischer's September 19, 1997, speech at the IMF–WB Annual Meeting in Hong Kong and at a March 9–10, 1998, seminar at the IMF he acknowledged that there was a strong case to be made for phased capital account liberalization where the macroeconomic framework and the financial sector were weak (Fischer, 1997).

During the period where some control is desirable, Fischer argued that these controls should be market-based (as in Chile today) and should be gradually phased out as the macroeconomy improves. In view of these considerations, the IMF's Interim Committee was charged with examining the issue of amending the Institution's Articles of Agreement to allow phased capital account liberalization (Fischer, 1997; IMF Survey, 3/24/98). Fischer further noted in his speech at the January 1998 World Economic Forum in Davos, Switzerland, that the Chileans were to be commended for their efforts at curbing excessive reliance on short-term loans from abroad (NYT, 2/3/98). At the same venue in Davos, Joseph Stiglitz, chief economist at the World Bank, called for similar curbs on short-term foreign borrowing by emerging economies (NYT, 2/1/98).

The IMF's austerity solution to the crisis was attacked from many quarters as well.[13] For example, following the bailout of South Korea, economists Jeffrey Sachs and Paul Krugman and currency trader George Soros made well-publicized cases against the austerity measures prescribed by the IMF (NYT, 2/1/98).[14] Soros, in particular, argued that the crisis and the IMF's mishandling of it demonstrated that markets and the private sector alone could neither prevent nor resolve the crisis (Soros, 12/31/97).[15]

It remains unclear as to whether anything positive will ever result from these attacks on the IMF and the soul searching by some of the most prominent staff members of the IMF–WB. At the same time and in the same venues where phased capital account liberalization was discussed, the issue of amending the IMF's Articles of Agreement in order to include explicit jurisdiction over capital movements was also being debated (IMF Survey, 3/24/98). Thus, "rethinking the capital account" may simply result in a further increase in the IMF's influence over decision-making in emerging economies. Moreover, following the Mexican crisis, a similar search for lessons ultimately resulted in a mere reconsolidation of the institutions' conventional focus on sound macroeconomic management and the failed effort to prevent crises via the dissemination of better information. It is ironic, too, that in a study of the Mexican crisis written prior to the events of 1997–8, the WB (1995) contrasted the misuse of capital inflows by Mexico with the sound use of such resources by Southeast Asian governments!

The arguments developed in this chapter indicate that governments in emerging economies must take steps to limit the growth of hard currency-denominated foreign debt and control highly liquid portfolio investment flows, even at the cost of slowing economic growth. The kinds of restrictive measures that might be used to control portfolio investment flows are quite familiar, and so they will be described only briefly here.

Capital controls are one such measure that deserves serious consideration especially in light of the events of 1997–8. Capital controls augment policy autonomy (by restricting investors' ability to flee whenever a government pursues a policy of which they don't approve) and enhance state capacity. More germane to the present discussion, they also reduce macroeconomic instability by dampening capital inflows and outflows. Crotty and Epstein (1996) have made a particularly forceful case for the necessity and feasibility of such policies in emerging economies.

Although they have fallen from favor in economic theory, capital controls remain an important component of economic management in some emerging economies today. Measures currently in place in Chile and Colombia (often referred to as the "Chilean model") represent an extremely promising direction for policy. The measures balance the need for capital with the need to protect the economy from instability. In Colombia, foreign investors are free to engage in (less liquid) direct investment, but are precluded from purchasing debt instruments and corporate equity. As a consequence, foreign capital is much less able to flee Colombia en masse. In Chile, foreign investors may engage in portfolio invest-ment, but they must keep their cash in the country for at least one year (*Economist*, 4/8/95). Investors are therefore much more apt to base their invest-ment decisions on a company's long-term economic prospects than on the opportunity for short-term speculative gain. To the surprise of many orthodox economists, this model has been performing well. Indeed, Chile has not only suc-ceeded in securing large portfolio investment inflows, but has also remained largely unaffected by the Asian flu.

The Chilean model also offers valuable lessons on the matter of discouraging the kinds of private sector borrowing that contributed significantly to the current crisis. The Chilean government tries to discourage borrowers from taking on short-term foreign loans by imposing a kind of reserve requirement tax on loans with a maturity of less than one year. Borrowers who take on such loans are required to deposit 30 per cent of their loan proceeds in a non-interest-bearing account for a number of months. This measure has also proven beneficial to Chile in terms of reducing the risk potential of foreign borrowing, and deserves wide consideration elsewhere.

Many economists (Arestis and Sawyer, this volume; Felix, 1993; Grieve Smith, 1997; and essays in Haq, Kaul, and Grunberg, 1996) and important organizations like the UNCTAD have also proposed adapting James Tobin's proposal for a uniform global transactions tax on foreign currency trading (termed the "Tobin tax"). The Tobin tax is primarily intended to address the problem of foreign exchange market volatility caused by speculation in this market. But this approach would also offset some of the instability associated with international portfolio investment flows, as traders fleeing assets denom-inated in a country's currency would face the tax in their foreign exchange transactions. In this way, the Tobin tax would offset the extreme liquidity asso-ciated with portfolio investment, reduce the profitability of international "churning" of investment portfolios, and thereby provide developing countries with greater financial stability. Relying on market incentives, such a Tobin tax represents a very simple policy tool for lengthening the time horizon of interna-tional portfolio investment. But it would also provide new pools of finance that could be targeted to developing countries to compensate those harmed by finan-cial instability, and especially to finance long-term, real-sector development projects (as Felix (1993) has suggested).

Finally, it would also be advisable for governments in emerging economies to consider designing simple measures that might indicate (both to them and to investors) whether they are vulnerable to a crisis triggered by investor exit or a currency collapse.[16] Three such indicators might serve as "ex-ante circuit breakers"; these circuit breakers would make apparent when a country faced high levels of risk of currency depreciation and investor/lender flight. As a country approached the danger range, governments would implement measures to curb imports, slow the pace of foreign borrowing, slow the entry and exit of portfolio investment or limit the fluctuation of the domestic currency. There would have to be, say, three sets of thresholds for these indicators – for emerging economies at the lowest, medium and highest levels of development.

Two indicators of currency risk might be given by the ratio of official reserves to total short-term external obligations (the sum of accumulated foreign portfolio investment and short-term hard-currency foreign borrowing); and the ratio of official reserves to the current account deficit. A simple indicator of vulnerability to a lender withdrawal would be the ratio of official reserves to private and public foreign currency-denominated debt (with short-term obligations receiving greater weighting in the calculation). The vulnerability to portfolio investor exit could be measured by the ratio of total accumulated foreign portfolio investment to gross domestic capital formation. If a large proportion of domestic capital formation were financed by inward portfolio investment, this would provide an indication of the country's vulnerability to a reversal of those flows and its excessive reliance on a particularly liquid type of international capital flow. As a country approached the danger range, new capital inflows would have to "wait at the gate" until domestic capital formation increased by a certain level. Thus, this indicator would slow unsustainable growth in an emerging economy until a larger proportion of any increase in investment could be financed domestically. Given the experiences of 1997–8 and 1994–5 (in Mexico), slower growth may be a worthwhile price to pay in lieu of the instability created by a sudden exit of external finance. These indices are merely suggestive and preliminary in nature; further research will be undertaken to develop the appropriate trigger ranges and test these for particular countries.

Notes

1 Earlier versions of this chapter were presented at the conference on "Global Instability and World Economic Governance," Cambridge University, Cambridge, England, May 13, 1998, at the "Vietnam–US Workshop," Institute for International Relations, Hanoi, Vietnam, March 21–30, 1998, and at the Fortnightly Gathering on Development at the University of Denver, Graduate School of International Studies. Thanks to participants at these fora, and to George DeMartino, Martin Fetherstone, John Grieve Smith, Jonathan Michie and Tom Palley for their reactions to this chapter. The University of Denver Internationalization Program provided financial support for this research. The research assistance of Minu Palani was immensely helpful on this project.
2 This discussion of the Mexican crisis is drawn from Grabel (1996).
3 The literature extolling the virtues of the "Asian model" is voluminous. The now classic World Bank (1993) study lauding the model was an embarrassment to Bank officials following the events of 1997–8. The IMF–WB continued to praise the Asian model in

the 1996 *World Development Report.* Aspects of the Asian model were also lionized in the late 1980s and early 1990s by mainstream policy analysts and liberal and left academics (see the review in DeMartino, 1996). At the time of nearly universal enthusiasm for the Asian model, the work of a few dissenters is worthy of note (Bello and Rosenfeld, 1990; Hart-Landsberg, 1993; Burkett and Hart-Landsberg, 1996).

4 In 1996 the ratio of non-performing to total loans was 4 per cent in Malaysia, compared to 13 per cent in Thailand (FT, 10/8/97).

5 The Indonesian Central Bank had for many years a policy of depreciating the rupiah by about 4 per cent a year (NYT, 7/22/97).

6 It was widely held that that the Philippine government aggressively managed the value of the peso despite its claims to the contrary (*Economist,* 7/12/97).

7 In the aftermath of the crisis, the *chaebols* (like their Japanese counterparts, the *keiretsu*) became the institution that analysts loved to hate. Prior to the crisis, these same institutions were held in high regard by the legion of policy analysts and business consultants that were seeking to solve the US's economic slide by looking east.

8 Important exceptions to this are Chang (1998a, 1998b, 1997) and Crotty (1998) who have to date developed the best analyses of the causes of the crisis in South Korea.

9 In contradistinction to elsewhere in the region, these foreign loans financed investment in the export sector (rather than in real estate) (Chang, 1997).

10 In a much publicized speech, President-elect Kim Dae-jung announced that "national bankruptcy was imminent" (DP, 12/24/97).

11 As of this writing (June 1998), Russia appeared to be entering a second round of crisis.

12 Note that bank-based lending to Latin America did not resume following the debt difficulties of the 1980s. However, bonds issued by the Brazilian and the Mexican government were sold in large numbers to private investors.

13 US Treasury Secretary Robert Rubin was the most prominent defender of the IMF's bailout policies. Beginning with his January 21, 1998, speech at Georgetown University, Rubin defended the soundness of IMF policy and argued that its bailouts protect US economic and foreign policy interests as well as those of the investors who would be hurt by an emerging market crisis (*Treasury News,* 1/21/98).

14 The costs of Brazil's self-imposed austerity received a surprising degree of attention in the business press (NYT, 2/8/98).

15 In view of the IMF's mishandling of the crisis, Soros developed a rather odd proposal to prevent a recurrence. He proposed the creation of an International Credit Insurance Corporation (ICIC) as a sister institution to the IMF. The ICIC's principal task would be to guarantee international loans for a modest fee. Borrowing countries could only receive loan guarantees if they provided the ICIC with full information on all borrowings – insured or not, public and private. This proposal is predicated on the assumption that the crisis was caused by bad or insufficient information about the indebtedness of the private sector in Southeast Asia. However, the high degree of leveraging of the region's borrowers could hardly be considered a secret to the very lenders that were extending these loans.

16 Note that a group of economists associated with the IMF (as both consultants and employees) proposed the development of a new early warning system to improve upon the IMF's failed Special Data Dissemination Standard. It involved monitoring a very broad array of crisis indicators. These indicators included internal and external imbalances, problems in the domestic financial sector (including declining international reserves, currency appreciation, credit growth, money supply growth, increasing domestic inflation), the rate of real GDP growth, and political instability (IMF Survey, 8/18/97). Given the array of indicators proposed, it is doubtful that anything but mixed signals could be derived from such a cumbersome signaling procedure.

References

Arestis, P. and M. Sawyer. 1997. "How many cheers for the Tobin transactions tax?" *Cambridge Journal of Economics* 21: 753–68.

Bello, W. and S. Rosenfeld. 1990. *Dragons in Distress*. San Francisco: Food First Books.

Burkett, P. and M. Hart-Lansberg. 1996. "The use and abuse of Japan as a progressive model." In L. Panitch (ed.). *Are There Alternatives? Socialist Register 1996*. London: Merlin Press, 62–92.

Business Week (BW). 1997. "The rush to Russia." (March 24): 48–50.

Business Week. 1997. "A costly lesson for Malaysia." (September 22): 64.

Business Week. 1997. "Storm clouds over Asia's safe haven." (August 11): 23.

Business Week. 1997. "Caution: curves ahead." (December 29): 116.

Chang, H.-J. 1998a. "Reform for the long term in S. Korea," *International Herald Tribune* (February 13).

Chang, H.-J. 1998b. "Korea: the misunderstood crisis." *World Development*, forthcoming.

Chang, H.-J. 1997. "Perspective on Korea." *Los Angeles Times* (December 31).

Crotty, J. 1998. "The Korean crisis." Mimeo.

Crotty, J. and G. Epstein. 1996. "In defence of capital controls." In L. Panitch (ed.). *Are There Alternatives? Socialist Register 1996*. London: Merlin Press, 118–49.

Crotty, J., G. Epstein, and P. Kelley. 1998. "Multinational corporations, capital mobility and the global neo-liberal regime: effects on northern workers and on growth prospects in the developing world." Mimeo.

DeMartino, G. 1996. "Industrial policies versus competitiveness strategies: in pursuit of prosperity in the global economy." *International Papers in Political Economy*. 3: 2: 1–42.

Denver Post. 1997. "Russian economy in trouble." (December 6): 26A.

Denver Post. 1997. "South Korea, IMF work out details of $55b bailout." (December 4): 17A.

Denver Post. 1997. "S. Korea to abolish currency controls." (December 16): 6C.

Denver Post. 1997. "S. Korea asks to defer foreign payments." (December 24): 9C.

Economist. 1995. "The tequila hangover." (April 8): 65–6.

Economist. 1997. "Thailand gets the bill." (August 9): 31–2.

Economist. 1997. "Lifebelts on." (July 12): 62–3.

Economist. 1997."Asian currencies: more turbulence ahead." (August 23): 54.

Felix, D. 1993. "Developing countries and joint action to curb international financial volatility." *UNCTAD Bulletin* 21: 7–9.

Finance and Development. 1997. "Capital flow sustainability and speculative currency attacks." (December): 8–11.

Financial Times (FT). 1997. "Malaysian banking faces pain, not failure." (October 8).

Fischer, S. 1997. "Capital account liberalization and the role of the IMF." *IMF* (September 19) (transcript of speech delivered at the seminar, "Asia and the IMF," held in Hong Kong on September 19, 1997).

Grabel, I. 1996. "Marketing the third world: the contradictions of portfolio investment in the global economy." *World Development* 24: 11: 1761–76.

Grieve Smith, John. 1997. "Exchange rate instability and the Tobin tax." *Cambridge Journal of Economics* 21: 745–52.

Haq, M. ul, Kaul, I., and Grunberg, I. 1996. *The Tobin Tax: Coping with Financial Volatility*. Oxford: Oxford University Press.

Hart-Landsberg, M. 1993. *The Rush to Development*. New York: Monthly Review.

International Finance Corporation (IFC). Various years. *Emerging Stock Markets Factbook.* Washington, DC: IFC.

International Monetary Fund (IMF). Various years. *International Financial Statistics.* Washington, DC: IMF.

IMF Survey. 1998. "IMF accelerates disbursement to Korea; schedules high-level visit to Indonesia." 27: 1 (January 12): 1–2.

IMF Survey. 1998. "Indonesia announces comprehensive reforms; seeks to rehabilitate banking sector." 27: 3 (February 9): 33–4.

IMF Survey. 1998. "Seminar discusses the orderly path to capital account liberalization." 27: 6 (March 23): 81–4.

IMF Survey. 1997. "Range of indicators may provide warning system for currency crises." 26: 16 (August 18): 257–60.

Lopez Gallardo, Julio. 1997. "Economic crisis and recovery in Mexico: a post-Kaleckian perspective." *Economia Aplicada.* 45.

New York Times (NYT). 1998. "Indonesians die as riots over price rises widen." (February 15): A1.

New York Times. 1998. "Korea's other big problem: $300b in domestic debt." (February 10): A1.

New York Times. 1998. "The poor pay." (February 8) 3: 2.

New York Times. 1998. "Brazil's reformist chief rides a bucking bronco." (February 8): 1: 6.

New York Times. 1998. "Fail-safe strategies in a market era." (January 4): 4: 1.

New York Times. 1998. "A flight to rigor." (February 15): 3: 2.

New York Times. 1998. "Indonesia considers a radical shift for currency, hitching it to dollar." (February 10): C1.

New York Times. 1998. "IMF may be closer to lending-curb idea." (February 30): C4.

New York Times. 1998. "Study shows how world banks panicked over Asian troubles." (January 30): C1.

New York Times. 1998. "Central Europe and Latin markets may escape Asian crisis." (February 2): A3.

New York Times. 1998. "Partial halt by Indonesia on payments." (January 28): C1.

New York Times. 1998. "Second-guessing the economic doctor." (February 1): 3: 1.

New York Times. 1998. "Hong Kong isn't immune to Asian distress." (February 2): C2.

New York Times. 1998. "Indonesia introduces key banking changes." (January 27): C7.

New York Times. 1997. "Hong Kong stocks extend plunge." (September 2): D12.

New York Times. 1997. "A warning light largely ignored in Thai currency crisis." (August 1): D1.

New York Times. 1997. "Speculators press attack on South Asian countries." (July 22): D1.

New York Times. 1997. "A domino effect in Thailand." (September 21): D1.

New York Times. 1997. "Premier of Malaysia spars with currency dealer." (September 22): A1.

New York Times. 1997. "IMF, with the help of Asians, offers Thais $16b bailout." (August 12): A1.

New York Times. 1997. "Seoul hints it's closer to idea of IMF aid." (November 21): C5.

New York Times. 1997. "Brazil to raise taxes and cut spending sharply to restore confidence in its currency." (November 11): A9.

New York Times. 1997. "Indonesia shuts wobbly banks as a key part of its bailout." (November 2): A12.

New York Times. 1997."Bangkok is gripped by economic protest." (October 2): A15.

New York Times. 1997. "Wall Street sneezes and, this time, the Russians catch a chill." (October 29): A10.

New York Times. 1997. "Hong Kong's slide goes 6% deeper." (October 28): C25.

New York Times. 1997. "Drop in Europe and US are 2.3% to 3.6%." (October 24): A1.

New York Times. 1997. "The risks to America in Asia's plummeting markets." (October 24): C1.

New York Times. 1997. "Asian waves, US ripples: yes, the baht does stop here." (October 24): A1.

New York Times. 1997. "Defending fixed exchange rate at further cost to stocks." (October 24): C7.

New York Times. 1997. "Korean crisis: blame the lenders." (December 14): 5: 1.

Safire, W. 1998. "Crony capitalism." *New York Times* (February 10): 14.

Soros, G. 1997. "Avoiding a breakdown." *Financial Times* (December 31): 12.

Treasury News. 1998. "Address on the Asian financial situation to Georgetown University (Rubin, Robert)." (January 21).

Wall Street Journal (WSJ). 1997. "Southeast Asian banks contribute to bust in the economic boom." (October 6): A1.

Wall Street Journal. 1997. "Brazil's Cardoso still has a big job ahead.' (November 7): A19.

Wall Street Journal. 1997. "IMF aid could hurt Indonesian shares." (October 13): C1.

Wall Street Journal. 1997. "Indonesia's poor will suffer most as nation tightens its belt." (November 3): A1.

Wall Street Journal. 1997. "Asia's woes revive fears of capital flight." (November 7): A2.

Wall Street Journal. 1997. "Indonesia's currency is latest domino." (August 15): A15.

Wall Street Journal. 1997. "Asia's financial shock." (November 26): A11.

Wall Street Journal. 1997. "Russia's finances worsen, imperiling large IMF loan." (November 3): A1.

World Bank (WB). 1995. *Global Economic Prospects and the Developing Countries.* Washington, DC: WB.

World Bank. Various years. *Global Development Finance.* Washington, DC: WB.

World Bank. 1993. *The East Asian Miracle.* Oxford: Oxford University Press.

3 Stabilizing capital flows to developing countries

Stephany Griffith-Jones with Jenny Kimmis[1]

I Introduction

The deep integration of developing countries into the global economy has many advantages and positive effects.

In particular, capital flows to developing countries have clear and important benefits. The benefits are especially clear for foreign direct investment, which is not only more stable, but also brings technological know-how and access to markets. Other external flows also have important positive micro-economic effects, such as lowering the cost of capital for creditworthy firms. At a macro-economic level, foreign capital flows can complement domestic savings, leading to higher investment and growth; this latter positive macro-economic effect is very valuable for low-savings economies, but may be less clear for high-savings economies like those of East Asia.

However, large surges of short-term and potentially reversible capital flows to developing countries can also have very negative effects. First, these surges pose complex policy dilemmas for macro-economic management, as they can initially push key macro-economic variables, such as exchange rates and prices of assets like property and shares, away from what could be considered their long-term equilibrium. Second, and more important, these flows pose the risk of very sharp reversals. These reversals – particularly if they lead to currency and financial crises – can result in very serious losses of output, investment and employment, as well as increases in poverty.

In the case of the Asian crisis, the reversal of private capital flows has been really dramatic. According to figures from the Institute of International Finance, the five East Asian countries hardest hit by the crisis (South Korea, Indonesia, Malaysia, Thailand and the Philippines) experienced in a single year a turn-around of US$105 billion, reaching more than 10 per cent of the combined GDP of these economies; the shift was from an inflow of capital of +US$93 billion in 1996 to an estimated outflow of US$12 billion in 1997 (see Table 3.1). Most of this dramatic swing originated from commercial bank lending (which fell by US$76.8 billion), whilst foreign direct investment remained constant (see again Table 3.1).

This massive and sudden withdrawal of capital flows in itself caused a dramatic

Table 3.1 Five Asian economies' external financing (US $ billion)

	1996	1997	Change between 1996 and 1997
External financing, net	92.8	15.2	–77.6
Private flows, net	93.0	–12.1	–105.1
Equity investment	19.1	–4.5	–23.6
Direct equity	7.0	7.2	+0.2
Portfolio equity	12.1	–11.6	–23.7
Private creditors	74.0	–7.6	–81.6
Commercial banks	55.5	–21.3	–76.8
Non-bank private creditors	18.4	13.7	–4.7
Official flows, net	–0.2	27.2	+27.4

Source: Institute of International Finance 'Capital Flows to Emerging Economies', 29 January 1998, Washington, DC.

reduction in absorption, as well as currency crises. In Asia, violent devaluation and large increases in interest rates implied that the currency crises interacted with banking crises, which led to a contraction of bank lending. It is interesting that usually in developing countries (with Mexico in 1994–95 providing another good example), currency crises spill over into domestic financial crises and vice versa, whereas this does not happen very often in developed countries (Akyuz, 1998).

The combination of the reversal of capital flows, currency and domestic financial crises led in East Asia to a very severe economic crisis in countries that had been growing extremely rapidly for a very long period. According to the International Monetary Fund's April World Economic Outlook (1998), growth of GDP in the Asian NIC's – Hong Kong, Singapore, South Korea and Taiwan – will fall by 4.2 per cent in 1998 to a mere 1.8 per cent; for Thailand, Malaysia, Indonesia and the Philippines the decline is far more dramatic, as their combined GDP will fall by 8.1 percentage points, to –2.7 per cent.

In Mexico, gross domestic product fell by almost 7 per cent in 1995 in the wake of the peso crisis, with investment and consumption falling over 15 per cent during that year.

Within present arrangements, the volatility and reversibility of some categories of capital flows and their very negative effects implies that the costs of these flows to countries' development are seen as higher than their benefits, at least during important periods of time.

As a consequence, there is growing consensus that important changes need to be made in the international monetary system as a whole – and in recipient country policies – to avoid costly crises, as well as to manage them better if they do occur. Important economic authorities like Alan Greenspan, Chairman of the US Federal Reserve (*Financial Times*, 28 February 1998), and Joseph Stiglitz, Chief Economist of the World Bank (Stiglitz, 1998a and 1998b) as well as several important analysts, have called for such changes.

It seems urgent to:

1   identify the possible changes required to achieve this result;
2   evaluate the potential economic effects of such changes; and
3   define institutional developments that would be required to implement those changes.

This chapter attempts to contribute elements to the important on-going debate on this issue. Section II will explore further the causes of the East Asian crisis, focusing on those more relevant to the central issues of this chapter. Section III examines measures for crisis prevention. More emphasis will be placed on international measures, like better surveillance by the IMF and better regulation of capital by source countries and internationally; however, some of the market based policies that may need to be taken by recipient countries to discourage excessive surges of short-term capital flows is also evaluated. Section IV examines the measures to better manage international crises if they do occur, including the expanded role of the IMF as a lender of last resort and better debt work-out mechanisms. Section V concludes and summarises.

II Causes of the Asian crisis

A large literature is emerging emphasising from different perspectives the domestic causes of the Asian crisis, for example Boorman (1998), Corsetti, Pesenti and Roubini (1998), IMF (1997), Radelet and Sachs (1998) and Wade and Veneroso (1998). It is beyond the scope of this chapter to examine the varying domestic causes of the crisis. Three key points are, however, worth stressing (Stiglitz, 1997). First, the current account deficits in East Asia reflected private sector deficits. Second, the Asian crisis was a consequence of overinvestment (some or much of it misallocated) and not of overconsumption. Third, the most important cause of the crisis was a sharp deterioration in confidence, not of macro-economic fundamentals, which were mostly extremely strong.

Indeed, what seems most disturbing about the Asian crisis is that it happened to countries that had been so successful for a long period, not just in terms of economic growth but also in terms of great dynamism in their exports, low rates of inflation, high rates of savings and rather equitable distribution. Even though several of these countries had high balance of payments current account deficits, this had been seen as acceptable for quite a long time both by analysts and markets alike, for two reasons: first, these deficits were financing very high investment rates; second, as mentioned above, the current account deficits did not originate in fiscal deficits – on the contrary, the Asian economies had fiscal surpluses – but were caused by private sector deficits.

So what went wrong? Clearly there were problems in the Asian economies, including serious weaknesses in their domestic financial systems and in their governance (see below). However, there is another causal factor, which relates more to the international dimension, and in particular to the behaviour of international capital flows. Though really important, this aspect has not received sufficient systematic attention in analyses of the Asian crisis.

This explanation is based on certain imperfections of international capital markets, that have always been there, but whose impact has increased due to technological developments, which allow the wheels of international finance to turn far faster than before. As pointed out above, this highly mobile capital plays positive roles. However, it can have very problematic aspects. Paradoxically, these negative effects can be strongest for economies that either are – or are perceived as about to become – highly successful. We could call it the curse of the successful economy; more technically, we could call it 'financial Dutch disease'.

A successful economy – like those of the previously so-called Asian tigers – offers high yields and profits to international investors. If these investors can find ways to enter these economies, or if their entrance is facilitated by capital account liberalisation, they will rush in. This surge of capital inflows will affect key macro-economic variables. Exchange rates tend to become greatly overvalued; the prices of key assets – like shares and land – tend to rise significantly and quickly. As a result there is both an increase in real income (as imported goods become cheaper) and an increase in perceived wealth (as asset prices become at least temporarily higher), as well as a perceived increase in future income. Banks can increase lending, lifting liquidity constraints. As a result of these factors, individuals consume more; also private companies increase their investment.

The sum of these individual decisions has macro-economic implications. The current account of the balance of payments deteriorates, often quite rapidly, as both consumption and investment rise. Initially, this is not seen as a problem, as foreign lenders and investors are happy to continue lending/investing, given high profitability combined with the perception of low risk, as they are going into what is broadly seen as a successful economy.

Then, something changes. The change may be domestic or international. It may be economic or political. It may be an important change or a relatively small one. The key element is that this change *triggers a sharp modification in perceptions, leading to a large fall in confidence in the economy among internationally mobile investors*; these can be both foreign investors in the country or nationals able and willing to take their liquid assets out of the country.

The change of perceptions tends to be both large and quick. A country that was perceived as a successful economy or a successful reformer – for which no amount of praise was sufficient – suddenly is seen as fragile, risky and crisis prone. The change of perception tends to be far larger than the magnitude of the underlying change warrants. The frightening aspect is that there is a very strong element of self-fulfilling prophecy in the change of perception. Currency crises happen to a significant extent because lenders and investors fear they can happen. The fact that they first stop lending and investing and then pull out contributes greatly to making their worst nightmares come true. As a result, there can be much overshooting. Exchange rates can collapse, as can stock markets and property prices. Governments or central banks are forced to raise interest rates to defend the currency. As a result, banking systems become far more fragile than they were before, as previous weaknesses are magnified and new ones emerge.

An additional problem is contagion. Countries in the same region, or with weaknesses seen to be similar to the crisis country can also suffer from a parallel change of perception by investors. The crisis spreads to other countries, including to those with basically good economic fundamentals. The latter may suffer somewhat less, but may, if unlucky, be caught up in the whirlwind of deteriorating perceptions.

This pattern helps explain the currency and banking crises in the southern cone of Latin America in the early 1980s; it helps explain the Mexican peso crisis and the tequila effect. It also provides important elements to understand the 1997 Asian crises. Of course there are significant differences between these crises, and the previous ones throughout the centuries. But the boom–bust behaviour of short-term lenders and investors, driven not just by real trends (which they help shape), but by dramatic changes in perceptions, is a common denominator to these different crises.

There is a relevant academic literature which explains why capital and financial markets are special, in that – though generally functioning well – they are prone to important imperfections. Factors like asymmetric information and adverse selection play an important role in explaining these imperfections, given that financial markets are particularly information intensive (Stiglitz, 1994). Furthermore, as Keynes (1936) showed with his well-known metaphor of the beauty contest, there are strong incentives to follow the herd in financial markets, as each individual short-term investor, lender or fund manager tries to choose the investment or loan that he/she thinks likeliest to be chosen by other investors or lenders, as his colleagues' assessment will be a crucial element in determining short-term prices.

Also of relevance for understanding the Asian crisis is the concept self-fulfilling attacks, that is crises arising without obvious current policy inconsistencies (see Griffith-Jones 1998). In this model, speculative attacks are basically caused not by bad fundamentals, but by future expected shifts of macro-economic policies, which will be *caused* by the attack itself. In these models, the attitude of speculators and investors is crucial to whether an attack occurs. This implies multiple equilibria for exchange rates. The existence of self-fulfilling attacks and multiple equilibria implies that good macro-economic fundamentals are a very important necessary but not a sufficient condition for avoiding currency crises. Stiglitz (1998) illustrates this clearly by comparing small open economies to rowing boats on an open sea. Bad steering or even more leaky boats significantly increases – or makes inevitable – a disaster. However, the chances of being overturned are significant no matter how well the boats are constructed and steered.

As Wyplosz (1998) rightly argues, there is at present limited understanding of what triggers self-fulfilling attacks. As a consequence, self-fulfilling attacks are fundamentally unpredictable. It is interesting that the main explanations given by market actors for different recent crises (e.g. the Mexican peso crisis, crises in different Asian countries) tend to be rather different ones. As a result, developing countries' policy-makers face the daunting task of 'playing to moving goalposts', to avoid crises. Naturally there are conditions of vulnerability that can be identified (such as the ratio of short-term foreign exchange debts plus the stock of assets that can easily leave the country divided by the level of foreign exchange reserves, or high current account deficits). But such vulnerability indicators do not imply that a crisis will occur. Many countries have such high vulnerability indicators but do not have a crisis. On the other hand, some of these indicators may be relatively low and/or improving (e.g. the current account deficit was relatively low and improving in South Korea in 1997) and the country can still have a crisis. These patterns confirm the multiple-equilibrium character of currency and other crises, where a triggering event can cause a dramatic change of perception, make these vulnerability indicators become important, and precipitate a large change of investor and creditor flows.

Further research is required into conditions of vulnerability and nature of triggering events, to be able to predict risk of – and, above all, improve prevention of – currency crises. However, measures are also necessary to shelter developing countries from these volatile and unpredictable flows and their negative effects, whilst continuing to encourage more stable flows, especially if – as in the case of foreign direct investment – they bring other valuable benefits.

Domestic policies – at the macro-economic level, to the domestic financial sector, and the possible regulation of short-term capital inflows – can of course play an important role. However, they are difficult to implement perfectly. As a consequence, an international effort is also required to make costly currency crises in developing and transition countries less likely and to manage them better if they do occur.

In the nineteenth century, the rapid development of private banking implied frequent national banking crises. The establishment and development of national regulatory bodies and of central banks with lender of last resort facilities made such crises less frequent (Griffith-Jones and Lipton, 1987). Similarly, the rapid development of global capital and banking flows in the latter part of the twentieth century implies the need for new measures of global governance to regulate those flows. These will include better regulation of international credit and portfolio flows, as well as improvements of the lender of last resort facility and the possible development of international debt workout procedures. We now turn to these options.

III Crisis prevention

The IMF proposals

The Asian crisis has provoked a vast amount of discussion and reflection in the international community. It is hoped that lessons can be drawn on what needs to be done to reduce the probability of future crises. A number of interesting proposals are currently being discussed, both by the IMF and others. This section will focus on the three main proposals for crisis prevention being put forward by the

IMF: improvements to the quality of information supplied by countries to the IMF and the public, together with improved IMF surveillance; the strengthening of domestic financial systems by improving regulation and supervision and increasing financial sector transparency; and encouraging the 'prudent and properly sequenced' liberalisation of capital flows. These proposals will be examined below, and the analysis will show that while each of them has a role to play in strengthening the international financial system, it is unlikely that these measures alone could prevent future crises.

Improving the quality of information

The Asian crisis has led to calls for improvements to information disclosure, data dissemination and international surveillance. Similar demands were made in the wake of the Mexican peso crisis, when emphasis was placed on better information regarding national economic policy. The current emphasis is on improved data in other areas such as foreign exchange reserves, short-term foreign currency denominated debt, and the state of the financial system. The question of accurate information is made even more complex due to the increased use of off-balance sheet transactions such as forward contracts and other financial derivatives. The Asian crisis has highlighted this issue as the true foreign exchange positions of some countries were hidden by central bank derivative transactions and positions. Therefore, improved information on derivatives would be particularly useful, and the role of the IMF in improving this information is very valuable.

First, the IMF has stated that countries must be encouraged to improve the quality of information that they make available to the Fund and to the public (Camdessus, 1998a; Interim Committee, 1998). Transparency and the timely release of economic information provide the bare bones of crisis prevention. It is now clear that there were major deficiencies in the quality of information available to the markets on the countries most severely affected by the Asian crisis. Once the facts emerged, particularly data on foreign exchange reserves and short-term foreign denominated debt, the markets over-reacted and the crisis deepened.

In order to encourage transparency in, sometimes reluctant, emerging market economies it was proposed at the spring 1998 meeting of the IMF and the World Bank that the Fund could delay the completion of its annual Article IV health check of a country's economy if it is not satisfied with the information being disclosed. The IMF also wants to encourage more emerging market economies to make public the results of these consultations with the Fund through the issuance of Press Information Notices (PINS) on the IMF website.

Second, IMF surveillance needs to be tighter and more far-reaching. In particular, the financial sector needs to be examined in more detail. The IMF and the World Bank have recently been building up their financial sector surveillance capacity. At a recent G7 meeting in Washington, proposals to create new surveillance structures were made (discussed further below).

Third, efforts need to be made to improve transparency on the part of the IMF itself. The establishment of the Special Data Dissemination Standard (SDDS) in 1996 and the Dissemination Standard Bulletin Board (DSBB) on the IMF website, are testament to the Fund's commitment to improve data dissemination in the aftermath of the Mexican peso crisis. The IMF is looking at ways in which the SDDS could be broadened and strengthened, to include data on reserve related liabilities, central bank derivative transactions and positions, debt, particularly short-term debt, and the health of the financial sector (Interim Committee, 1998). However, some of these areas will involve problems concerning the international compatibility of reporting standards.

The Asian crisis has led to requests that the IMF be obliged to inform the markets when it thinks a country is heading for a crisis. The dangers of 'whistle blowing' are clear: it could compromise the Fund's position as confidential advisor to member countries, and a public warning may provoke the very crisis that it is trying to prevent. However, the recent meeting of the IMF's Interim Committee proposed developing a 'tiered response' whereby the Fund would give increasingly strong, and ultimately public, warnings to countries which it believed were heading for trouble (Interim Committee, 1998).

While all commentators on the Asian crisis are agreed that improved information disclosure and tighter surveillance would be helpful, these changes are not sufficient to prevent future crises. In the first place, the attempts to implement greater transparency in the aftermath of the Mexican crisis have revealed the difficulties involved. Yet getting data on public finances is much easier than obtaining information on private capital flows. As Stiglitz states:

> In a world where private-to-private capital flows are increasingly important, we will need to recognize that monitoring and surveillance are going to be especially challenging. The growing use of derivatives is increasingly making the full disclosure of relevant information, or at least the full interpretation of the disclosed information, even more difficult.
>
> (Stiglitz, 1998, p. 8)

In addition to the problems of obtaining and interpreting information on private capital flows, there are the difficulties involved in obtaining and interpreting information on the financial sector. First, criteria for assessing the strength of bank and non-bank financial sector institutions are far from standard across countries, making any interpretation very difficult. Second, information on the state of the financial sector can be misleading as the health of financial institutions will deteriorate in a crisis.

Moreover, even if information and transparency were to be greatly improved, it is doubtful that this will necessarily lead to better investment decisions and the removal of the threat of market over-reactions. It has been shown that in the lead up to the Asian crisis, investors and lenders were well aware of some of the problems the worst-hit countries were experiencing (see for example Wade and Veneroso, 1998, and Stiglitz, 1998). Yet they did not adjust their lending and investment until the crisis hit. A World Bank report points out that while most of the lending was done by seemingly well-regulated institutions in the advanced countries:

> foreign lenders and investors were not restrained by inadequate financial statements, high short-term debt, or the unhedged foreign exchange exposure present in the financing structure of east Asian banks and firms.
>
> (World Bank, Global Development Finance 1998 report cited in the *Financial Times*, 25 March 1998, p. 18)

As discussed above, this apparent anomaly can be put down to the herd behaviour of market participants. An analysis of the Mexican peso crisis showed that the problems associated with market over-optimism (or 'irrational exuberance' as Greenspan calls it) followed by market over-pessimism, were more to do with the behaviour of fund managers than with the lack of information available (Griffith-Jones, 1996). Keynes' analogy of the beauty contest shows how success for international investors, often operating in unfamiliar markets, depends on accurately judging what average opinion will be (Griffith-Jones, 1998). Their incentive structure leads to herd behaviour, as their reputation will be damaged if they lose money while others make profits, but they will not suffer if they incur losses together with other market participants. Therefore, investors invariably base their decisions on the general perception of the market, rather than on a systematic analysis of economic fundamentals.

It is often argued that markets judge countries according to their fundamentals, and crises usually occur because of some change in fundamentals caused by external shocks or policy mistakes. Both the peso crisis and the Asian crisis have led to warnings on the importance of sound economic fundamentals in emerging market economies. However, in the case of both Mexico and the Asian countries, there were no changes to fundamentals significant enough to account for the severity of crises (see Stiglitz, 1998, p. 2; Rodrik, 1998, p. 5; Fischer, 1998, p. 9; Wolf, 1998; and Wyplosz, 1998).

Strengthening domestic financial systems

Problems in the domestic financial systems of the worse affected countries are central to the IMF analysis of the Asian crisis (IMF, 1997, and Fischer, 1998). The main problems are believed to be: weak financial institutions; inadequate bank regulation and supervision; and the relations between government, banks and corporations (referred to as 'crony capitalism'). Financial sector weakness has often been a contributing factor for countries experiencing macro-economic difficulties. Therefore, strengthening domestic financial systems is a core element of the IMF strategy for crisis prevention. The updated IMF *World Economic Outlook* published in December 1997 states:

> recent events clearly demonstrate the crucial importance of strong financial institutions operated in accordance with established principles of sound

banking and of rigorous transparency in the provision of economic and financial information. In this context, the emerging market countries need to move as quickly as possible to adopt the core principles on banking supervision.

(IMF, 1997, p. 45)

A number of publications have examined how domestic financial systems could be strengthened. In 1997, the Basle Committee on Banking Supervision published its 'Core Principles for Effective Banking Supervision', developed by a working group consisting of representatives of the Basle Committee and emerging market countries.[2] In 1998, the IMF published *Towards a Framework for Financial Stability* which was designed as a first step in building a framework that could be used in the Fund's surveillance of its members' financial sectors. The IMF's work on financial systems has focused on the banking system, due to its primary role as financial intermediary in many member countries and the limits of staff expertise. However other institutions, such as the International Organisation of Securities Commissions (IOSCO), have been compiling 'best practices' for their sectors of the financial system.[3]

The key aspects of a sound financial system outlined in *Towards a Framework for Financial Stability* include: transparency of the financial system; competent management; effective risk control systems; adequate capital requirements; lender-of-last-resort facilities; prudential regulation; a supervisory authority with sufficient autonomy, authority, and capacity; and supervision of cross-border banking (IMF, 1998).

The role of the IMF in the surveillance of domestic financial systems has also come under scrutiny recently. Limitations of staff resources and expertise mean that IMF surveillance in this area would normally focus on identifying weaknesses in the financial systems of member countries which could have a significant impact on the macro-economic situation. The Fund, as it stands, cannot oversee the regulatory and supervisory authorities in each country, or address problems in other areas of the financial system (IMF, 1998, p. 1).

As we saw above, the Fund and the World Bank have been increasing their financial sector surveillance capacity. At the G7 meeting in April 1998, Canada and Britain proposed establishing a joint surveillance unit from the IMF and the World Bank. The proposed unit would be responsible for designing financial sector reform strategies in crisis situations and for carrying out surveillance of national financial regimes in non-crisis countries.

However, establishing effective risk management and sound regulatory and supervisory systems in all IMF member countries would be a huge task. As Rodrik notes:

Putting in place an adequate set of prudential and regulatory controls to prevent moral hazard and excessive risk-taking in the domestic banking system is a lot easier said than done. Even the most advanced countries fall considerably short of the ideal, as their bank regulators will readily tell you.

(Rodrik, 1998, p. 7)

Stiglitz echoes these concerns when he writes:

> Building robust financial systems is a long and difficult process. In the mean-time, we need to be realistic and recognize that developing countries have less capacity for financial regulation and greater vulnerability to shocks.
>
> (Stiglitz, 1998, p. 8)

The reform of the domestic financial sector in the Asian countries and elsewhere will, therefore, be lengthy and complex. Additionally, as noted above, the state of the financial sector is likely to deteriorate in a crisis. Therefore, in countries which exhibit signs of weakness, it might be prudent for the regulating authorities to consider the likely effects of major economic changes such as would occur in a currency crisis, on the quality of bank assets. This could be done by running simulations which predict the impact of changes to the exchange rate, interest rates, and value of property and shares given as guarantees to loans. Furthermore, the current emphasis of the IMF, for reasons cited above, is on improvements to the banking sector, particularly to regulation and supervision. Yet analyses of the Asian Crisis have shown that much of the foreign borrowing was by the non-bank private sector: one-third in South Korea, about 60 per cent in Malaysia and Thailand, and around two-thirds in Indonesia (Akyuz, 1998, p. 3). However, it would be extremely difficult to regulate the foreign borrowing of private companies, as Stiglitz notes:

> No country can, does, or probably should regulate individual corporations at the level of detail that would be required to prevent the foreign exchange and maturity mismatches that arose.
>
> (Stiglitz, 1998, p. 3)

Prudent capital account liberalisation

The third strand in the IMF crisis prevention strategy concerns encouraging countries to liberalise capital flows in 'a prudent and properly sequenced way' (IMF, 1998, p. 4). Capital account liberalisation involves both costs and benefits. The main benefits include: the increased availability of finance for trade and investment in recipient countries; the international diversification of risky assets; and increased efficiency in domestic financial systems. However, the costs can also be substantial and include: macro-economic instability due to the speculative inflow of foreign capital, and the loss of policy autonomy for liberalising countries.

In the IMF analysis, capital account liberalisation is problematic when macro-economic conditions are not adequate, or when it is not accompanied by reforms to the domestic financial system. Camdessus states that capital account liberalisation should be 'bold in its vision, cautious in its implementation' (Camdessus, 1998b, p. 4). He outlines the basic necessary conditions for success as follows: a sound macro-economic policy framework; reforms to the financial system; that the opening of the capital account should be phased to take account of the country's macro-economic situation and the state of domestic reforms; and timely and accurate information disclosure.

The Asian crisis has highlighted the problems that can result when fragile emerging market economies open their capital accounts. The sometimes irrational behaviour of market participants can have deeply damaging effects on countries which have seen little change in their economic fundamentals. The IMF position, that capital account liberalisation should be prudent, and phased to take account of prevailing economic conditions, appears to be sensible. McKinnon and others have stated that full capital account liberalisation should be the last step, after the consolidation of other liberalising measures and the strengthening of the domestic financial system (McKinnon, 1991). Countries should also be able to reverse liberalisation measures if a change in the macro-economic situation calls for it. In particular, countries should be able to use market-based measures to discourage excessive surges of short-term flows as has been the case in Chile (see below).

The three main proposals examined here, improvements to the quality of information and surveillance, strengthening domestic financial systems, and the prudent liberalisation of capital flows, would all contribute to strengthening the international financial system. Shaping an effective crisis prevention strategy, however, will require sharper tools.

Regulating and/or taxing capital inflows

National measures

This section will focus more on suggestions for international measures to discourage excessive surges of short-term and easily reversible capital and debt flows. However, we will start by examining measures that recipient countries can take to discourage such surges. Indeed, some countries (e.g. Chile and Colombia) have implemented measures (such as taxes and non-remunerated reserve requirements on flows during a fixed period) to discourage excessive surges of short-term capital flows. Their aim has been threefold:

1   To change the structure of capital inflows in order to increase the share within total capital flows of foreign direct investment and long-term loans, and above all to decrease the share of short-term and potentially reversible flows, by discouraging the latter. The lower level of short-term flows makes the country less vulnerable to currency crises.

2   To increase the autonomy of domestic monetary policy, as measures such as non-remunerated reserve requirements allow the recipient country to maintain higher national interest rates than the international ones; this is useful for controlling inflation and curbing excessive growth of aggregate demand – without attracting excessive capital inflows.

3   To curb large over-valuation of the exchange rate, caused by a surge, which

discourages growth of exports and poses the risk of growing and unsustainable current account deficits.

Studies in the mid-1990s (e.g. Ffrench-Davis and Griffith-Jones, 1995) showed how measures to discourage inflows – in countries like Chile and Colombia – have been a contributory factor to a relatively more successful management of capital inflows. Furthermore, these measures to discourage short-term inflows are widely seen as one of several reasons (with prudent macro-economic management being perhaps the main one) why Chile and Colombia were amongst the few countries in Latin America to be relatively unaffected by the tequila crisis in 1994–1995 and by the 1997–1998 Asian crisis. In the case of Chile, there is econometric and other evidence that the disincentives to short-term inflows have contributed fairly significantly to reduce the inflow of short-term, interest arbitraging funds, and their proportion of total capital inflows (Agosin, 1996; Budnevich and Le Fort, 1997). Also, Chilean policy-makers saw as important that – at a time of declining US interest rates in the early 1990s and a booming economy in Chile – the Central Bank was able to increase rather than lower interest rates in order to maintain macro-economic equilibrium (personal communication with Ricardo Ffrench-Davis, then Chief Economist at the Central Bank). There is also evidence that total capital flows to Chile were lower than they would have otherwise been (though a clear counterfactual is always difficult) and that as a consequence the resulting strengthening of the currency has been less than it would have otherwise been.

Two of the attractive features of the Chilean measures are: that they are market-based, rather than quantitative (Fischer, 1997), and that they apply to practically all short-term flows, thus simplifying administrative procedures and reducing possibilities of evasion, even though some evasion is naturally inevitable. Colombia has a similar, though more complex, approach to Chile's. Its measures are also broadly seen as successful, particularly in discouraging short-term flows and improving the term structure of total capital flows. It is interesting that the IMF (1995), the World Bank (1997) and the BIS (1995) (that is, all the major international financial institutions) now explicitly recognise that – though having some limitations and minor micro-economic disadvantages – market measures taken by recipient governments to discourage short-term capital flows do play a positive role, if they are part of a package of policy measures that include sound macro-economic fundamentals as well as a strong and well-regulated domestic financial system. This support for recipient countries discouraging short-term flows during surges as a useful measure has grown since the Asian crisis (Wolf, 1998; Rodrik, 1998; Radelet and Sachs, 1998).

There is therefore a growing consensus – further strengthened after the Asian crisis – that, though no panacea, discouraging short-term flows by recipient countries is one of several useful policy instruments for better management of capital flows and for reducing the risk of currency crises. It would therefore seem advisable for recipient countries to implement such a policy during periods of surges, and for international institutions like the IMF to encourage countries adopting such measures, in a temporary way, at times when countries receive excessive inflows of short-term capital and when other key conditions, e.g. good macro-economic fundamentals, are in place.

International measures

The question, however, needs to be asked whether measures to discourage excessive short-term capital inflows by recipient countries are enough to deal with the problem of capital surges and the risk of their reversal. There seem to be at least three strong reasons making complementary action by source countries necessary. First, not all major recipient countries will be willing to discourage short-term capital inflows, and some may even encourage them. A recent example of the latter are the tax and regulatory measures taken in Thailand to encourage the Bangkok International Banking Facility, which de facto encouraged short-term borrowing (Boorman, 1998). Second, even those recipient countries – like Chile, Colombia and Malaysia – which have deployed a battery of measures to discourage short-term capital inflows have on occasions found these measures insufficient to stem very massive inflows. Third, if one or several major emerging countries experience attacks on their currencies, which also result in difficulties in servicing their debt in full, it is far more probable than in the past that those countries will be forced to seek official funding to allow them to continue servicing their foreign exchange obligations in full, rather than being able – as in the past – to restructure such obligations. As the IMF (1995) pointed out, one important reason for the latter is the difficulty of restructuring securitised exposures owned by a diversity of investors. Because international official funding plays such a large role in providing finance during such crises, to avoid moral hazard, there is a clear need for international and/or source country regulation that will discourage excessive short-term capital inflows that may be reversed, contributing to a costly currency crisis. If such international and/or source country regulation is not developed, international private investors and creditors will continue to assume excessive risks, in the knowledge that they will be bailed out if the situation becomes critical. This is the classical moral hazard problem.

As a consequence, it is important to complete and improve international prudential supervision and regulation, to adapt it to the new scale and nature of private flows. Indeed, it is essential to fill existing regulatory gaps. Calls for improved supervision and regulation of capital flows to emerging markets internationally and/or by source countries began to be heard after the Asian crisis. For example, Martin Wolf (1998) wrote in the *Financial Times* 'After the crisis, the question can no longer be whether these flows should be regulated in some way. It can only be how.' In the same spirit, the G-24 in their April 1998 statement called for the creation of a task force that, amongst other aspects, would examine: 'more effective surveillance of the policies of major industrialised countries affecting key international monetary and financial variables, including capital flows'. Soros (1997) has argued forcefully that international capital and credit flows need to be regulated.

There are two types of flows to emerging markets where additional regulation and supervision seems particularly necessary, as they seem insufficiently regulated and their surges, as well as outflows, have played a particularly prominent role in sparking off recent currency crises. One of these is short-term bank loans; the other is easily reversible portfolio flows.

As regards short-term bank loans, they played a particularly important role before and during the Asian currency crises, especially in some countries, such as South Korea. In principle, bank loans (including short-term ones) are already regulated by industrial countries' central banks or their other regulators; these national regulations are co-ordinated by the Basle Committee. Such regulations include requirements for provisioning against potential future losses on lending to emerging countries (with a particularly detailed methodology developed in the Bank of England with its provisioning matrix) and capital adequacy requirements. However, existing regulations were not enough to discourage excessive short-term bank lending to several of the Asian countries. A key reason was that until just before the crisis most of these Asian countries (and particularly countries like South Korea) were seen by everybody including regulators as creditworthy (for evidence see again Radelet and Sachs, 1998). This was caused not just by asymmetries of information and disaster myopia (Griffith-Jones, 1998) but also by the excellent record of the East Asian countries described above. Another, perhaps somewhat secondary but also important reason, seems to have been current regulatory practice.[4] This implies that for non-OECD countries (which included South Korea until recently) loans of residual maturity of up to one year have a weighting of only 20 per cent for capital adequacy purposes, whilst loans over one year have a weighting of 100 per cent for capital adequacy purposes. As a result of this rule, short-term lending is more profitable for international banks. Therefore, to banks' economic preference for lending short-term, especially in situations of perceived increased risk, as this allows them to have more liquid assets that can be more easily not renewed if the situation deteriorates, is added a regulatory bias that also encourages short-term lending. The capital adequacy weighting differential appears too large in favour of short-term loans for non-OECD countries, resulting in excessive incentives for short-term lending. A narrowing of this differential may therefore be desirable.

Further measures to discourage excessive surges of short-term bank loans to emerging markets as suggested by Witteveen (1998) also requires further study. However, care must be taken that any measures adopted to discourage excessive short-term loans do not affect directly or indirectly, trade credit, as this is essential.

As regards portfolio flows to emerging markets, there is at present no regulatory framework in source countries or internationally, for taking account of market or credit risks on flows originating in institutional investors, such as mutual funds (and indeed more broadly for flows originating in non-bank institutions). This is an important regulatory gap that needs to be urgently filled, both to protect retail investors in developed countries and to protect developing countries from the negative effects of excessively large and potentially volatile portfolio flows.

As regards retail investors from developed countries, the need to protect them by regulation remains, in spite of important efforts being made to improve information by the regulatory authorities, especially in the US (see d'Arista and Griffith-Jones, 1998). The key reason is that it is practically impossible to improve sufficiently information and disclosure for retail investors on risk/return for their investments in emerging markets, because of the conceptual complexities involved, and especially given that the problems of asymmetric information and principal agency are particularly large for this category of investments (Mishkin, 1996).

As regards emerging market countries, the Asian crisis confirms what was already clearly visible in the Mexican peso crisis. Institutional investors, like mutual funds, given the very liquid nature of their investments can play an important role in contributing to currency crises. It seems important to fill this regulatory gap and introduce source country regulation to protect their domestic investors (especially the less informed retail investors), and discourage excessive surges of portfolio flows to emerging markets. This could perhaps best be achieved by risk-weighted cash requirements for institutional investors, such as mutual funds. These cash requirements would be placed as interest-bearing deposits in commercial banks. It should be stressed that this proposal is in the mainstream of current regulatory thinking, which sees risk-weighting as the key element in regulation (for an authoritative statement from the US Federal Reserve Board, see Phillips, 1998).

Introducing a risk-weighted cash requirement for mutual funds (and perhaps other institutional investors) would require that standards be provided by regulatory authorities. In the United States, these standards would result from consultations among the Securities and Exchange Commission with the Federal Reserve Board and the Treasury. In the UK, the standards would result from consultations between the Securities Investment Board, with the Bank of England and the Treasury. Weight should be given to the views of market analysts such as credit rating agencies, as well as particularly to the views of international agencies such as the IMF and BIS, with a long expertise in assessing countries' macro-economic performance. This would provide guidelines for defining macro-economic risk and for its measurement in determining the appropriate level of cash reserves. Thus, cash reserves would vary according to the macro-economic risks of different countries.

The guidelines for macro-economic risk (which would determine the cash requirements) would take into account such variables as the ratio of a country's current account deficit (or surplus) to GDP, the level of its external debt to GDP, the maturity structure of that debt, the fragility of the banking system, and other country risk factors. Factors such as custody-related risks (which already greatly concern securities regulators) could be included where relevant. It is important that quite sophisticated analysis is used, to avoid simplistic criteria stigmatising countries unnecessarily and arbitrarily. The views of the Central Bank, the Treasury, the IMF and the BIS should be helpful in this respect, especially given the long experience of foreign exchange crises and their causes that the international community has acquired.

The fact that the level of required cash reserves capital charge would vary with the level of perceived 'macro-economic risk' would make it relatively more profitable to invest more in countries with good fundamentals and relatively less profitable to invest in countries with more problematic macro or financial sector fundamentals. If macro-economic or financial sector fundamentals in a particular country deteriorate, investment in them would decline *gradually*, which hopefully would force an early correction of macro-economic policy, and, once this happened, a resumption of flows would take place; this smoothing of flows would hopefully discourage the massive and sudden reversals of flows that sparked off the Mexican peso and Asian currency crises, making such costly crises less likely. Though the requirement for cash reserves on mutual funds' assets invested in emerging markets could increase somewhat the cost of raising foreign capital for them, this would be compensated by the benefit of a more stable supply of funds, at a more stable cost. Similarly, retail investors in developed countries could get slightly lower yields, but be assured of far lower risks and lower volatility. Given the dominant role and rapid growth of institutional investors in the US and UK, this proposal – a risk-weighted cash requirement capital charge on mutual funds – could be adopted first in these two countries without creating significant competitive disadvantages. However, once implemented in the major countries – like the US and the UK – efforts to harmonise such measures internationally would need to be given urgent priority for discussion at the global level by the International Organisation of Securities' Regulators (IOSCO), so as to prevent investments by mutual funds being channelled through off-shore intermediaries that did not impose these cash requirements.

The suggested measures would follow a similar process as adopted first by G-10 central banks individually, on provisioning and capital adequacy on bank loans, which were then co-ordinated for all G-10 countries in the Basle Committee; the procedure would be similar, and the mechanism would be based on the same principle as capital adequacy, but would be clearly adapted to suit the institutional features of mutual funds, where shareholder capital backs 100 per cent of invested assets.

Finally, it is important to stress that additional regulation of mutual funds should be symmetrical with regulation of other institutions (e.g. banks) and other potentially volatile flows, e.g. excessive short-term bank credit, discussed above. Emphasis on regulation of institutional investors like mutual funds is necessary because they are clearly under-regulated, in comparison with other financial institutions, principally because their growth is so recent, particularly in relation to their increased investment in emerging markets.

It can be concluded that though better disclosure of risk is both difficult and very valuable, practical difficulties which have been analytically illuminated by the theory of asymmetrics imply that better information and disclosure needs to be complemented by other measures to both achieve better investor protection and diminish potential volatility of flows, which is particularly damaging for developing countries. A complementary measure to improve disclosure – risk-weighted cash requirements – have been discussed. Naturally other proposals – or variations of the present proposal – could be considered. What is clearly important is that meaningful measures should be taken to help stabilise capital flows to emerging markets. It is also important to stress that, given the evolution of the markets, past strategies, such as prohibiting investment in certain markets, are clearly no longer appropriate. Such prescriptive rules could have potentially negative effects on investors (who could lose profitable opportunities) and some emerging market economies, as their access to portfolio flows could be curtailed either in general, or – even worse – abruptly in times of macro-economic difficulties. The central proposals made here, of a risk-weighted approach – via capital charge cash requirements – would seem better as changes in cash requirements would be more gradual, thus contributing to smooth flows, which is the desired objective for the developing economy, and which would also give greater protection to developed country investors. Furthermore, risk-weighted cash requirements for institutional investors are consistent with modern mainstream regulatory thinking which sees risk weighting as the key element in regulation.

The above proposals have certain important similarities (especially in their objectives) with Soros' 1998 interesting proposal. The latter may be considered more radical because it implies setting up and funding a new institution, the International Credit Insurance Corporation (ICIC) which may provoke resistance. According to Soros' proposal, this new authority would guarantee international loans for a modest fee. On the basis of detailed data on countries' total borrowing, and an analysis of the macro-economic conditions in the countries concerned, this authority would set a ceiling on the amounts it is willing to insure. Up to those amounts the countries concerned would be able to access international capital markets at prime rates. Beyond these, 'the creditors would have to beware' (Soros, 1998) as there would be no cover. Like the other above proposal, Soros' idea has the important virtue that it would tend to cap excessive surges of capital flows while encouraging moderate flows, as the ICIC would not just perform an insurance, but also a signalling role. The proposal as made seems to refer more to international loans, but it could also possibly be extended to other flows, like portfolio ones. The key problem of Soros' proposal may be a serious moral hazard, unless the fee charged is high enough to appropriately cover risks of non-payment; the latter risk is of course hard to estimate ex-ante. However, the Soros proposal is interesting because if implemented it would smooth flows, encouraging them up to a 'reasonable' level, and discouraging them beyond that. It is also of interest because it explicitly tries to tackle imperfections in international credit markets, and in particular herd behaviour.

It would seem desirable to complement measures for improving and completing international prudential supervision for credit and capital markets as described above with a measure of international taxation. A measure that deserves attention is Tobin's proposal to levy an international uniform tax on spot transactions in foreign exchange. This proposal, initially made by James Tobin in 1972, has received much attention recently, particularly given turbulence on foreign exchange markets, both in Europe (1992) and in the emerging markets. Kaul, Grunberg and ul

Haq (1996) explore the issues in depth; Kenen (1996) in that volume in particular shows the practical feasibility of such a tax. Tobin's proposal is for a very low tax on all currency transactions. The aim would be to slow down speculative, short-term capital flows movements (which would be more affected as by definition they cross borders often, and would be taxed every time), while having only a marginal effect on long-term flows. This would achieve two objectives; it would increase the autonomy of national authorities for monetary and macro-economic policy, with a bit more independence from the effects of international money markets. Such an autonomy would be particularly valuable for LDCs, to the extent that their economies adapt less easily to external shocks and because their thinner financial markets are more vulnerable to the impact of external capital inflows and outflows. The second objective of the tax is to make exchange rates reflect to a larger degree long-run fundamentals relative to short-range expectations and risk. Volatility – in particular departures from fundamentals – would be diminished. So would the likelihood of currency crises.

This proposal is different from the others listed above, in that it may seem more radical. However, there is a widespread feeling, even in private circles, that financial liberalisation may have proceeded too far or at least too fast, and that financial liberalisation carried to the extreme may even risk damaging the far more important trade liberalisation whose benefits are far more universally recognised. Furthermore, a new tax with potentially high yields would be attractive to fiscally constrained governments. Part of the proceeds could also fund public goods like poverty alleviation and environment spending, especially in poorer countries. Therefore, a small tax on financial flows – which particularly discourages short-term flows – could be a welcome development. It could be introduced on a temporary basis for a fixed period, for example five years. This would be consistent with the fairly widespread perception that financial fragility and systematic risk are particularly high in the current stage of 'transition' from regulated freer financial markets.

It can be concluded that one or several measures need to be taken internationally to make currency crises in emerging markets far less likely, and therefore ensure the efficient operation of the market economy in emerging markets, which should be a basis for sustained development. The objective of crises avoidance seems to require some discouragement and/or regulation of excessive and potentially unsustainable short-term inflows. Such measures would be most effective if they are applied both by source and recipient countries, if they avoid discouraging more long-term flows, if the rules designed are simple and clearly targeted at unsustainable flows and if they are complemented by good policies in the emerging economies.

As in medicine, so with currency crises; prevention is far better than cure. Therefore, it seems desirable to particularly emphasise crisis prevention measures. However, if prevention fails and major currency crises do unfortunately occur, measures need to be in place to manage them as well as possible. It is to this that we turn in the next section.

IV Crisis management

The lender of last resort

The first response when a large currency crisis starts unfolding in one or more countries is to activate quickly a sufficiently large 'international lender of last resort' to provide the important public good of stability. The key institution in this has been the International Monetary Fund, both through its own resources and its catalytic role in attracting other resources.

A number of issues arise relating to the IMF's role as lender of last resort. The main ones seem to be: timing, scale, conditionality and ways to avoid moral hazard. We will discuss these briefly.

The issue of timing is crucial, as currency crises happen so quickly. Though the IMF and the international financial community have made important efforts to develop emergency procedures to speed up significantly the Fund's response in moments of currency crises, the response is still not fast enough. This implies that a currency crisis is able to unfold for a couple of weeks, before a financing package can be put in place. As markets move so fast and overact so much, a great deal of damage can occur in that period (e.g. there can be much overshooting of the exchange rate). Also, due to contagion the crisis can spread to other countries, adding to costs and problems.

The best solution seems to be to build on a suggestion made in a 1994 IMF paper ('Short-term Financing Facility'), and have preventive programmes; indeed, such a facility seems to have been established for the Philippines in early 1998. What this implies is that a request for a country's right to borrow from the IMF could be made before a crisis happens, for example during the time of an Article IV consultation. The country would only draw on this facility if a crisis occurred, but could do so immediately when it starts. This would, however, imply that the Fund would have a 'Shadow programme' with the country, and therefore impose some policy conditionality, focusing on conditions that would make a currency crisis less likely. The Fund's conditionality would naturally be less tough than in the middle of a crisis, as far less draconian measures would be required.

The country would have to accept conditionality even while it was not receiving disbursements; however, the country would have the very important advantage of an automatic right to draw off a large credit (or at least a first tranche) immediately when a crisis started; naturally, the drawing of the credit would be accompanied by an immediate report to the Fund's board, but *no* need for board approval. This procedure would have the *great advantage* for the country (and the international community) that the immediate activation of the facility would reassure the markets more quickly, thus hopefully reducing the scale of the crisis and its cost.

A second crucial issue is the scale of the lending, by the IMF and others. Bagehot's (1873) classic advice on national lenders of last resort was that – to be effective in convincing markets – such a facility must be able to 'lend freely', that is virtually open-ended, or at least extremely large. The massive scale for an international lender of last resort, given the scale of assets in the private markets, poses a serious challenge for governments and central banks of the major countries. This challenge is made more difficult by the resistance of the US Congress to providing further resources to the IMF, which are clearly necessary.

An additional serious problem, that has been insufficiently discussed, is that when such large volumes of IMF – as well as World Bank and Regional Development Bank – funding is channelled towards middle-income countries in crisis, funding available from those institutions for low-income countries can fall drastically. This is a very negative indirect effect of currency crises.

Two types of measures can help alleviate the pressure on the IMF and governments as international lender of last resort. The first one is to reduce the likelihood of currency crises, by giving high priority to adopting measures along the lines discussed in section III above. In particular it is necessary to limit moral hazard. Countries are not really subject to so much moral hazard, due to the dramatic economic, social and political costs of a currency crisis. Moral hazard, however, affects lenders, investors and fund managers; for this reason, it is essential that this moral hazard is curbed by appropriate preventive measures by source countries as well as internationally to regulate and/or discourage excessive easily reversible flows to emerging markets which could later precipitate a crisis, that would require an international lender of last resort.

The second measure to reduce the need for international public funding, is to attempt to involve the private sector in providing some of the liquidity required for the lender of last-resort facility. Reportedly, this has already been suggested in an IMF confidential report. This would imply adopting the experience of the 1980s debt crisis, when the IMF assembled financing packages that included concerted or 'involuntary' lending from creditor banks. However, as mentioned above, this may be somewhat more difficult, given the diversity of actors and the greater securitisation of instruments. This also makes it more important to develop orderly work-out procedures, as this will reduce the required scale for international lending of lender of last resort.

It is interesting that some countries (e.g. Argentina) have recently already themselves arranged stand-by facilities with international banks, only to be used in case of a currency crisis. This facility, however, has not yet been tested.

A final issue is the nature of IMF conditionality that should accompany the large financial packages, linked to currency crises. A number of criticisms have arisen of IMF conditionality. For example, Feldstein (1998) has argued that IMF conditionality has been too intrusive and too comprehensive, trying to make dramatic changes in very short periods. Radelet and Sachs (1998) have further argued that the conditionality has not been appropriate in several important aspects, (e.g. bank closures, tightening of fiscal policy, excessive emphasis on full debt repayment) and that even some of these measures and their pace have 'added to, rather than ameliorated, the panic'. Their critique seems particularly strong on the abrupt shutting down of financial institutions without a more comprehensive programme for financial sector reform and no deposit insurance in place, which in Thailand and Indonesia only deepened the panic.

On macro-economic policy, the key new challenge for IMF (and country) pro-grammes is to design appropriate macro-economic responses for currency crises that mainly originate in private sector imbalances (higher private investment than private savings), and not, as traditionally IMF packages were accustomed to dealing with, public sector imbalances, reflected in fiscal deficits. Therefore the tra-ditional IMF response – tightening fiscal policy – may either be totally inappropriate or insufficient. New elements need to be introduced, in the new context of private sector-led deficits, like counter-cyclic macro-economic policy; greater focus has to be placed not just in post-crisis macro-management, but in prudent fiscal and monetary management during periods of abundant capital inflows; this could for example even include cyclically adjusted taxation to curb excessive growth of private spending. Domestic prudential regulation of the finan-cial sector could also include anti-cyclical elements; this could include stricter prudential regulation of short-term foreign exposure by banks. It could also imply limiting the value of assets (e.g. real estate) allowed to be used as guarantees for loans, when the value of such assets can fall significantly if a currency and finan-cial crisis occurs.

Orderly workouts

Official lending during crises in heavily indebted countries can lead to moral hazard problems. In terms of borrowers, this could lead to excessive risk-taking or the danger that countries might pursue imprudent economic policies, believing that they would be bailed out in the event of a crisis. However, this is extremely unlikely given the huge cost to a country of a currency crisis (Strauss-Kahn, 1998). The risk of moral hazard is more on the lenders' side, as bail-outs mean that they do not have to bear the full risks of their investment decisions. Equally, a belief that a bail-out is likely in the future could discourage lenders from carry-ing out adequate risk appraisals.

In the absence of orderly debt workout procedures, the alternative to official financial intervention would be to continue with the drawn-out negotiations of the type seen in the 1980s. In the aftermath of the 1980s debt crisis countries were denied access to international capital markets for a number of years, which had serious consequences for economic growth. Therefore a system is required which can bring about the rapid resolution of crises, while limiting the problems of moral hazard. There is now a general consensus among the international com-munity that ways need to be found to involve private sector creditors at an early stage in crisis resolution in order to achieve equitable burden sharing *vis-à-vis* the official sector – in what Fischer has termed 'the bail-in question' (Fischer, 1998, p. 16; see also Interim Committee, 1998, p. 3).

This issue was also intensely debated after the Mexican peso crisis.[5] At that time, it was recognised that recent changes to the international financial system would affect the nature of future sovereign liquidity crises. The key changes were the increased globalisation of financial markets, changes in the composition of capital flows to emerging market countries, with an increase in debt in the form of securities, and a decrease in the likelihood that existing creditors would be pre-pared to offer new financing to a country experiencing a sovereign debt crisis (Group of Ten, 1996, p. 3).

Discussions at the time focused on ways to improve the existing mechanisms for dealing with such crises while minimising moral hazard for both creditors and debtors. Yet despite a great deal of support for some of the proposals put forward, the discussions did not result in any significant changes. The level of official financing used in the Asian crisis far exceeded that needed in Mexico, and in spite of official intervention the crisis has been more severe. Stiglitz has noted:

> In spite of repeated resolutions that lenders should bear more of the cost of their risky decisions, the moral hazard problem in the 1990s is, if anything, larger, not smaller than it was in the 1980s.
>
> (Stiglitz, 1998b)

Therefore in the wake of the Asian crisis, this issue has emerged again and the IMF, among others, is reviewing the proposals discussed in the aftermath of the peso crisis which included: the establishment of international bankruptcy pro-cedures; changes in the provisions of loan contracts and bond covenants; and IMF-supported debt moratoria (see Group of Ten, 1996, and Eichengreen and Portes, 1995). Each of these proposals has advantages and disadvantages.

First, it has been suggested that the features of bankruptcy procedures within countries could be applied to sovereign debt. International bankruptcy proced-ures, it is argued, could prevent the problems which arise when individual creditors race to press their claims, giving countries the chance to restructure exist-ing debts and secure new financing. However, this idea is unlikely to be put into practice given the apparently insurmountable legal difficulties involved. Even if it were possible to establish, it is difficult to imagine that an international bankruptcy court could have powers corresponding to national bankruptcy courts; with regards to creditors for example, to set aside existing contracts and to compel them to accept restructuring, and in terms of debtors, to seize collateral or to replace wayward governments (Eichengreen and Portes, 1995). Moreover, some level of official involvement in the resolution of severe crises is necessary, given the problems associated with containing systemic risk (Group of Ten, 1996).

Second, it has been proposed that changes should be made in the provision of loan contracts and bond covenants to both private and official borrowers. Such changes could facilitate orderly crisis resolution by encouraging dialogue between debtors and creditors, and among creditors, and by preventing dissident investors from holding up the settlement (Eichengreen and Portes, 1995). Provisions in loan contracts and bond covenants would provide for the collective representation of debt holders; allow a majority of creditors to alter the terms of payment through qualified majority voting; and require sharing among creditors of assets received from the debtor (Group of Ten, 1996, p. 14).

The third proposal is that IMF-supported debt moratoria could form the basis of orderly crisis resolution in exceptional circumstances (Group of Ten, 1996;

Wyplosz, 1998; and Eichengreen and Portes, 1995). Eichengreen and Portes (1995) suggest that the IMF should undertake a signalling function, advising when a unilateral payment standstill would be justified. The IMF sanction would mean that a government which received approval for a standstill would not risk its future access to credit. Equally, it is argued, moral hazard would be limited because of the possibility that the IMF would not sanction a moratorium. The Group of Ten (1996) stressed that while a suspension of payments may be necessary in extreme cases, there should not be any formal mechanism for signalling IMF approval.

Objections to an IMF-supported suspension of payments are based on the moral hazard problem and on disapproval of interfering with the efficient operation of the market. It has been argued that such a proposal could distort incentives and lead to excessive borrowing. However, it seems unlikely that countries would take excessive risks because of the possibility of a debt moratorium given the extremely painful consequences for a country which experiences a crisis. Furthermore, as Wyplosz (1998) points out, a suspension of payments would reduce the moral hazard that encourages lending by financial institutions that expect to be bailed out by an IMF-led rescue. Here, however, the danger would be that IMF-sanctioned moratoria might throw out the baby of capital flows to emerging markets in general with the bath water of more speculative or less sustainable flows (Griffith-Jones, 1996, p. 75).

There are also objections to debt moratoria based on the argument that the cost of capital could rise for all borrowers if they were used too often. Moreover, the issue of contagion implies that the involvement of the private sector in the resolution of the problems of one country could lead to capital outflows from other countries (Fischer, 1998, p. 16). Reportedly, the possibility of an IMF-supported orderly workout in one Asian country was not adopted because of fears that the crisis could spread to other regions. Such fears may always be there and inhibit the use of IMF-sanctioned payment standstills.

Despite the inherent difficulties, however, the international community is agreed that there is a need for new procedures for the resolution of crises in heavily indebted countries. The experience of the 1980s and 1990s has shown that, with the changes to the character of international financial markets, the existing mechanisms for crisis resolution are no longer adequate.

The principal benefit from the establishment of orderly workout procedures would be that priority could be given to dealing with the domestic implications of a crisis, rather than to paying back investors and creditors. This would be of particular value in situations where the basic fundamentals of the country concerned are sound, and the problem is more one of illiquidity than insolvency. In such cases, as Wyplosz (1998) points out, the weakness is usually a structural problem, such as high debt or a weak banking system, which will take time to be corrected. For such corrections to be worked through, it is imperative that the economic environment be as stable as possible, for as Wyplosz argues:

> Structural changes are easier and less costly when the economy is growing. It

is essential therefore that the priority be given to preventing the economy from being severely hit by the crisis.

(Wyplosz, 1998, p. 18)

V Conclusions

The international community has been reflecting on lessons emerging from the Asian crisis and what steps need to be taken to improve crisis prevention and crisis management in the new globalised economy. The IMF has played a central role in these discussions, putting forward its proposals for strengthening 'the architecture of the international monetary system'. While there is a general consensus that the ideas being put forward by the IMF are valuable, many now believe that more far-reaching reforms to the international financial system are necessary.

In terms of crisis prevention, the key IMF proposals put forward are: improving the availability and transparency of information regarding economic data and policies to both the Fund and the public, together with strengthening IMF surveillance; strengthening domestic financial systems, by improving regulation and supervision; and encouraging the orderly and properly sequenced liberalisation of capital flows. Earlier in this chapter we examined these proposals and showed that while they represent necessary steps toward a stronger international financial system, they would not be sufficient to prevent future crises. Key problems areas, such as the irrational behaviour of market participants and the difficulties of implementing financial sector reform in emerging market countries, represent major obstacles. Furthermore, while more prudent capital account liberalisation in emerging market countries would undoubtedly be welcome, many now believe that these sometimes fragile economies need to be protected from the full force of international finance. This could be done by one or several measures that better regulate or tax short-term capital flows, nationally and/or internationally.

At a national level, there seems to be growing consensus that market-based measures to discourage excessive surges of short-term capital flows are desirable, as part of a package of measures of good management of capital flows, which clearly includes prudent monetary and fiscal policies, as well as a well-supervised domestic financial system. The Chilean system of non-remunerated reserve requirements on inflows up to one year seem to work particularly well, even though they have some micro-economic costs.

Internationally, prudential regulation of short-term capital flows also may need to be improved, and completed, where gaps exist. In this context, two types of capital flows seem particularly relevant. One is short-term bank loans, whose regulation may need to be modified, as the current system provides strong regulatory incentives towards more short-term loans and less for long-term loans. Portfolio flows are at present totally unregulated by source countries, if they originated in non-bank institutions, like institutional investors.

Risk-weighted cash requirements for mutual funds in source countries – varying with macro-economic evolution in developing countries – may be an appropriate way to smooth such flows, which will be beneficial for developing countries. An alternative mechanism – that would achieve a similar objective – is the creation of a guarantee institution, that for a fee would guarantee flows to emerging markets, up to a limit. Another idea worth considering is that of a very small international tax on all foreign exchange transactions (known as the Tobin tax), that would also help discourage short-term flows without having any major effect on desirable long-term flows.

Though top priority needs to be given to crises prevention, measures also need to be put in place to improve crises management. They include improving existing mechanisms – led by the International Monetary Fund – for a lender of last resort. Improvements relate first to the necessary speed of such lending, given the incredible pace at which markets move; approval of shadow programmes before a crisis occurs, with loans activated as soon as one breaks out, may be an attractive option. The scale of existing facilities and IMF resources needs to be increased, given the large level of private funds flowing through international markets. To enhance the level of official facilities, the prospect of co-financing with the private sector – and particularly with private banks – needs to be explored.

Finally, the issue of appropriate conditionality attached to financial packages needs to be revised, so that the conditionality is best targeted to restoring market confidence, with minimum damage to growth in the countries.

Also there is now a general consensus among the international community that new ways need to be found to involve the private sector in crisis resolution in order to achieve equitable burden sharing with regard to the official sector, limit the problems of moral hazard and reduce the size of official financing required. This chapter has outlined some of the proposals for orderly debt workouts currently being reviewed: the establishment of international bankruptcy procedures; changes in the provisions of loan contracts and bond covenants; and IMF-supported debt moratoria. Examination of the possible benefits and shortcomings of these proposals suggests that despite the objections raised, international dialogue on these issues needs to be stepped up.

The policy debate in these areas needs to lead urgently to new policy measures and mechanisms, so as to avoid costly currency crises happening again and to manage them better if unfortunately they do happen. Given the complexity of the issues involved, the policy debate and actions need to be underpinned by improved knowledge.

Further work is required to understand better than we currently do:

1   How international capital and credit markets work. This will include, for example, better understanding of how decisions are made by different categories of bankers, fund managers and other actors to enter and leave countries. What explains domestic investors' behaviour? Are some foreign investors/lenders more volatile than others? What determines whether contagion from one country to others occurs? What explains the path of contagion?

2   What policy mechanisms could best be deployed nationally and internationally to prevent currency crises in developing countries? This would include

more detailed study of measures outlined above, but could also include others, like self-regulatory mechanisms within the financial industry and changes to the incentive systems of fund managers. The costs and benefits of different mechanisms need to be carefully assessed, together with the complex issues of implementation.

3   Finally there is the question of which existing international institutions are best suited for carrying out the different tasks, and whether there are any institutional gaps to be filled? How can co-ordination – between international institutions and between them and national authorities – best be improved? How can co-ordination between international public and private institutions most fruitfully be improved?

Notes

1   This chapter is based on a paper prepared for a Conference on Global Instability and World Economic Governance, held at Robinson College, Cambridge, on 13 May 1998. It draws on work undertaken for the Expert Group Meeting of the Commonwealth Secretariat in London on 15–17 June 1998. I appreciate the financial support of the Commonwealth Secretariat and the valuable suggestions of Aziz Ali Mohammed and Rumman Faruqi.
2   'Core Principles for Effective Banking Supervision' is annexed to the main text in IMF (1998).
3   IOSCO's 'Principles and Recommendations for the Regulation and Supervision of Securities Markets' is annexed to the main text in IMF (1998).
4   Communication with Colin Miles, Bank of England.
5   See, for example, the Group of Ten (1996) and Eichengreen and Portes (1995).

References

Agosin, M. 1996. 'El retorno de los capitales extranjeros a Chile', *El Trimestre Economico*, Mexico.
Akyuz, Y. 1998. *The East Asian Financial Crisis: Back to the Future?*
    http: //www.unicc.org/unctad/en/pressref/prasia98.htm
d'Arista, J. and Griffith-Jones, S. 1998 (forthcoming). 'The boom of portfolio flows to "emerging markets" and its regulatory implications', mimeo, IDS.
Bagehot, W. 1873. *Lombard Street: A Description of the Money Market* (London, reprinted John Murray, 1917).
Bank for International Settlements (BIS). 1995. *65th Annual Report* (Basle, BIS).
Boorman, J. 1998. 'Reflections on the Asian crisis: causes, culprits, and consequences', paper prepared for the FONDAD conference on 'Coping with financial crises in developing and transition countries: regulatory and supervisory challenges in a new era of global finance', March.
Budnevich, C. and Le Fort, G. 1997. 'Capital account regulations and macro-economic policy: two Latin American experiences', Banco Central de Chile. March. *Documento de Trabajo 06* (Santiago, Chile).
Camdessus, M. 1998a. 'Is the Asian crisis over?', address by Michel Camdessus at the National Press Club, 2 April, Washington, DC.
    http: //www.imf.org/external/np/speeches/1998/040298.HTM
Camdessus, M. 1998b. 'Capital account liberalization and the role of the Fund', remarks by

Michel Camdessus at the IMF Seminar on Capital Account Liberalization, 9 March, Washington, DC.

http: //www.imf.org/external/np/speeches/1998/030998.HTM

Chote, R. 1998. 'Crystal balls in Washington', in the *Financial Times*, 17 April 1998, p. 19.

Corsetti, G., Pesenti, P. and Roubini, N. 1998. 'What caused the Asian currency and financial crisis?', *Asian Crisis Homepage*, March.

http: //www.stern.nyu.edu/~nroubini/asia/AsianCrisis.pdf

Eichengreen, B. and Portes, R. 1995. *Crisis? What Crisis? Orderly Workouts for Sovereign Debtors* (London, CEPR).

Feldstein, M. 1998. 'Refocusing the IMF', *Foreign Affairs*, vol. 77, no. 2, pp. 20–33.

Ffrench-Davis, R. and Griffith-Jones, S. (eds). 1995. *Surges in Capital Flows to Latin America* (Boulder, Lynne Reinner).

Fischer, S. 1997. 'Capital account liberalization and the role of the IMF', 19 September.

http: //www.imf.org/external/np/apd/asia/FISCHER.htm

Fischer, S. 1998. 'The IMF and the Asian crisis', 20 March, Los Angeles.

http: //www.imf.org/external/np/speeches/1998/032098.HTM

Greenspan, A. 1998. *Financial Times*, 28 February.

Griffith-Jones, S. 1996. 'How can future currency crises be prevented or better managed?', in Jan Joost Teunissen (ed.) *Can Currency Crises Be Prevented or Better Managed?* (The Hague, FONDAD).

Griffith-Jones, S. 1998 (forthcoming). *Global Capital Flows* (London, Macmillan).

Griffith-Jones, S. and Lipton, M. 1987. 'International lender of last resort: are changes required?', in Z. Ros and S. Motamen (eds) *International Debt and Central Banking in the 1980s* (London, Macmillan).

Group of Ten. 1996. *The Resolution of Sovereign Liquidity Crises*, A Report to the Ministers and Governors prepared under the auspices of the Deputies, May.

IMF. 1995. *International Capital Markets: Developments, Prospects and Key Policy Issues* (Washington, International Monetary Fund).

IMF. 1997. *World Economic Outlook: Interim Assessment, December 1997* (Washington, International Monetary Fund).

IMF. 1998. *Toward a Framework for Financial Stability*, Prepared by a Staff Team led by David Folkerts-Landau and Carl-Johan Lindgren (Washington, International Monetary Fund).

Interim Committee of the Board of Governors of the IMF. 1998. *Communiqué*, 16 April 1998.

http: //www.imf.org/external/np/cm/1998/041698a.htm

Kaul, I., Grunberg, I. and ul Haq, M. (eds). 1996. *The Tobin Tax: Coping with Financial Volatility* (New York, Oxford University Press).

Kenen, P. 1996. 'The feasibility of taxing foreign exchange transations', in I. Kaul, I. Grunberg and M. ul Haq (eds) *The Tobin Tax: Coping with Financial Volatility* (New York, Oxford Univeristy Press).

Keynes, John M. 1936. *The General Theory of Employment, Interest and Money* (Cambridge, Cambridge University Press).

Khan, M. and Reinhart, C. 1995. 'Macro-economic management in APEC economies: the response to capital flows', in M. Khan and C. Reinhart (eds) *Capital Flows in the APEC Region*. Occasional paper 122, IMF, Washington, DC, March.

Mishkin, F. 1996. 'Understanding financial crises: a developing country perspective', *Proceedings of the World Bank Annual Conference on Development Economics*, pp. 29–77.

McKinnon, R. 1991. *The Order of Economic Liberalisation: Financial Control in the Transition to a Market Economy* (Baltimore, Johns Hopkins University Press).

Phillips, S. 1998. 'Risk weighted regulation'. Paper presented at FONDAD Conference. Holland. March.

Radelet, S. and Sachs, J. 1998. 'The onset of the East Asian financial crisis', first draft, 10 February.
http: //www.hiid.harvard.edu/pub/other/eaonset.pdf

Rodrik, D. 1998. 'Who needs capital account convertibility?', University of Harvard.
http: //www.nber.org/~drodrik/essay.PDF

Soros, G. 1997. 'Avoiding a breakdown', *Financial Times*, 31 December, p. 12.

Stiglitz, J. 1994. 'The role of the state in financial markets', Proceedings of the World Bank Annual Conference on Development Economics, IBRD, pp. 19–61.

Stiglitz, Joseph. 1997. 'Statement to the meeting of Finance Ministers of ASEAN *plus* 6 with the IMF and the World Bank, Kuala Lumpur', 1 December.
http: //www.worldbank.org/html/extdr/extme/jssp120197.htm

Stiglitz, J. 1998. 'The role of international financial institutions in the current global economy', address to the Chicago Council on Foreign Relations, 27 February, Chicago.
http: //www.worldbank.org/html/extdr/extme/jssp022798.htm

Strauss-Kahn, D. 1998. 'A fix, not a fudge', personal view, *Financial Times*, 17 April.

Wade, R. and Veneroso, F. 1998. 'The Asian financial crisis: the unrecognized risk of the IMF's Asia package', draft manuscript, Russell Sage Foundation, 1 February.

Witteveen, H. 1998. 'Economic globalisation in a broader, long-term perspective: some serious concerns', in J.J. Teunissen (ed.) *The Policy Challenges of Global Financial Regulation* (The Hague, FONDAD).

Wolf, M. 1998. 'Flows and blows', *Financial Times*, 3 March, p. 22.

World Bank. 1997. *Private Capital Flows to Developing Countries* (Washington DC, World Bank)

Wyplosz, C. 1998. *Globalised Financial Markets and Financial Crises* (London, CEPR).

4 International finance and global deflation

There is an alternative

Thomas I. Palley

Introduction

It is often said that geologists learn most about the earth's crust from extreme events such as earthquakes and volcanoes. A similar principle probably applies for economists, and it is illustrated by the financial crisis which erupted in east Asia in mid-1997.

The crisis and the IMF's initial response revealed two important things. First, the new international economic order is unstable and susceptible to financial crashes that carry the risk of global deflation. Second, the IMF is imbued with an economic philosophy that impedes achieving international financial stability and widely shared economic prosperity. This philosophy has given rise to an economic outlook that recommends fiscal austerity, financial liberalization, and export-led growth irrespective of circumstance. Over time, such a policy configuration stands to aggravate the problem of financial instability and trigger global deflation.

The revealed instability of the international financial system and the IMF's unduly austere initial response in turn reveal two clear needs. One is to remedy the underlying structural weaknesses that afflict the international financial system. The other is to reform the IMF.

At the systemic level, the fundamental problem concerns speculative "hot" money that chases yield and capital appreciation without regard to risk. The task is to make this money "cold," in the sense of getting investors to invest on the basis of economic fundamentals. Bail out critics argue that the only reliable mechanism is market discipline. Investors must eat their losses: bail outs merely encourage more risk taking by leading investors to believe that they will be bailed out when they get into trouble. There is logic to this argument, and bail outs that leave the system unchanged will produce this outcome. However, we can do better. Appropriately crafted market rules can turn hot money into cold money, while avoiding the periodic economic crashes that are the inevitable accompaniment of market discipline.

The other need is to reform the IMF. Though the IMF was forced to dilute its demands for austerity in east Asia, its initial response revealed the true color of its spots. Without fundamental reform of the IMF, there can be no confidence that it will not resort to the same policies in subsequent crises. Moreover, next time, the political leverage provided by the IMF's request for increased capital may not be available to get it to reverse course. The IMF remains committed to a policy of financial liberalization and expanded capital mobility. In pursuing this policy it has been driven by the myth of a "natural" market that can be achieved by abolishing controls on capital movements. However, rather than creating a natural market, this policy has merely created an unstable market that needlessly endangers livelihoods and prosperity. IMF reform is therefore needed if the existing policy dynamic is to be turned around.

The origins of the east Asian crisis

Though the IMF sought to place the blame for the crisis on excessive east Asian government intervention, the real cause lies in international capital markets. These markets permitted excessive short term foreign currency denominated lending, and they also encouraged extensive foreign portfolio investment. In combination with uncontrolled international capital mobility, this produced a combustible mix.

Globalization of finance has encouraged a taste for "emerging markets." In the early 1990s, this new taste was rewarded with spectacular returns, which attracted even larger flows of funds and produced a herd-driven move by investors and banks into east Asia. Moreover, this development was actively promoted by the IMF, which encouraged governments to eliminate controls, remove domestic ownership restrictions, and open domestic financial markets.

Portfolio investors hold equities denominated in local currencies, and are therefore concerned with the exchange rate since it determines the dollar value of their investments. Believing that the exchange rate was about to fall, equity investors in east Asia sought to protect their funds by selling out and repatriating them back home. However, this selling then drove the exchange rate down. In doing so, it increased the burden of foreign debts which are denominated in foreign currency, thereby pushing east Asia toward insolvency. Since much of east Asia's debts were of a short term nature, with the prospect of repayment not far off, this gave portfolio investors additional reason to sell. In this fashion, east Asia found itself locked in a spiral of exchange rate depreciation.

Having created an east Asian asset price bubble in the first half of the 1990s, international capital markets created a debt-deflation when they reversed themselves. The region had borrowed billions of dollars, and the decline in exchange rates increased the burden of these debts. The prospect of corporate bankruptcies then prompted foreign investors to continue bailing out. Given the increase in burden of debts, the supply of credit evaporated, thereby disastrously reducing economic activity and providing additional reasons to exit. In this fashion, the rush for the exits created a vicious cycle. Declining exchange rates worsened countries' debt burdens and lowered credit ratings, which in turn reduced credit availability, raised interest rates and lowered economic activity, which gave investors additional "fundamental" reasons to exit.

Globalization and the new danger of global deflation

The hallmark of globalization is increased international trade and financial flows. These flows have in turn produced an increase in economic interdependence. The east Asian crisis of 1997 revealed that entire regions can now be pulled down, but it is also possible that world economic interdependence is sufficiently advanced that regional downturns have acquired the potential to threaten all regions through an expanded global transmission mechanism.

There are a number of channels to this expanded transmission mechanism. One is international trade. Here the effects work though a combination of exchange rate depreciation and economic recession which together impact exports and imports, thereby transmitting shocks across countries. The international trade channel has always been present, but globalization has increased its relative significance by increasing exports and imports as a share of GDP. This is illustrated in Table 4.1 which shows how countries have become significantly more "open" since the 1960s, as measured by exports and imports as a share of GDP.

This international trade transmission mechanism may have been further strengthened by the development of regional trading blocs which have

Table 4.1 Openness of OECD countries, 1966–1995

	1966 (%)	*1995 (%)*	*Change (1966–1995) (%)*
United States	9.9	23.6	138
Canada	39.1	72.3	95
Japan	19.4	16.8 [a]	–13
Germany	51.1 [b]	63.4 [a]	24
United Kingdom	37.8	57.3	52
France	25.0	44.5	78
Italy	28.1	43.2 [a]	54
Austria	51.4	76.2	48
Belgium	73.5	137.2 [a]	87
Denmark	58.5	63.3	8
Finland	41.3	67.5	63
Netherlands	89.8	100.0	11
Norway	83.2	70.6	–15
Portugal	54.1	61.0 [a]	13
Spain	20.2	47.3	134
Sweden	43.8	75.3	72
Switzerland	58.7	66.9	14
G-7	30.1	45.9	53
Europe	51.2	69.6	36

Source: Author's calculations using IMF statistics. G-7 and Europe computed as simple average.

Notes
Openness = [Exports + Imports]/GDP.
a 1994 data.
b 1979 data.

accompanied globalization. When crisis strikes, entire regions can now be pulled down and this potentially amplifies disturbances through a cascade effect. Thus, an economic disruption in country A pulls down neighboring country B, and the combined disruption is then sufficient to pull down country C which is located in another region. The potential for such a cascade effect is illustrated by the US economy: in 1997 almost 30 per cent of US exports were directed to the east Asia region (Japan, China, Singapore, Taiwan, Hong Kong, South Korea, Thailand, Indonesia, Malaysia and the Philippines).

A second transmission channel is global commodity markets. Here the mechanism is commodity price deflation which reduces incomes of commodity-producing countries, thereby lowering their demand for exports from the industrialized world. Commodity price developments in late 1997 and early 1998 suggest that region-alization may have also strengthened this channel. Thus, markets recognized that east Asia is a major industrial basin and large consumer of primary commodities, and the implications of recession were therefore quickly reflected in lower prices for key commodities such as nickel, copper, and oil. However, balancing this defla-tionary effect is the fact that consumers in industrialized countries benefit from lower commodity prices which serves to increase their domestic spending power.

Even more important than the export demand effect of commodity markets is the potential for these markets to spread financial contagion. As commodity prices fall, commodity export earnings also fall. Since many commodity exporting coun-tries are hard currency debtors, these countries could start to face debt repayment problems that generate their own east Asian-style currency runs. Examples of indebted countries that are vulnerable to such an outcome are Chile which is exposed to the price of copper, and Mexico and Russia which are both exposed to the price of oil.

The international trade channel also has the potential for spreading financial con-tagion. Over the last decade, developing countries have been encouraged to adopt export-led growth policies. Such policies have set up a dangerous rivalry whereby countries compete for demand in industrialized countries, and it may have inad-vertently recreated the problem of competitive devaluation that afflicted the world economy in the 1930s. Thus, when one country suffers an extensive depreciation, financial markets soon shift their pressure on to the currencies of export rivals real-izing that those rivals now face difficulty maintaining their export competitiveness. In this fashion, future spirals of competitive devaluation could easily develop.[1]

Production shifting is a fourth channel now operating to transmit economic dis-turbances. Opening of international markets and increased mobility of capital have contributed to increased foreign direct investment flows. As a result, firms can increasingly engage in production shifting and investment diversion in response to large scale currency realignments. This production shifting channel is a new supply-side feature of globalization, and it stands to amplify the future effects of financial crises.

Related to this production-shifting channel is the fact that industrialized coun-try domestic labor markets are probably more fragile as a result of globalization. This is particularly true of the US economy in which nominal wages are more flexible owing to the decline in trade union membership, a phenomenon which is itself significantly attributable to globalization. Thus, declining transactions costs and increased mobility of physical and financial capital have enabled US business to shift unionized manufacturing jobs overseas or to "sun belt" states where labor laws make union organizing difficult. This development has increased worker economic insecurity, shifted bargaining power toward business, and made nominal wages more flexible.

The increase in nominal wage flexibility takes on significance when it is linked with increased household indebtedness (another feature that is particularly evident in the US economy). Wages are now more likely to fall in recessions, and household nominal income is also more volatile because a greater share of compensation derives from overtime hours and profit-sharing plans. The combination of downward flexibility of household nominal income and increased household indebtedness means that industrialized economies may have become more vulnerable to their own debt-deflation traps. The mechanism is as follows: falling household income renders heavily leveraged households increasingly insolvent, thereby worsening the problem of aggregate demand, destabilizing the banking sector, and cutting off the creation of credit. There are hints that the US recession of 1990 partook of such a process.

The expanded trade channel also interacts with the emergence of increased financial fragility within industrialized countries. The initial impact of the trade channel operates on the manufacturing sector, and especially export-oriented and import-competing sectors. Given increased export involvement, manufacturing sector profitability is more vulnerable to foreign disturbances, and falling profitability can cause a cutback in investment spending that spreads economic contraction more widely.

Declining profitability also has the potential to trigger a stock market decline. In industrialized countries, particularly the US, more households are now invested in the stock market and stocks are also more highly valued. Households are therefore more exposed to stock market fluctuations, and this has probably increased the magnitude of the stock market wealth effect on consumption spending. Consequently, future stock market downturns can be expected to have larger macroeconomic effects than in the past.

In sum, globalization has expanded the conventional international trade transmission mechanism. It has also promoted a restoration of *laissez-faire* price flexibility in commodity markets, product markets and labor markets. When linked with increased household indebtedness and increased household exposure to stock markets, these developments suggest that the world economy may have become more vulnerable to debt-deflations triggered by financial market crashes.

Capital mobility and the new problem of capital account governance

The above discussion of the international transmission mechanism reveals how globalization has widened the international propagation of financial shocks and made domestic economies more susceptible to deflation. This means minimizing the frequency and containing the scale of such shocks has become an urgent task.

Rather than being read in isolation, the east Asian crisis should be read as part of an on-going history of economic dislocation emerging out of international money markets. In 1994, Mexico was subject to a financial crisis rooted in unsustainable macroeconomic policies which international capital markets had bankrolled. In 1992, the British pound and Swedish krona were both subjected to speculative attack. The UK was forced to leave the European exchange rate mechanism, while Sweden was forced to raise interest rates thereby initiating a period of permanently higher unemployment. In the mid-1980s the US dollar was significantly over-valued, leading to a major deindustrialization of the American economy. A similar problem afflicted the British economy in the early 1980s. France has defensively tied its interest rates to German rates since the 1980s in order to protect against currency disorder and imported inflation, but the result has been massive unemployment. Finally, in 1982 there was an international debt crisis amongst developing countries.

International financial markets are deeply implicated in each of these crises. With regard to east Asia and Mexico, they allowed excessive short term foreign currency denominated lending. In the case of the Reagan dollar and Thatcher sterling over-valuations, portfolio flows responded to tight domestic monetary policy in a fashion that appreciated the exchange rate and caused deindustrialization. In the case of France, the government had to capitulate to the threat of an exit of financial capital and raise interest rates. International financial flows have either directly contributed to the making of instability, or they have acted in a way that has frustrated the conduct of domestic monetary policy.

In the post-Bretton Woods globalized economy, capital account governance rather than exchange rate management has become the critical problem. This marks a change from the Bretton Woods era when capital controls and relatively unintegrated financial markets meant that exchange rate management was the issue. Back then the problem was how to facilitate exchange rate realignments in response to balance of payments difficulties engendered by underlying country differences in productivity growth and inflation rates. Those problems are now taken care of by flexible exchange rates, but capital mobility threatens to undermine countries' abilities to conduct domestic monetary policy and developing countries' potential to grow. Though exchange rate fluctuations remain the most visible sign of crisis, they are the symptom of underlying deficiencies in the system of capital account governance. It is to this issue that policy makers must therefore direct their attention.

However, any redesign of the international financial architecture must also preserve the benefits of capital mobility. Just as national capital markets bring benefits of improved allocation of scarce capital, so too do international capital markets. Lender nations are made better off by being given access to the globally highest rate of return, while borrower countries are also made better off by getting access to lower cost foreign capital which enables them to undertake more investment. Portfolio holders are also given increased opportunities for portfolio diversification. The ensuing reduction in risk then enables them to adopt more high return/high risk projects, and this rebalancing of portfolios raises total rates of return (Obstfeld, 1994). These are real benefits that stem from voluntary exchange in expanded capital markets, and they must be preserved.

Finally, though crisis may provide the opening for reform, crisis must not be the exclusive focus of reform. The new financial architecture should certainly be designed to prevent the emergence of crisis, but equally important is that it work to promote a pro-growth full employment environment through the provision of widely accessible credit that is available on reasonable terms. In sum, the goal is the prevention of crisis, the preservation of the benefits of capital mobility, and the promotion of a pro-growth global economic environment.

Changing lender behavior: Tobin taxes, speed bumps and hedging

The revealed instability of the international financial system and its proclivity to frustrate expansionary domestic economic policy mean that there is a need to fix the system. One dimension of the problem concerns lender behavior. Though the IMF has sought to blame the east Asia crisis on excessive and unwise foreign borrowing, the reality is that the fault lies with lenders whose chase for yield resulted in an over-extension of credit. One accepted fact in economics is that borrowers have a proclivity to over-borrow, and well-functioning credit markets therefore place the onus of control exclusively in the hands of lenders. When credit markets fail, the *prima facie* case is always against lenders. The only time when lenders are excused is when there has been major fraud that could not have reasonably been detected. This is not the case for east Asia where countries' policies and procedures have been long established.

The chase for yield by both banks and portfolio investors is the root of the problem. Additional dimensions of the problem concern destabilizing exchange rate fluctuations and uncovered foreign currency denominated lending. All three dimensions need to be addressed.

East Asia's crisis has shown that the IMF's existing model of financial liberalization, predicated upon free capital flows, foreign portfolio investment and short term foreign currency denominated borrowing, is unstable and vulnerable to movements in the exchange rate. Such movements can be initiated either for reasons associated with economic fundamentals, or for completely speculative motives. Whereas the former are desirable since they contribute to economic balance, the latter are undesirable and can cause the system to collapse precipitously. The reason is that speculatively induced expectations of a declining exchange rate provide a rational pretext for individual portfolio investors to sell out. By selling out they protect the dollar value of their investment, but when they sell out this initiates a further fall in the exchange rate, thereby generating a vicious spiral.

A new mechanism is therefore needed to prevent such speculatively induced collapses. The natural candidate is the Tobin tax (Tobin, 1978), whereby a small tax (perhaps 0.1 per cent) is placed on all foreign exchange (FX) dealings. Such a tax would be sufficiently large to discourage speculative FX trading, but would not be large enough to discourage investors who are acting on the basis of economic fundamentals. Reducing speculative trading in this fashion would take a lot of noise out of the system, thereby reducing the likelihood of a speculatively induced rush for the exit such as has occurred in east Asia.

The crisis has also shown that foreign portfolio investment is extremely sensitive to exchange rate movements, be they driven by speculation or fundamentals. Investors are concerned with rate of return, and this is affected by the exchange rate. Once foreign portfolio investors begin to believe that the exchange rate will fall, they have good reason to sell. This then pushes the exchange rate further down, so that their actions become self-reinforcing. This same self-reinforcing tendency also holds with the development of asset price bubbles, when portfolio investors rush in and bid up asset prices and the exchange rate, thereby generating extravagant returns that attract the herd. New mechanisms are therefore needed to stop ill-considered financial inflows and sudden financial outflows.

The natural mechanism to stop such flows is "speed bumps", such as those that have been used to good effect by the Chilean monetary authorities. Such speed bumps work by having investors commit to a minimum stay (perhaps 12 months) when they bring money in. Attention has been focused on how speed bumps protect from sudden outflows because investors cannot withdraw their money at will. However, speed bumps have additional constructive incentive effects. Knowing that there are speed bumps, investors will think carefully before committing their funds. Instead of simply chasing yield, investors will take account of the risk that they might find themselves stuck in the midst of a crisis, unable to withdraw their funds.

Just as there are beneficial incentive effects on investors, so too there are beneficial incentive effects on policy makers. Given the presence of speed bumps, investors will demand risk premiums from countries where policy is unstable. Consequently, countries that want to obtain low cost credit will have an incentive to put in place stable policies so as to lower the risk premium they are charged.

A third element of lender failure concerns the existence of uncovered foreign currency denominated loans. The US is not exposed to this problem because it borrows in dollars. However, developing countries cannot borrow in their own currency, and are therefore exposed to increases in debt burdens resulting from foreign exchange fluctuations. Traditionally, the responsibility for protecting against such effects has lain with borrowers. However, hedging is expensive, and borrowers therefore have an incentive not to do so because creditors bear the loss in the event of default: once again, the fundamental economics of credit markets asserts itself. Unfortunately, the scale of international lending is now so large that the system is afflicted by a "too big to fail" problem whereby taxpayers are being forced (indirectly through IMF bail outs) to bear the losses. Creditors are therefore passing on their losses, and this has given rise to yield chasing and an explosion of uncovered risk that threatens to get ever larger.

A mechanism for correcting this situation is therefore needed. The economics of credit markets suggests that, rather than relying on debtors to hedge their borrowings, monetary authorities must instead insist that lenders hedge their loans against exchange rate risks on behalf of borrowers. As noted above, hedging is expensive and this will cause the cost of credit to rise. However, the risk is there, and it therefore needs to be priced in. Credit should not be subsidized as it now is through the provision of a bail-out safety net paid for by taxpayers. These new hedging regulations would apply to both bank loans and bond issues. Thus, when bonds are issued, they would also be required to be fully hedged as part of the terms of issue.

Changing borrower behavior: transparency, openness and labor rights

Reforming lender behavior is one part of fixing the system. However, borrower behavior also matters. The IMF has emphasized the problem of political corruption and economic cronyism which has given rise to misallocation of borrowed resources. It has advanced two solutions. One is to increase market transparency by requiring improved accounting and reporting standards. The second is to increase the extent of financial liberalization by giving foreign companies increased domestic market access. The argument is that market competition will compete cronyism away.

This belief is mistaken. The reality is that these behaviors are politically sponsored, and changing them requires political reform. All future bail outs (as well as the existing IMF programs in over seventy developing countries) should therefore require that governments abide by internationally recognized human and labor rights. This is the ethically correct course, but there is also a profound economic argument.

Ending cronyism and political corruption demands political reform that puts in place the countervailing forces needed to block such behavior. Human and labor rights are the foundation of such reforms. Crony capitalism distorts the behaviors of borrowers: it also distorts the actions of lenders, who all too easily get sucked into its malpractices. It is this logic that has prompted the OECD to adopt the Convention on Combatting Bribery (1997). Bribery distorts economic outcomes and reduces welfare, and hence the push to outlaw it. Political cronyism has the same effect, but the only way to end it is by establishing well-functioning democracies predicated on human and labor rights.

Fair and free markets cannot function in a corrupt and unconstrained polity. Under the 1994 Frank–Sanders law, US executive directors to the World Bank and IMF are already required to use the voice and vote of the US to urge their respective institutions to adopt policies that encourage borrowing countries to guarantee internationally recognized worker rights. It is now a matter of urgent public policy that the Frank–Sanders provision become part of standard IMF conditionality. The problems in east Asia have clearly revealed that this is a necessary ingredient for well-functioning international capital markets.

Another economic advantage of insisting on human and labor rights concerns economic growth and wages. Palley (1998a) documents how countries that have instituted improved rights of free association have grown significantly faster in the ensuing five-year period. Rodrik (1998) documents how greater democracy goes hand-in-hand with higher wages. This can help transform developing economies from being export dependent into mature economies in which their own citizens are the principal consumers. The current emphasis on export-led growth has given rise to a situation in which a few countries run large trade surpluses, and drain demand from the global economy. This chase for exports is contributing to global deflation. Having wages rise in newly industrialized countries would remedy this by creating the conditions whereby these countries could grow their industrial capacities on the basis of their own domestic demand.

Reasserting domestic monetary control: asset-based reserve requirements, requirements on foreign currency short sales, and Tobin taxes

A key consequence of increased capital mobility and the globalization of financial markets has been a tendency for domestic monetary authorities to lose control over interest rates. This loss of control is evident in France's adoption of the *Franc fort* policy, and in Sweden's forced adoption of higher interest rates in 1992 to defend the krona. Capital mobility allows financial capital to vote with its feet and veto policy it does not like. In general, financial interests prefer mildly deflationary policies as this preserves the value of financial assets. As a result, rather than lowering global interest rates, capital mobility may have contributed to institutionalizing deflationary monetary policy.

One policy for restoring domestic monetary control is the adoption of asset-based reserve requirements (ABRR). Existing reserve requirement regimes focus on the liability side (LBRR), and are an outgrowth of earlier concerns with depositor bank runs. Deposit insurance and the lender of last-resort function have now taken care of this problem, rendering LBRR obsolete. The new policy problem is how to regain control over interest rates for purposes of managing the domestic economy.

ABRR give monetary authorities a means of differentially affecting the cost of credit across sectors (Palley, 1997), thereby allowing them to cool individual sectors without cooling the entire economy. More importantly, the borrower cost of credit can be raised (by increasing reserve requirements) without raising money market interest rates. Thus, tighter monetary policy need not be accompanied by an inflow of foreign capital and exchange rate appreciation, such as happened in the US in the 1980s.

A second proposal (Eichengreen and Wyplosz, 1993) is that short sales of currency by individuals and corporate nationals be accompanied by placement of a non-interest-bearing deposit with the central bank equal to 50 per cent of their value. The regulation would also apply against foreign subsidiaries operating in the monetary authorities' jurisdiction, and against foreign subsidiaries and affiliates of all corporate nationals. This would reduce currency speculation by raising its cost, and it is workable because there are good reasons to believe that most

FX short sales come from domestic nationals since their income flows are denominated in the currency they are selling which significantly reduces their exchange risk.

The move to risk-based equity requirements also needs to be carefully reconsidered. This move has been prompted by a desire to minimize yield chasing. However, it risks destabilizing the system. This is because financial institutions suffer loan losses in bad times, which wipes out equity. Loan quality also deteriorates then. Consequently, financial institutions will have to raise more equity in bad times, but this is exactly when it is most difficult to do so. As a result, risk-based capital requirements could unleash a destabilizing dynamic, that squeezes the financial sector in bad times, thereby worsening asset price deflation and exacerbating credit contraction. This could transform shallow recessions into deep recessions.

In this regard, ABRR are a better instrument of control. These requirements can be calibrated according to the riskiness of assets, thereby addressing the moral hazard problem. However, when loans default, the reserve requirements on them are released, which mitigates any liquidity pressure financial institutions may be feeling. This helps preserve asset values and prevents unnecessary credit contraction.

Finally, not only are Tobin taxes good for mitigating currency speculation, they are also good for reasserting domestic monetary control. The Keynesian problem of loss of control over interest rates arises because of interest rate arbitrage, which has funds flowing from low rate centers to high rate centers. Tobin taxes introduce a small wedge that prevents complete arbitrage, and this creates a space for differences in cross-country interest rates.

Changing IMF policy: restoring an equitable pro-growth agenda

The final piece of the policy puzzle concerns IMF policy. The crisis in east Asia has revealed that the IMF is imbued with an economic mentality that impedes achieving financial stability and widely shared prosperity. This mentality is predicated upon the economics of fiscal austerity, financial liberalization, and export-led growth: it risks exacerbating the problems of financial instability and global deflation.

The danger posed by the IMF's current stance is illustrated by its initial response to the east Asian crisis (Palley, 1998b). Despite the fact that both South Korea and Thailand had consistently displayed fiscal responsibility, and even run sustained budget surpluses, the IMF arrived on the scene and immediately demanded government spending cuts and higher taxes. Coming on top of an already dire collapse in economic activity, such a recipe would inevitably have deepened east Asia's recession. Concerted opposition by the IMF's critics forced it to backtrack on fiscal austerity, but the IMF's plan still requires countries to aim for large trade surpluses that threaten to export deflation. One country's surplus is another's deficit, and this means that all countries cannot engage in export-led growth. Rather, countries must seek to develop their own domestic markets. However, as a country grows and sucks in imports, others must grow and take its exports or else it will become balance of payments constrained. Hence the need for an expansionary global regime.

The bottom line is that the IMF's policy combination of fiscal austerity plus devaluation engenders worldwide wage competition and deflation as countries seek to export their way out of problems. Side-by-side, the IMF's continued push for financial liberalization, unaccompanied by appropriate systemic reform to the domestic and international financial system, promotes financial fragility and entrenches moral hazard.

Reforming the IMF is therefore critical for two reasons. First, because current IMF policies are counter-productive; second, because the IMF's institutional standing means that it can importantly influence whether and how the international financial order is reformed.

Sachs (1997) recently documented how the IMF has stabilization programs in 75 countries. These countries comprise half the developing world. South Korea, the world's eleventh largest economy, has now been added to this list. The IMF has actively promoted the existing international financial order, but rather than seeing the proliferation of stabilization programs as evidence of design failure, the IMF sees it as vindicating its own existence.

The IMF's intellectual framework promotes financial instability, but there is no means to get it to change. The incentives are wrong. The east Asian bail out involves more than $100 billion, and its massive scale contributes to further growth in the size and import of the IMF. It is not the institution of the IMF that is wrong. An institution such as the IMF will always be needed to provide liquidity to the international financial system in times of financial crisis. Moreover, it should be remembered that the IMF was created under the Bretton Woods agreement in an era of progressive economic policy. Rather, it is the IMF's policies of economic austerity and inappropriately designed financial liberalization that are wrong. In the case of South Korea, the IMF persistently encouraged the South Koreans to open their economy. The Koreans did this, and in doing so they made themselves vulnerable to the type of bank run which they are now suffering. The lesson is clear. If countries are to engage in financial opening, then these moves must be accompanied by international reforms that render "cold" international capital flows. In the absence of these reforms, such openings can prove highly dangerous. The IMF has completely failed to appreciate this.

Overcoming these obstacles requires institutional reform. Just as the IMF has insisted on increased transparency in government and in financial markets, so too its decision making should be made transparent. The IMF also needs to engage in self-conscious institutional reform. There is too little diversity of economic opinion within the IMF, and this has promoted a closed state of mind. The consequences of this were evident in the wrong-headed call for fiscal austerity in South Korea and Thailand.

Though the IMF retreated on these policies, its original response revealed its true color. This time round, critics were able to get it to change its policies because the IMF needed political support for increasing its capitalization. In the absence of this, it is unlikely it would have changed its stance, and such leverage may not be available in future. Internal and external institutional reform is therefore essential: there must be greater intellectual diversity within the IMF, and the IMF must be subjected to regular open external monitoring by participant governments.

Finally, as one of the developing world's largest creditors, the IMF must consider the matter of debt relief. Debt service burdens now hinder much of the developing world from following an equitable pro-growth agenda. They also force the third world to focus on export-led growth, which has contributed to deteriorating terms of trade, as well as causing job loss in developed countries. Debt relief is a means of getting out of this box.

Paying for such debt relief is a third way in which Tobin taxes can help since they would raise billions of dollars, some of which could be used to finance a Marshall Plan for the third world.

Conclusion: rediscovering imaginative regulation

The inter-war years were a period of economic depression and competitive devaluation. In the immediate post-war era, the Bretton Woods system prevented competitive devaluation, while governments pursued Keynesian demand management policies that ensured full employment. However, in 1973 the Bretton Woods system broke down because of its inability to deal with repeated instances of balance of payments disequilibrium.

The system of flexible exchange rates that replaced Bretton Woods addressed the problem of balance of payments disequilibrium. However, this system has itself fallen prey to the emergence of unrestrained international capital mobility which has introduced a new set of capital account management problems. Governments can no longer conduct effective stabilization policy because financial markets veto policies they do not like. Side-by-side, the scourge of competitive devaluation has re-emerged owing to speculative herd-driven investor behavior in financial markets. Such behavior generates asset price bubbles that are financed by international capital inflows. However, once the bubble bursts, countries are forced to undergo massive devaluations to generate the foreign currency earnings needed to repay earlier borrowing, thereby triggering the competitive devaluation process.

Reform of international money markets has become an urgent priority. Such reform must aim to change both lender and borrower behavior while preserving capital markets' abilities to efficiently allocate scarce capital. It must also aim to restore control to domestic monetary authorities and promote a pro-growth economic environment.

Unfortunately, there has been a colossal failure of imagination amongst policy makers that has prevented this from happening. This failure is illustrated by Chairman Greenspan's speech to the Economic Club of New York which reiterated the IMF mantra that the only thing policy makers can do is push for fiscal austerity and more financial liberalization.[2] This is economic fatalism, whereby the right to control economic destiny is rendered subservient to the dictates of global capital markets.

Regulation is difficult, and it requires imagination. Moreover, regulation needs to be updated. Effective regulation places constraints on profit-maximizing firms and prevents them from doing what they would like to do. They therefore have an incentive to seek out ways to evade regulation, and over time they inevitably succeed in doing so. In effect, good regulation always sows the seeds of its own destruction. This is the Rosetta stone of all good regulators.

Over time, financial markets will undoubtedly innovate in ways that evade the above package of regulations. This in no way invalidates the package; instead, it merely affirms that regulation is an on-going process that needs to be continually updated. Sometimes regulators are lucky enough to get ahead of their market rivals, as illustrated by the successful financial regulations of the New Deal. Sometimes, regulators merely manage to keep abreast of the game. However, there is never an excuse for capitulating and surrendering the public interest to the dictates of the market.

Notes

1 It is easy to create a counter-factual scenario whereby the depreciations which have afflicted east Asia spread to other countries as they try to maintain export competitiveness. China and Hong Kong face the prospect of reduced international competitiveness, and Brazil which is Latin America's industrial giant faces similar problems. Once landed in Latin America, Argentina and Mexico could then readily become victims of a competitive devaluation spiral. Chile is also vulnerable since 40 per cent of its exports go to east Asia, and copper which is its major export has fallen in price.
2 Speech to the Economic Club of New York, December 2, 1997.

References

Eichengreen, B., and Wyplosz, C. (1993), "The Unstable EMS," unpublished paper, presented to the Brookings Panel on Economic Activity.

Obstfeld, M. (1994), "Risk-Taking, Global Diversification, and Growth," *American Economic Review*, 84, 1310–29.

OECD (1997), *Convention on Combatting Bribery*, Paris.

Palley, T.I. (1997), "Asset Based Reserve Requirements: An Unappreciated Instrument of Monetary Control," Technical Working Paper, T007, AFL-CIO Public Policy Department, Washington, DC.

Palley, T.I. (1998a), "The Beneficial Effects of Core Labor Standards on Economic Growth," AFL-CIO Public Policy Department, Washington, DC.

Palley, T.I. (1998b), "Unnecessary Austerity: A Case Study of the Initial IMF Rescue Packages for Thailand and South Korea," AFL-CIO Public Policy Department, Washington, DC.

Rodrik, D. (1998), "Democracies Pay Higher Wages," NBER Working Paper 6364.

Sachs, J. (1997), "Power Unto Itself," *Financial Times*, December 11.

Tobin, J. (1978), "A Proposal for International Monetary Reform," *Eastern Economic Journal*, 4, 153–9.

Part II
Global instability

5 Creating international credit rules and the Multilateral Agreement on Investment

What are the alternatives?[1]

Elissa Braunstein and Gerald Epstein

I Introduction

International relations of production, mediated either by the market or through the internal transactions of multinational corporations (MNCs), are spreading rapidly to most parts of the world. This process of "globalization," though exaggerated by some analysts, should not, on the other hand, be dismissed as just more of the same.[2] While by some measures, the internationalization of production is no more extensive now than in 1913 (see the discussion and data below), this comparison is misleading. First of all, considering the standards of living and economic and political rights of workers and communities, 1913 can hardly be hailed as a reassuring benchmark. Second, the role of national governments and the welfare state in much of the world is fundamentally different and greater now than it was in 1913.[3] Hence, the world has never before experienced 1913 levels of globalization with 1990s' levels and types of government intervention. Are they compatible with each other? Are they sustainable?

These questions are at the heart of the analysis of international economic property relations and governance structures. For as globalization has proceeded, MNCs, financial institutions, and governments have accelerated the pace of constructing this architecture. The creation of the World Trade Organization (WTO), the European Monetary Union, and the North American Free Trade Agreement (NAFTA) are only three of the most important developments in these attempts. Since the mid-1990s, negotiations have taken place at the Organization of Economic Cooperation and Development (OECD) to formulate the so-called Multilateral Agreement on Investment, establishing property rights and governance structures for international capital movements – foreign direct investment (FDI) as well as portfolio investment.

As was the case in the creation of capitalism, these international initiatives have been led by capitalists. In the current era, these capitalists are mostly large banks and businesses, which have attempted to create an edifice to their liking. And similarly, as with the establishment of national property relations and nation states, this process is hotly contested by different groups of capitalists and wealth owners. In the current case of the creation of international economic relations, these conflicts often take the form of disagreements among banks and corporations from different nations, and therefore among national governments, who, depending on the country's level of development and other aspects of their economic position, fight over the form of the international governance structure.

In a much weaker position in the construction of this new system are labor and communities. In many developing countries, workers and citizens have very little power because of the relatively authoritarian nature of their governments, and because the developing country governments themselves have been marginalized in the negotiating process. In the developed capitalist economies, workers are not without power. Since democratic governments are creating this new structure, labor and the citizenry have some power to influence the position taken by governments. But, in this context, they are at a severe disadvantage in the sense that labor organizations have lost power *vis-à-vis* business in national politics over the last twenty-five years or so in virtually every major industrialized country. So citizens' power to organize the state to support their interests in these negotiations is weak. In the rise of national capitalism, labor formed organizations on the same geographical basis as capital to fight over the creation of property rights and the state. But now, the geographical context is more global, whereas labor organization is still primarily national.

Increasingly stepping into the breach are non-governmental organizations (NGOs), which have become organized internationally and are contesting the business-led creation of this new world governance structure. While these NGOs cannot match the wealth and power of the corporations, they have had some successes and are likely to have more.

In this chapter we analyze these issues of international governance with respect to capital flows, more particularly with an emphasis on MNC production and FDI; the concrete context for our discussion is the Multilateral Agreement on Investment (MAI). The chapter is organized as follows. In the next section we present some data on the evolution of globalization with special reference to FDI. In section III, we introduce the MAI and a framework for understanding the nature of the MAI. In section IV we consider its effects, and in section V we propose an alternative to the MAI. An appendix presents a simple economic model to help analyze the functions and effects of agreements like the MAI.

We first conclude that the MAI and similar initiatives have two main effects: (1) to create a new set of *international* property relations and governance structures, and (2) to fundamentally change *national* property relations and governance to the benefit of MNCs but at the expense of citizens, labor and communities. Because of its domestic policy intents and impacts, it is a mistake to see the MAI as simply a benign vehicle for structuring international economic relations.

Second, we conclude that unless labor, citizens and national governments want to dramatically reverse the level of international economic interaction, they will have to fight for an alternative set of international structures. Just strengthening the state will not suffice because of the already existing market power of global finance and MNCs.

Finally, however, we argue that promoting national, regional and/or international policies to expand aggregate demand and strengthen national controls over capital flows will also be a necessary part of any transition to citizens' governance over capital. Because without these, citizens and labor are less likely to get the political power they need to defend themselves against the political and economic attacks of business on a global scale.[4]

II International capital flows: some stylized facts

The context of globalization

The term "globalization" has no common, widely agreed upon meaning.[5] We define it quite simply as follows: globalization is the widening and deepening of international economic interactions (Milberg, 1998). Note that this definition does not say these relations are necessarily international *market* relations. This is because it is a mistake to see globalization as synonymous with marketization and economic liberalization. Economic liberalization is one form globalization can take, and indeed, that is precisely its form in the current era – globalization is occurring in a neo-liberal regime. But one can imagine international economic relations that are not dominated by pure market relations, but, rather, are embedded in rich social structures of governance.[6] Indeed, as we will argue below, many of the problems which appear to stem from globalization are really problems associated with globalization in the neo-liberal regime of deregulation and *laissez-faire*.

The paradox confronting many analyses of globalization is that while the changes upon us seem revolutionary, much of the data suggest that what we are experiencing is, in fact, not unprecedented. Table 5.1 presents some measures of international economic relations. As the table suggests, by some measures, globalization in 1913 was just as extensive as it is in the 1990s. The stock of FDI was 9 per cent of world output in 1913 and just a shade bit higher in the 1990s at 10.1 per cent. The stock of overseas assets was 1.9 per cent of world exports in 1913 and 2.1 per cent in the 1990s. Yet some things have changed quite dramatically. Whereas manufacturing was primarily an occupation of the rich countries in the early twentieth century, by the late twentieth century manufacturing had become a large share of exports in many parts of the world, high wage and low wage. To take the most dramatic case: whereas in 1913 Asia exported 21.2 per cent of its output, by the 1990s it was exporting 73.4 per cent. This world competition in exports from poor countries is surely a key difference between globalization then and now. Second, recently there has been an acceleration in portfolio investment that is probably historically unparalleled. Funds raised on international financial markets were only 0.5 per cent of world exports in 1950 and were up to 20 per cent in the 1990s, and this is probably an underestimate, given that these data exclude financial options and other derivatives.

But it is the change in context for globalization that is most dramatic and most

Table 5.1 Measures of globalization, 1913–1996

	1913	1950	1990s
World exports/GDP (%)	8.7	7.0	13.5
Manufacturing exports as percentage of total exports			
Asia	21.2	25.3	73.4
Latin America	3.2	2.3	48.7
FDI (stock) relative to world output	9.0	4.4	10.1
World overseas assets/exports (%)[a]	1.9	n.a.	2.1
Funds raised on international financial markets			
as percentage of world exports	n.a.	0.5	20.0

Source: Baker, Epstein and Pollin (1998).

Note
a World overseas assets/world exports: 1885: 2.2; 1938: 1.6.

Table 5.2 Central government expenditures as a share of national income (C) and military expenditure as a share of central government expenditure (M), 1870–1994 (%)

	1870		1914		1950		1994	
	C	M	C	M	C	M	C	M
France	15.0	34.3	11.8	28.8	33.2	42.5	47.2	5.6
Germany	5.5	—	7.0	—	—	23.7	34.0	5.9
Great Britain	5.0	—	8.0	25.0	39.2	13.1	42.7	10.1
Sweden	5.3	—	7.5	—	21.3	20.0	51.0	5.3
US	4.7	32.6	2.4	69.1	17.3	50.2	22.0	18.0

Sources: Authors' calculations, from UN (1997).

important. Since the 1940s, when the modern welfare state came into being, globalization and marketization on a world scale, which had been severely curtailed by depression and war, accelerated rapidly, as seen by comparing the Table 5.1 data for 1950 and the 1990s. This acceleration is all the more dramatic when placed against the numbers of Table 5.2. Table 5.2 shows that in 1870 and 1914, government spending was a very small fraction of national income, and of that small fraction, a quarter to one-half was spent on the military. In 1994, by contrast, central governments spent a much larger amount relative to the size of their economies (by a factor of seven or eight), and most of that was being spent on programs other than the military, such as education and transfer payments. It is this context for globalization which is so new and so problematic: we have not seen 1913 levels of globalization with 1990s' levels of the welfare state and social protection.

Foreign direct investment and multinational corporations

In this chapter we focus on FDI and MNCs.[7] FDI has been growing in recent years far faster than world trade (see Table 5.3). The bulk of the stock of FDI is

Table 5.3 Indicators of growth of international economic activity, 1964–1994 (average annual % change)

Period	World export volume	World FDI flows	International bank loans	World real GDP
1964–1973	9.2	—	34.0	4.6
1973–1980	4.6	14.8	26.7	3.6
1980–1985	2.4	4.9	12.0	2.6
1985–1994	6.7	14.3	12.0	3.2

Sources: Crotty, Epstein and Kelly (1998); UNCTAD (1997a: Table 24, p. 71).

Table 5.4 Regional distribution of the stock of inward FDI, 1980 and 1996

Inward stock of FDI as a % of the total:	1980	1996
Developed	78	70
US	17	20
European Union	39	38
Developing	22	28
Latin America	10	10
Asia	10	17
Hong Kong and China	0.4	5.5

Source: UNCTAD (1997b: Annex table B.3 and authors' calculations).

among the world's wealthier countries ("the North"), but the amount going from the "North" to the "South" has been increasing in recent years (see Table 5.4). The most astounding change is the rapid increase of flows to Asia, which increased its share of the world's stock of inward FDI from 10 to 17 per cent between 1980 and 1996. Note the spectacular rise in China and Hong Kong, which has increased its share of the world's stock of inward FDI from 0.4 per cent in 1980 to 5.5 per cent in 1996.

More generally, a handful of developing countries in Asia and Latin America, and a number of countries in Eastern Europe and the former Soviet Union, are beginning to see rapid increases in FDI; but still, on the whole FDI predominantly flows among the OECD countries. Hence, it is no accident that the major initiative to create a multilateral legal structure for FDI is being negotiated at the OECD.

III The international credit regime and the Multilateral Agreement on Investment

The MAI is an international economic agreement designed to limit the power of governments to restrict and regulate foreign investment, both FDI and portfolio investment.[8] Its principles are based on those embodied in the investment provisions of the North American Free Trade Agreement, but the MAI amplifies these provisions and, unlike NAFTA, which only applies to the US, Mexico and Canada, would apply first to all OECD countries, and then to countries outside the OECD which could become signatories.

The key provisions of the agreement include:

1   *National treatment,* which requires countries to treat foreign investors at least as well as domestic firms, but, in the words of the OECD, "[Countries] have no *obligation* to grant foreign investors more favourable treatment."[9]

2   *Most favored nation (MFN)* status, which requires governments to treat all foreign countries and all foreign investors the same with respect to regulatory laws.

3   *Limiting performance requirements,* which are any laws that require investors to invest in the local economy or to meet social or environmental goals in exchange for market access.

4   *Limiting the ability of governments to restrict the repatriation of profits and the movement of capital,* thus ensuring that corporations and individuals can move their assets more easily.

5   *Banning uncompensated expropriation of assets.* The MAI would require governments, when they deprive foreign investors of any portion of their property, to compensate the investors immediately and in full. Expropriation would be defined not just as the outright seizure of a property but could also include governmental actions "tantamount to expropriation". Thus, certain forms of regulation could be argued to be expropriation, potentially requiring governments to compensate investors for lost revenue.

6   *"Roll-back" and "standstill" provisions* that require nations to eliminate laws violating MAI rules and to refrain from passing any such laws in the future. State and local, as well as federal laws, would probably be affected, though many existing laws specifically acknowledged by "reservations" to the agreement will be exempted.

7   *Investor-to-state dispute resolution* that would enable private investors and corporations to sue national governments and seek monetary compensation when they believe a law, practice or policy violates investors' rights as established in the agreement. This provision is a significant departure from most previous international agreements, save NAFTA, and is perhaps the most important aspect of the MAI. Previous agreements, such as the General Agreement on Tariffs and Trade, only allow governments to bring complaints against other governments, whereas this provision would allow corporations to sue governments over these issues.

It is important to note that the MAI does not include any binding language on the *responsibilities* of corporations or any mechanisms to enforce those responsibilities.

Negotiations on the MAI began in May 1995 and were originally scheduled to be completed by May 1997; the deadline was then extended for another year, and then extended again. As we discuss below, the major sticking point in the negotiations from the point of view of the negotiators is the question of access; some countries, including France, do not want to give foreign investors access to all sectors of their economies. If completed, the MAI will be presented to the governments of OECD countries for approval; developing nations will also be encouraged to join.

Immediately, the question arises: why is such a treaty being negotiated? Since foreign investment is a market phenomenon, why can't the market simply operate on its own without governments getting involved? There are three answers: (1) access, (2) enforcement, and (3) rolling back the state.

Access

By signing on to the MAI, countries would agree to open up virtually all sectors of their economies to FDI. Countries now limit foreign investment in various economic sectors for a variety of reasons: to protect domestic ownership of militarily sensitive production, or to protect the viability of certain forms of indigenous production, for example the French film industry. In this sense, access involves many of the same issues as are involved in trade agreements, such as how much to protect domestic industry, and therefore reflects competition among rival capitalists.

It has a further dimension, however. Open access might also force governments to offer government-owned sectors to foreign investment. Whether this is a good thing depends on a large number of factors including how "socially" efficient the industries are currently run, and how they would be run if they were turned over to private ownership. In many cases, social control over production in some sectors of the economy is likely to be curtailed by the agreement.

These issues of access constitute some of the most contentious from the point of view of the negotiators, and help to account for some of the continuing delays in reaching agreement. However, apart from the issue of government-controlled sectors, these conflicts are primarily inter-capitalist rivalry. Of far more concern to workers and citizens generally are the other two aspects of the MAI: enforcement and rolling back the state.

Enforcement

All relations of authority, including property relations, need some kind of enforcement mechanism to operate. Walrasian economics, the dominant version of mainstream economics until the last decade or so, was built on the idea that enforcement was unproblematic. For Marx, as for modern post-Marxian and so-called analytical institutional economics, one of the central problems of economics is to get others to behave in ways that aren't always in their best interest: to labor when the boss isn't watching; to not expropriate or excessively tax or regulate foreign investment; or to not be excessively risky with borrowed money (Bowles and Gintis, 1990). Legal structures and courts provide *exogenous enforcement* of transactions in cases where transactions (or contracts) are relatively transparent. But since you can't always know which future contingencies might arise, or even what the other contracting party is up to all of the time, contracts often require *endogenous enforcement* mechanisms as well. Endogenous enforcement results in things like paying workers high wages so they don't want to lose their jobs and thus work harder (employment rents). Without sufficient exogenous or endogenous enforcement, many types of economic relations will not function well, and can even cease to exist. The more powerful the mechanisms of exogenous enforcement, the less costly and necessary are endogenous forms.

These considerations are especially important in credit relations where it is difficult to monitor the use to which credit is put and where, because of the fungible nature of credit, it is easy to divert credit from its presumed use. Collateral is a central mechanism of endogenous enforcement in credit relations.

Enforcement is much more problematic in the realm of international investment than in that of domestic investment, because although there are powerful court enforcement mechanisms at the national level, such legal structures are absent at the international level. Moreover, seizing collateral from a sovereign nation is fraught with the same problems of force and enforcement entailed in the international lending to begin with. How, then, can international lenders and investors be assured that there will be a sufficient likelihood that they will be repaid? Without such mechanisms of enforcement, international lending and investment will be relatively low or non-existent.

Building on the seminal work of Lipson (1986), Epstein and Gintis (1992) develop the idea of an international credit regime (ICR): an international institutional structure that provides the enforcement investors need to make foreign investment. This ICR consists of an enforcement structure and a repayment structure. The former is the set of institutions that creditors use to enforce repayment, such as the IMF and the US government; the latter is the set of arrangements or policies that debtor countries use to convince creditors that they will not interfere with investments, such as an outward-oriented trade policy that makes debtors vulnerable to trade sanctions. Agreements such as the MAI can be interpreted as elements of an ICR, enabling creditors to sanction recalcitrant debtors, and providing structures for debtors to make themselves vulnerable to such sanctions in order to convince creditors that they, the debtors, will not interfere with creditors' investments.

The North American Free Trade Agreement, while one of the most significant multilateral treaties offering investment protection, is by no means the only such recent agreement. The number of bilateral investment treaties (BITs) for the protection and promotion of international investment has increased extremely rapidly in recent years. In 1960, there were 75 such treaties in existence; by the end of the 1980s, the number had jumped to 386. By January 1, 1997, there were 1,330 BITs in existence, involving 162 countries (UNCTAD, 1997b: 19).

Countries have been interested in entering into such agreements for many reasons. Perhaps the most important, the disintegration of the Soviet Union and the evident discrediting of its economic model, along with decades of attempted sabotage of alternative development models by the US and international organizations, dramatically enhanced the TINA view prevalent among today's governments: there is no alternative to integration into the world economy.

Hence, there has been a large increase in both developed and developing countries' openness to MNCs, and increased willingness on the part of developing countries to enter into treaties to protect foreign investment.[10]

The MAI strengthens the BITs and reinforces pressures for liberalization. The key difference between the MAI and the BITs is the investor-to-state-resolution provisions of the MAI. These allow corporations to sue governments at any level if they think that the agreement has been violated, whereas in BITs, only governments can seek redress. This provision of the MAI provides a gargantuan increase in the international enforcement power of MNCs. With their deep pockets, they would be able to intimidate governments by simply threatening to take them to court over real or perceived interference with their prerogatives.

Rolling back the state

The ability of MNCs to sue states for imposing regulations and performance requirements could provide them with a powerful tool to fight government controls and regulations, a tool they could never have expected to wield through their national and local governments alone. In this sense, the MAI provides a Trojan horse, having nothing to do with international investment per se, by which domestic and foreign corporations can get leverage over national policies and fight against the ability of democratic governments to regulate the prerogatives of property owners. The issue is different from that portrayed by some populist opponents: it's not that foreigners are usurping national sovereignty. Rather, through the use of an international treaty, it is capital, both domestic and foreign, usurping the rights of citizens and workers in their attempts to influence government policy.[11]

IV Analyzing the MAI

The benefits of MAI

What about the positive benefits that MAI proponents argue might accrue to citizens from more investment, jobs and technology transfer? The MAI will be beneficial to the extent that it increases the quantity or quality of real investment; so for purposes of discussion it is helpful to ask whether the rules are: (1) investment-creating, (2) investment-enhancing, and/or (3) income (or rent) redistributing. We begin by considering investment within the OECD, and then extend the analysis to developing countries.

Investment creation

It is an important empirical question as to how much new real investment will be generated as a result of the MAI within the OECD. There is already a substantial amount of FDI within the OECD from other OECD countries. It seems unlikely that changing the rules along the lines of the MAI would generate a great deal of new investment. Even if it did, the domestic investment forgone would have to be netted out. This effect is likely to be large because of the relatively closed nature of the OECD countries as a group with respect to FDI: if a UK company invests in Germany, it is probably not investing in the UK or Ireland. So, truly new investment would only be forthcoming if the MAI raised the profitability of investment per se, and not simply made one location more profitable than another. It is likely that the MAI would succeed in doing so only to the extent that it would shift rents from other activities (point 3 below) or eliminate truly socially wasteful rules and regulations. The burden of proof must surely be on the promoters of the MAI to demonstrate that it would have that effect, but most of the promotional literature is so vague that the question has not even been properly posed.

Investment-enhancing

The MAI could yield benefits if, by eliminating inefficient rules and regulations, it could improve the quality of investment, either by improving access to more profitable sectors, or by allowing more effective use among already targeted sectors. Those who believe that the MAI will promote privatization of inefficient government sectors, or will eliminate socially inefficient performance requirements, are banking on this positive effect. Again, there has been very little in the way of a rigorous attempt to estimate these effects.

Rent (or income) redistributing

By altering the distribution of power between workers and citizens on the one hand, and corporations on the other, the MAI could simply redistribute income from workers and citizens to firms, either of this generation, or, by harming the environment, from future generations. By enhancing the bargaining power of firms relative to citizens, the MAI makes it more likely that firms will capture what gains there are to be had from any increase in investment that occurs.

We suspect that, at least within the OECD, this will be the major impact of the MAI.

If the MAI were extended to less developed countries, the analysis of potential benefits is more complicated.[12] The case for the MAI leading to new investment in developing countries is stronger than that made for increased investment within OECD countries, but under the terms of the MAI, which outlaw performance requirements and other government regulation, this may be a pyrrhic victory. Under the rules of the MAI, even if financial flows arrive, they may not benefit the domestic economy.

For FDI to enhance economic development, it must fit within the overall development strategy (Dunning, 1994). But liberalization itself, and the investment treaties that accompany it, often make it more difficult for developing economies to utilize FDI to their best advantage. The early and more recent experiences of the East Asian NICs suggest the flaws in this liberalization approach. Education, infrastructure and other public services played a central role in their development strategies and contributed to decades of success by fostering environments favorable to both domestic and foreign investment. Moreover, this region attracted FDI despite the presence of some of the most restrictive investment regimes in the world. It has only been in the recent context of the liberalization of financial flows in East Asia that crises have emerged, indicating the potential costs to developing countries that the liberalized atmosphere specified in the MAI might bring.

To the extent that the MAI increases or enhances foreign investment in developing countries, we argue constraints imposed on developing country governments make it extremely difficult to capture the benefits of increased FDI and portfolio investment, and are likely to result in merely a redistribution of what benefits are created away from host countries to multinational investors.

What is the evidence? Capital mobility and state tax competition[13]

If the goal of the MAI and other similar treaties is to dramatically reduce enforcement costs and create a relatively seamless market for foreign investment, then, if it is successful, what will the effect be? One way to consider this question is to study regional interactions in the United States, a vast market with separate jurisdictions. Here we focus on tax and subsidy competition for corporate investment.

Sometimes called the "War Among the States," the competition among US states for investment and jobs may well be a microcosm of what is emerging in the global arena. With the increased mobility of capital across geographic regions has come heightened competition among US states to attract and retain corporate investment. This competition is obvious in the rush of deals offering multi-million dollar tax breaks and incentives to large corporations in return for in-state investments, as well as in the proliferation of state tax credit programs for firms looking for new production sites. Notable among the numerous large incentive packages offered, the state of Indiana provided $300 million in incentives to United Airlines, South Carolina doled out $135 million in incentives to BMW, Alabama agreed to a $253 million dollar incentives package for the Daimler-Benz Corporation, and Kentucky gave the Defasco Company (a steel producer) $140 million. Some of these high priced deals have aimed not at attracting investment, but simply at keeping corporations from leaving the state; for instance, Sears Roebuck received almost a quarter of a billion dollars in grants and tax breaks from the state of Illinois in 1986 when that corporation threatened to move out of the state.[14]

States have also increasingly written business incentive programs into their tax codes to attract footloose firms. According to Mancon Inc., a firm that tracks business incentive programs, the number of individual state programs across the US offering tax breaks in the form of investment tax credits, jobs creation tax credits and property tax abatements has grown from 450 to over 700 in just the last two years.[15] States have also expanded their activities to market these tax breaks to mobile corporations. The average budget of state development agencies (which oversee efforts to attract companies with these incentive packages) has grown from about $18 million in 1986 to about $35 million in 1994.[16]

Although exact figures are difficult to attain, the corporate tax credits and other financial incentives with which states compete for new investment result in billions of dollars in foregone state revenues each year, certainly playing a significant role in the dramatic fall in the rate at which states have collected taxes from corporations in the 1980s and 1990s. The effective state tax rate on corporate income has fallen from 7.5 per cent in 1980 to 4.7 per cent in 1994. This decline has not come about because of a lowering of the states' statutory rates (which have actually risen on average between 1982 and 1994), but from tax rule changes, including the expansion of corporate tax credits proffered by the states.[17]

The fall in corporate tax collections put additional pressure on state governments, which have cut public services while struggling to balance budgets in the 1980s and 1990s. If corporations were paying at the 1980 effective tax rate in 1994, the states would have received 60 per cent more in corporate taxes that year, or another $15 billion in revenues. With the decline in revenues from corporate tax dollars has come a shift of the tax burden to individuals. Between 1980 and 1994 the share of total state revenues coming from corporate income taxes fell by almost 3 points (from 9.7 per cent to 6.8 per cent), while the share coming from personal income taxes rose by 4.4 points (from 27.1 per cent to 31.5 per cent).

Competitive business incentive policies by the states have a natural propensity to expand. As one state institutes a new tax break or subsidy, other states feel compelled to expand their incentive packages. The frantic competition among the states rewards firms for being mobile as the gains from relocating become ever higher. In this way, the growth of incentives may even further encourage the capital mobility that has driven the proliferation of these competitive programs in the first place.

In fact, past studies have shown that tax incentives have generally been either ineffective or relatively unimportant in determining the location decisions of firms (Carlton, 1983; Waits and Heffernon, 1994). A study by Head, Ries and Swenson (1994) suggests that these kinds of state incentive programs have now become so widespread that they basically offset each other in attracting new investment. Thus, the proliferation of "beggar thy neighbor" incentive programs since the late 1980s may not have actually generated any significant change in the distribution of production among states. For many states, the end result has probably been a "race to the bottom," with little gain in jobs, less corporate tax revenues for the states, and fewer public services and higher taxes for the public.[18]

Ending this competitive downward spiral would allow states to use the billions of dollars in funds now being siphoned off by special incentives to mobile corporations on the promotion of sound economic development – good physical infrastructure, high quality education and a well-trained workforce. A cooperative regime in which states competed with each other on the basis of these factors – rather than low corporate taxes or wages – could be key to putting states on the path of a high wage "climb to the top" as they confront a new world of rising corporate mobility.

This type of competitive bidding for mobile capital is a practice that extends well beyond the United States, and with similar consequences. Hence a *global* treaty, rather than purely national policies or agreements within specific regions, is of central importance for any alternative international governance structure.

V Alternatives to neo-liberal governance of FDI

If we are correct, that the type of globalization represented by the MAI is on balance harmful to the majority of workers and citizens, then what are the alternatives to the MAI and similar attempts to construct an international credit regime?

One alternative is to roll back globalization. Countries could put up various protective barriers to trade, FDI and portfolio flows. Is this a feasible and desirable strategy? We think the answer is yes and no. Certain forms of globalization have very negative effects such as speculative, short-term capital inflows and outflows; these transactions can and should be restricted. International trade in general can often have very strong net benefits. FDI is much more of a mixed bag, and ought to be regulated more on a case-by-case basis, but international competition for investment may undermine a country's ability to regulate FDI in this way. As a result, international arrangements which can underpin a leveling up, rather than a race to the bottom or a rolling back of the state, are necessary to the proper regulation of FDI and capital flows generally.

What would such an alternative set of arrangements look like? Using the framework outlined in section III above, the goals of such arrangements would be two-fold: (1) to reduce the conflict between the needs of workers and citizens and the incentives facing corporations, and (2) to reduce the power bias currently in favor of corporations relative to citizens and workers so that corporations will not be able to ratchet down legitimate and desirable social protections. There are two other goals which we have not discussed explicitly but which are important to keep in mind: (3) environmental protection (in addition to social protection) – reminding us that the goal is not to maximize foreign investment but to optimize it by taking into account true social costs, and (4) contributing to or at least not interfering with poverty reduction in the poorer countries of the world. Social protection in industrialized countries should not unduly interfere with productive and efficient transfers of resources to poorer countries that will actually benefit those at the lower rungs of the world income distribution.

We see the architectural layout for reaching these goals as a structure akin to a building, complete with *floors, windows, meeting rooms,* and *elevators,* and every building needs good *insurance.*

Floors

To prevent the leveling-down process, international floors on key variables and policies are required. These should include:

- *International tax floors.* This floor would outlaw tax and subsidy bidding for FDI to stave off a race to the bottom. Special dispensations could be made for particularly poor or disadvantaged regions where lower productivity levels need to be offset beyond what lower wage rates can provide.
- *Regulation floors.* Similarly, any offer of substantial regulatory reduction ought to be approved by a commission, housed in an appropriate international institution such as the ILO, UNCTAD or the WTO. These would include labor and environmental regulations.
- *Minimum wage floors.* A set of international minimum wages that apply to MNCs ought to be negotiated among countries. These minima should be high enough to contribute to poor workers' living standards, but should not be so high as to unnecessarily choke off investment.[19]

To make these floors operate properly, two other parts of the building are necessary: *windows* and *meeting rooms*.

Windows

Rules are required to make MNC and government operations more transparent. Today, it is extremely difficult to grapple with tax, regulatory and subsidy abuse because many of these policies are kept secret. Firms and governments should be required to reveal all tax, subsidy and regulatory treatment given to a corporation. This information should be easily accessible to the public.

Meeting rooms

To create, administer, and alter these floors, international governing bodies must be democratically organized. They should represent not only national governments, but have members of labor unions and NGOs on their bodies, making it more likely that there will be true representation of citizens.[20] As it is, the only groups besides governments that sit around the negotiating table are corporations.

Elevators

These rules of the game will not be sufficient to reduce the pressure for leveling down without elevators. Elevators are policies and institutions that maintain sufficient levels of aggregate demand, providing more security and employment for workers and citizens. Without adequate demand, temptations to violate floors out of desperation will become overwhelming, and workers will lose the bargaining power that comes with low levels of unemployment. Policies to maintain aggregate demand can be implemented at both the international and domestic levels. They include expansionary monetary policy at the domestic and regional levels, with circuit breakers such as short-term capital controls to prevent excessive exchange rate instability.[21]

Insurance

In exchange for abiding by these principles, an international body could be established to insure corporations against expropriation. This insurance would be the carrot that would help convince corporations to abide by these rules. It could also provide a worker-friendly enforcement regime that would underpin an adequate flow of FDI.

VI Conclusion

More citizen- and labor-friendly rules of the game are both feasible and necessary to reduce and even reverse "race to the bottom" pressures emanating from globalization. Those pressures stem both from the external economic forces that result from globalization, and also from attempts by corporations to use the new political and legal architecture being created to undermine national and local democratic rights.

While there are likely to be genuine and even significant benefits from some aspects of globalization, proponents of the MAI and other international agreements fail to demonstrate such benefits, often simply falling back on ideological or tautological claims. In fact, the economic effects of the currently negotiated MAI are likely to be negative, in both the developed and developing world. Much further research is necessary, however, before the costs and benefits of such agreements can be known with any certainty.

The most hopeful aspect of the newly emerging globalization is the ways in which citizens and labor groups in many parts of the world are mobilizing and joining forces to criticize, oppose and develop new alternatives to the neo-liberal architecture being constructed by corporate-influenced governments. These efforts, for the most part, are taking what we believe to be the appropriate steps of not simply trying to retreat behind the walls of nation states, a strategy which we argue is likely to fail, but proposing new international structures for regulating international economic interactions. At the same time, more control of short-term capital and other aspects of globalization is needed at the national level to enhance the power of these global coalitions to influence the emerging rules of the game.

Appendix: a simple model of the effects of the MAI on social welfare

In this section we develop a simple (and indeed, a simplistic) model to illustrate the impact of the MAI. The model uses as its framework the basic idea that as globalization increases, there will be two opposing tendencies operating on the policy structures of domestic economies. On the one hand, there will be pressures toward a "race to the bottom," that is pressures for cutting the role of the government, including the social protections of the welfare state, in order to allow firms to be more competitive and to help the country compete as a site for foreign investment (Barnet and Cavanaugh, 1994). On the other hand, there will be pressures for the government to take on more responsibilities as globalization creates losers as well as winners, and as it generates more insecurity by accelerating the pace of change. These pressures will tend to enlarge the size of the state and the amount of social protection (Rodrik, 1997).

These opposite pressures can operate simultaneously: the demand for more social protection, à la Rodrik, and the race to the bottom, or the declining willingness of capital to supply protection as openness increases. Figure 5.1 illustrates these in a simple diagram, the supply and demand for social protection. The "demand for social protection" is upward sloping, reflecting the fact that as openness to the international economy increases, citizens and workers will need more social protection to protect them from the vagaries of the market. The "supply of social protection" represents firms' willingness to pay taxes to support government social protections, as well as the willingness firms have to provide these at the firm level, including the toleration of unions, the payment of health benefits, and other firm-level benefits. The line G represents the exogenously given level of globalization, reflecting firms' exit options as well as the pressure on firms coming from trade competition.

A shift out in G represents an exogenous increase in the level of globalization, that is, an enhancement in the exit options available to firms, as well as an increase in the international competition facing domestic firms. As G shifts out, a wedge develops between the social protection that citizens and workers need, and that which capital wants to provide (Figure 5.1). This sets up a power struggle for institutional change which could take place at the level of the state or the level of the firm or both. Where the economy will end up depends on the relative power of the two groups, the institutional structures in place, and significantly, the level of globalization itself. Figure 5.2 illustrates this relationship between globalization and the outcome of the bargaining process over social protection in the case where the higher the level of globalization, the closer the outcome will be to those desired by capital (the "supply" curve). This outcome is illustrated by the "contract curve," which represents the locus of bargains settled on as globalization increases. By enhancing the exit options of firms, globalization enhances their power relative to citizens, workers and the state. This allows firms to win a better deal in the struggle for social protection represented (see Crotty and Epstein, 1996; and Crotty, Epstein and Kelly, 1998).

We can use this simple apparatus to illustrate the effects of the MAI. By increasing the power of the international enforcement structure, the MAI will cause a shift out in the G line, the exogenous level of globalization, hence widening the gap between the needs of citizens and that of firms. This is the enforcement effect. But the MAI will also have a second effect (see Figure 5.3). By reducing the power of central and local governments, it will reduce the effective demand for social protection that citizens can generate and therefore will lower the level of social protections that they will receive. This is illustrated by a shift downward of the demand for social protection curve. This is the "Trojan horse" effect.

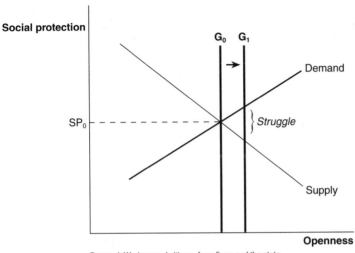

Figure 5.1 Demand for and supply of social protection

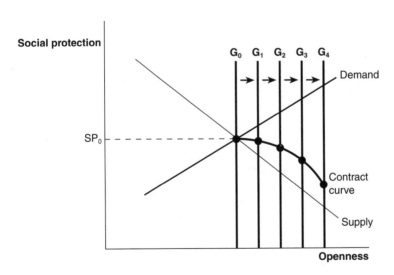

Figure 5.2 Effects of globalization on social protection when it favors capital's bargaining power

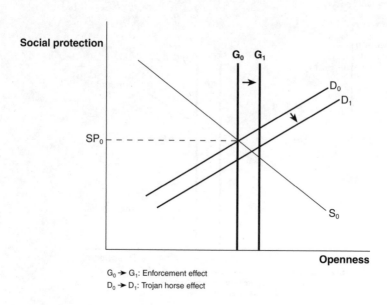

$G_0 \rightarrow G_1$: Enforcement effect
$D_0 \rightarrow D_1$: Trojan horse effect

Figure 5.3 The effects of the MAI

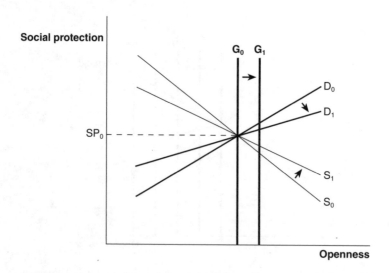

Figure 5.4 The effect of increases in aggregate demand on social protection

Note that the supply of social protection may be upward sloping. Through agglomeration effects and economies of scale, more openness may be associated with greater demands for infrastructure, education, and high performance work structures on the part of firms (see Milberg, 1998). By generating a "climb to the top" these effects may moderate or even eliminate the negative impacts of globalization. But as long as the need for social protection increases at a faster rate than the supply (the slope of the demand curve is higher than that of the supply curve), the same dilemma, though quantitatively smaller, will still exist.

This framework is also useful for illustrating how alternatives to the MAI might work. "Elevators" such as increases in aggregate demand would shift (or rotate) down the demand for social protection curve because the greater availability of jobs would increase security; increases in aggregate demand would also shift up (rotate up) the supply curve because by increasing export markets, it would reduce the pressure on firms and governments to cut jobs. (See Figure 5.4.) Both effects reduce the scope of social struggle and bar against the leveling-down process that might come with globalization. "Floors" rotate the demand for social protection curve down, as citizens require less social protection for any given level of openness. They can also have bargaining power effects, moving the contract curve of Figure 5.2 closer to the needs of citizens rather than firms.

Notes

1 The authors thank James Burke and Trish Kelly for their significant contributions. They are not responsible for errors, however.
2 See Hirst and Thompson (1996) and Sutcliffe and Glyn (1998).
3 For more discussion of these points, see Baker, Epstein and Pollin (1998).
4 See Crotty and Epstein (1996) and Crotty, Epstein and Kelly (1998) for discussions of various aspects of these issues.
5 See Hirst and Thompson (1996) and Baker, Epstein and Pollin (1998) for a discussion of various definitions of globalization.
6 This is the point made by Block (1973) in his classic book on the international monetary system. See also the excellent book by Helleiner (1994) on the same subject.
7 It is important to distinguish between FDI and MNCs because the latter engage in international production relations through means broader than FDI, for example, by joint ventures and outsourcing.
8 The following description of the MAI draws heavily on the work of the Preamble Center for Public Policy in Washington. See their web site [www.RTK.NET:80/ preamble/mai/keyprovs.html]. Also see OECD (1996).
9 (OECD, 1997, italics added.) On the question of whether countries can treat foreign investors better than domestic firms, calls to the OECD did not turn up anyone who would answer this question. After reviewing materials from their offices and the MAI itself, it seems that nowhere does the MAI bar countries from treating foreign investors better than locals.
10 This section draws on Crotty, Epstein and Kelly (1998).
11 On these points, see the excellent information being put out on the MAI by NGOs such as the Preamble Center for Public Policy, and Public Citizen's Global Trade Watch.
12 This section benefited from the contributions of Trish Kelly.

13 Our thanks to James Burke, who contributed most of this section on state tax competition.
14 The figures for these incentive deals are from the *Washington Post*, August 20, 1995, p. A1.
15 Telephone conversation with Anthony Misino at Mancon.
16 *Wall Street Journal*, March 8, 1995, p. A2.
17 Statutory tax rates for the states can be found in the *Directory of Incentives for Business Investment and Development in the US* and in *American Business Climate and Economic Profiles*.
18 A report by the Federal Reserve Bank of Minneapolis, entitled *Congress Should End the Economic War Among the States* (1994), decried the tax competition among US states and locales for investment by large companies. The Bank argued that competition lowers domestic tax revenues below desired levels and may distort the location of domestic investment (see also Holmes, 1995).
19 See Pollin and Luce (1998) on "living wage legislation"; this can be extended to the international level.
20 These representatives should be drawn from both the developed and developing world so that outcomes are the result of an inclusive negotiating process.
21 See Pollin (1998).

References

Baker, Dean, Gerald Epstein and Robert Pollin. 1998. "Introduction," in Dean Baker, Gerald Epstein and Robert Pollin, eds, *Globalization and Progressive Economic Policy*. Cambridge, UK: Cambridge University Press.

Barnet, Richard and John Cavanaugh. 1994. *Global Dreams; Imperial Corporations and the New World Order*. New York: Simon and Schuster.

Block, Fred. 1973. *The Origin of International Monetary Disorder*. Berkeley: University of California Press.

Bowles, Samuel and Herbert Gintis. 1990. "Contested Exchange: New Micro-Foundations for the Political Economy of Capitalism," *Politics and Society* 18(2): 165–222.

Carlton, Dennis. 1983. "The Location and Employment Choices of New Firms: An Econometric Model with Discrete and Continuous Endogenous Variables," *Journal of Economics and Statistics* 65: 440–449.

Crotty, James and Gerald Epstein. 1996. "In Defense of Capital Controls," *Socialist Register*: 118–149.

Crotty, James, Gerald Epstein and Trish Kelly. 1998. "Multinational Corporations and the Neo-Liberal Regime," in Dean Baker, Gerald Epstein and Robert Pollin, eds, *Globalization and Progressive Economic Policy*. Cambridge, UK: Cambridge University Press.

Dunning, John H. 1994. "Re-evaluating the Benefits of Foreign Direct Investment," *Transnational Corporations* 3(1): 23–51.

Epstein, Gerald and Herbert Gintis. 1992. "International Capital Markets and the Limits of National Economic Policy," in Tariq Banuri and Juliet Schor, eds, *Financial Openness and National Autonomy*. Oxford: Clarendon Press.

Federal Reserve Bank of Minneapolis. 1994. "Congress Should End the Economic War Among the States," *Annual Report*. Minneapolis: Federal Reserve Bank of Minneapolis.

Head, C. Keith, John C. Ries and Deborah L. Swenson. 1994. "The Attraction of Foreign Manufacturing Investments: Investment Promotion and Agglomeration Economies," NBER Paper no. 4878.

Helleiner, Eric. 1994. *States and the Resurgence of Global Finance*. Ithaca: Cornell University Press.

Hirst, Paul and Grahame Thompson. 1996. *Globalization in Question.* Cambridge: Polity Press.

Holmes, Thomas J. 1995. "Analyzing a Proposal to Ban State Tax Breaks to Businesses," *Federal Reserve Bank of Minneapolis Quarterly Review:* 29–39.

Lipson, Charles. 1986. *Standing Guard.* Berkeley: University of California Press.

Milberg, William. 1998. "Technological Change, Social Policy and International Competitiveness," working paper on Globalization, Labor Markets and Social Policy. New School for Social Research, New York.

OECD. 1997. "The Multilateral Agreement on Investment," OECD Policy Brief no. 2–1997.

OECD. 1996. *Towards Multilateral Investment Rules.* Paris: OECD.

Pollin, Robert. 1998. "Can Domestic Expansionary Policies Succeed in a Globally Integrated Environment? A Consideration of Alternatives," in Dean Baker, Gerald Epstein and Robert Pollin, eds, *Globalization and Progressive Economic Policy.* Cambridge, UK: Cambridge University Press.

Pollin, Robert and Stephanie Luce. 1998. *The Living Wage: What It Is and Why We Need It.* New York: The New Press.

Rodrik, Dani. 1997. "Has Globalization Gone Too Far?" Washington, D.C.: Institute for International Economics.

Sutcliffe, Bob and Andrew Glyn. 1998. "Still Underwhelmed: Indicators of Globalization and their Misinterpretation," *Boston Review.*

United Nations. 1997. *Human Development Report.* New York: United Nations.

UNCTAD. 1997a. *Trade and Development Report.* New York: United Nations.

UNCTAD. 1997b. *World Investment Report.* New York: United Nations.

Waits, Mary Jo and Rick Heffernon. 1994. "Business Incentives: How to Get What the Public Pays For," *Spectrum,* Summer: 34–40.

6 World trade liberalisation

National autonomy and global regulation

Avadhoot Nadkarni

With the conclusion of the Uruguay Round of multilateral trade negotiations, the multilateral trading system has, under the aegis of the World Trade Organisation, become all pervasive. This is leading to, in some sense, a loss of domestic sovereignty over areas of policy which had hitherto been jealously guarded in the national realms. At the same time, global structures are being visualised for managing the spill-over of the trade policy regime into other realms of policy.

Loss of national autonomy and the transfer of power to supranational structures are, of course, in the present context, two sides of the same coin. Yet the more important question is not whether, or even how, national autonomy is being sacrificed, but to what kind of global structures is power to be transferred as a consequence of world trade liberalisation. This chapter, therefore, deals not only with the issue of the loss of national autonomy due to the emergence of an all-pervading multilateral trading system, but also with the question of the global structures. Three kinds of structures are distinguished, those which *are developing* in the multilateral trading system, those which *are sought to be developed* by modifications of this system, and those which, in our view, *should be developed,* independently of the multilateral trading system.

The chapter is divided into four sections. Section I brings out the extent to which trade policy has over the years become broader in scope influencing areas that were hitherto in the realms of domestic policy. The remaining sections deal with the issue of global regulation. Section II discusses the concept of global governance that is implicit in the WTO model of trade liberalisation. The model gives primacy to the needs of an open non-discriminatory trade system over all other considerations. We illustrate this with reference to the relationship between trade and the environment. Section III brings out the northern non-governmental organisations (NGO) model for managing the interaction of trade policy with social and environmental policy. This model relies on social and environmental clauses within the multilateral trading system in the pursuit of broader social and environmental objectives and, in some sense, seems to be in favour of the strengthening of the global structures that are emerging out of a system whose primary purpose is trade liberalisation. Section IV attempts a critique of this approach and suggests that desired structures of global governance will have to take cognisance of broader policies, like global redistribution policies, and go beyond the multilateral trading system.

I Trade liberalisation and the loss of national autonomy

The experience of world trade liberalisation over the last few years seems to have led to an erosion of national autonomy for the following reasons:

1. The international trade policy regime has become much wider in its reach, covering areas which had hitherto been an exclusive preserve of domestic policy regimes.
2. With the establishment of the World Trade Organisation (WTO), the obligations of national governments to the multilateral trading system (MTS) are being more effectively enforced.
3. Given their obligations to the MTS, national governments seem unable to deal with the problems created by the expansion of international trade and the all-pervading character of the MTS. Moreover, it is being perceived that legitimate objectives of other policy areas (the social and environmental spheres, for example) are being increasingly subordinated to the requirements of an 'open, unrestricted and non-discriminatory' trading system.

Increasing scope of the multilateral trading system

The MTS under the WTO has come a long way since the time it merely provided a multilateral forum for tariff negotiations under successive rounds of GATT. Tariffs on products traded between industrial countries reached a historical low in the 1970s and, under the impetus of the economic difficulties of the period, protectionism in the form of non-tariff barriers gained grounds. The Kennedy Round and, in particular, the Tokyo Round turned their attention to non-tariff barriers to trade. Unlike tariff measures which essentially operate at the border, many of the so-called non-tariff measures operate within the domestic economies and any attempt at codification of these measures essentially impinges on the powers of the national governments to deal with domestic policy matters. The Tokyo Round negotiated six codes on non-tariff measures, viz., the standards code, the subsidies code, the customs valuation code, the anti-dumping code, the Agreement on Import Licensing Procedures and the Agreement on Government Procurement. All these codes, except perhaps the one on customs valuation, attempt in varying degrees to discipline measures that are not necessarily border measures, and thus have implications for the powers of national governments in areas which were hitherto outside the purview of the MTS.

Under the provisions of the Tokyo Round, governments were, however, able to choose to a large extent which of these agreements they would join. This freedom was no longer available at the conclusion of the Uruguay Rounds. Under the 'take-it-or-leave-it' arrangements, countries had to accede to all the so-called

Annex 1, 2, 3 multilateral agreements of the WTO. Governments had a choice only in the matter of joining the so-called plurilateral agreements in Annex 4 of the WTO Agreement.[1] The implications are clear: countries had no option but to bring under the scrutiny of the MTS their regulations in matters like technical standards and subsidies.

The Marrakech Agreement concluding the Uruguay Round succeeded in increasing the scope of the MTS in more important ways than codification of non-tariff barriers. All of this had implications for what governments could hitherto more or less freely do in the respective areas. We note below some of these important extensions of the MTS:

1   The Agreement on Sanitary and Phyto-Sanitary Measures has clear implications for the ability of governments to set health-related food standards in their domestic jurisdictions.

2   The trade in sensitive sectors like agriculture and textiles and clothing was made GATT consistent. This has long-run implications for the domestic support and export subsidies that advanced country governments can provide to the agricultural sector; as also for the protection they can offer through quota restrictions on imports of labour-intensive products like textiles and clothing. Social implications in the developed countries would be tremendous if the built-in negotiations in agriculture, slated for the year 2000, produce substantive results and if the dismantling of the Multi-Fibre Agreement proceeds as scheduled. (It is this realisation that has generated the feeling in some quarters in the developing countries that there will be, in one way or the other, a default on the implementation of the Agreement on Textiles and Clothing.)

3   Trade in services was brought under the aegis of the MTS through the General Agreement on Trade in Services (GATS). In some of its provisions, GATS goes beyond GATT in circumscribing the powers of national governments. The enshrining of the right to establishment under GATS for the purpose of domestic delivery of services, however circumscribed in itself, could be a pointer to the ways in which things could shape in the future.

4   Domestic legislation providing intellectual property protection is to be made WTO-consistent through the Agreement on Trade-Related Aspects of Intellectual Property Rights. Legislation providing the required private patent, copyright and trademark rights have always been in place in the advanced countries. Governments in the third world would have to substantially change their intellectual property protection regimes to make them TRIP-consistent. The private property rights that would thereby be created could further have adverse implications to the rights of local communities as distinct from the rights of national governments.

5   Even investment measures that were hitherto freely adopted, especially by the developing country governments in regulating investment, have, through the Agreement on TRIMS, been brought under the aegis of the

WTO to the extent that these measures could have trade implications. Measures like local-content requirement and foreign-exchange requirement have been made GATT-inconsistent and hence no longer available to these governments.

The missing clauses and annexes of the WTO Agreement

It is true that the TRIMS Agreement is a much narrower version of a full-fledged agreement on investment that was being visualised on par with the multilateral agreements on trade in goods, the GATS, and the Agreement on TRIPS. In the event, partly because of the opposition from some quarters to such an agreement being under the WTO, what came in was the Agreement on TRIMS as one of the multilateral agreements on trade in goods and not an independent multilateral agreement on investment in its own right; though GATS has its own provisions on investment in conjunction with the right of establishment.[2]

The issue of investment is, however, far from dead in the WTO. It has been kept alive through the establishment of a working group on trade and investment at the first ministerial meeting of the WTO in Singapore in 1996. The relationship between trade and investment continues as a new issue in the WTO along with a large number of so-called new issues. Largely because of new forms of interaction between trade policy and other policy areas, a large number of issues have been arising around the MTS. These issues include the relationships between trade on the one hand and investment, environment, labour standards, competition, and even illicit payments, on the other.[3] As these issues mature beyond the stage of working groups through negotiating mandates, WTO Agreement is expected to be augmented with new clauses and whole new annexes. Each of these clauses and agreements will further circumscribe the domestic policy options of the Contracting Party governments in dealing with the areas covered by these agreements.

Stricter enforcement of the obligations

The increasing scope of the MTS is, in a way, a continuation of a trend initiated by the Tokyo Round codes to discipline non-tariff barriers; though, as we have noted above, governments then had an option not to accede to these codes. What is new under the present dispensation, though, is that the WTO Agreement has definite provisions to enforce its annexed agreements. This is secured through two means.

Contracting Parties have a definite obligation to adopt legislation to make their systems consistent with the provisions of the WTO Agreements in a definite timeframe and, in the meantime, to report all inconsistent measures. Liberal time-frames have been provided in many cases especially since many of the changes sought are of a fundamental nature.

The implementation is effectively controlled through the WTO dispute settlement procedure. It provides final and binding decisions. Whereas previously Contracting Parties have been able to ignore panel rulings through the exercise of an effective veto, the decisions of the WTO panels and appellate bodies cannot be ignored except by providing compensation to the affected party.

Inability of national governments to deal with trade-related problems

The proof of the pudding is, of course, in the eating, and the WTO recipe would not have been visualised as affecting national autonomies if national governments dealt with domestic problems that are seen as having been engendered by liberalisation of trade and investment, and the solution was not seen as being impeded by obligations to the WTO. Examples of such problems abound.

In the economic sphere, the problem of unemployment in Europe and that of falling real wages in the US is frequently attributed to trade and investment liberalisation and competition from low-wage economies. In the non-economic sphere foremost examples are provided by inability of governments to enforce health and animal welfare standards. The US–EU beef hormone dispute is the case in point so far as health standards are concerned. In the realm of animal welfare, the tuna–dolphin disputes provide the classic examples. So does the issue in the EU about 'battery' eggs and 'free-range' eggs.

Loss of national sovereignty: some caveats

Not all the perceived loss of autonomy in dealing with these problems is real. More often than not, the balance of domestic interests groups may require a government to abstain from taking the necessary measures to safeguard jobs and wages. Keeping protectionist interests at bay has actually been identified as one of the important functions served by a rule-based MTS (Hoekman and Kostecki, 1995). Also, a clear distinction needs to be made between measures sought to be enforced within national jurisdictions and those which could have extra-territorial implications.[4] It could be argued that what is important is national sovereignty over matters in one's own jurisdiction and that national sovereignty over extra-territorial matters is a contradiction in terms; though, admittedly, it is the opening up of trade which leads to a blurring of these distinctions.[5]

Nor can all the problems be attributed entirely to the working of the MTS. Clearly not all of the unemployment in Europe or the fall in real wages in the US can be attributed to trade, whether with developing or developed countries. Fundamental forces, such as changes in technology, are at work.

There are also other considerations involved. At some level, this alleged loss of national autonomy represents a voluntary surrender of autonomy by sovereign governments in return for presumed national benefits obtained in other areas, although these may benefit different sections of their respective populations. For another, national sovereignty need not in itself be sacrosanct in a world where, more often than not, such sovereignty is forged at a tremendous cost to local communities and through a sacrifice of local autonomy. There is currently no dearth of examples of such sacrifices extracted in the interest of international trade. This suggests that any discussion of loss of national autonomy through trade liberal-isation, should pay attention to the distribution of benefits both between and within countries.

The more important question therefore is not whether national autonomies are being sacrificed but to what kind of global structures is power sought to be trans-ferred as a consequence of world trade liberalisation. It is to the consideration of this question that we turn in the following sections of the chapter.

II The neo-liberal perspective on global regulation

The conflicts between the trade policy regime and other policy areas has given rise to a need for developing global institutional mechanisms for dealing with these conflicts. Thus Cottier (1998) discusses the WTO in the context of the need to develop institutions with 'constitutional' functions of 'balancing a variety of equally legitimate interests and policies'. It would be illustrative to examine the response of the multilateral trading system to the postulation of such conflicts before we look at the concept of global regulation and governance that seems to be emerging in the WTO.

Two responses, at two different levels, can be identified in the multilateral trading system in dealing with conflicts that inevitably arise between the needs of trade liberalisation and other policy objectives:

1   an outright denial that, in principle, a conflict of objectives exists; and
2   an assertion, in practice, of the primacy of the needs of the multilateral trading system.

Attempts have thus been made to show that, in principle, the conflict between trade liberalisation and other policy areas is minimal, or even that the relationships are not one of conflict but of mutual benefit. In practice, in the event of any con-flict of the trade system with other policy areas, the interests of the trade system have been consistently upheld through the dispute settlement process of the WTO. We illustrate this with reference to the areas of interaction between trade and environment. All issues of relationship between trade and environment can be discussed under the following three categories:[6]

1   environmental effects of trade liberalisation;
2   use of trade measures to secure multilateral environmental objective;
3   trade effects of national environmental regulations and environment-related product standards.

The denial of conflict is clearly seen in the case of the environmental effects of trade liberalisation and trade measures in pursuit of multilateral environmental objectives, where the primacy of the needs of the trading system is asserted in set-tlement of disputes about national environmental regulations and product-related environmental standards.

Environmental effects of trade liberalisation

Important in this context are the Ministerial Decision on Environment establishing the Committee on Trade and Environment (CTE), the Report of the CTE adopted for the First WTO Ministerial Meeting and, of course, the work of the WTO Secretariat.

The CTE was established, through the above-mentioned ministerial decision, along with the WTO in January 1994. The decision clearly noted that there should not be nor need be any policy contradiction between upholding and safeguarding an open, equitable and non-discriminatory multilateral trading system on the one hand and acting for the protection of the environment on the other.

The discussions in the CTE have clearly been guided by this neo-liberal sentiment expressed in the Ministerial Decision establishing it. As noted by the Committee in its Report adopted for the First Ministerial Conference in Singapore in 1996:

> The two areas of policy-making are both important and they should be mutually supportive in order to promote sustainable development. Discussions have demonstrated that the multilateral trading system has the capacity to further integrate environmental considerations and enhance its contribution to the promotion of sustainable development without undermining its open, equitable and non-discriminating character [Para. 167].

Economic growth is postulated as the main link between trade liberalisation and environmental protection. Trade liberalisation is supposed to be a powerful engine of economic growth as shown by the performance of outward-oriented economies in contrast to that of inward-looking ones. Growth itself helps environmental protection in two ways. First, it leads to alleviation of poverty supposed to be the single most potent source of environmental degradation and, second, it provides resources that can be devoted to environmental protection. Trade liberalisation achieves all this by getting the prices right. Pricing failures, working through market access restrictions, domestic support policies and export subsidies, are supposed to be a major cause of environmental degradation. Getting prices right thus not only leads to more rapid growth with indirect benefits to the environment, but also has direct beneficial consequences to the environment through efficient allocation of resources.

This principle, of course, also guides the work undertaken in the WTO Secretariat on the relationship between trade and environment. A note prepared by the Secretariat 'Environmental Benefits of Removing Trade Restrictions and Distortions' enumerates existing trade restrictions and distortions and the environmental benefits of removing these restrictions in seven sectors, viz., agriculture, fisheries, forestry, energy, non-ferrous metals, textiles and clothing, and leather.

The Director-General of the WTO speaks of a newly emerging consensus that trade liberalisation and environmental protection are not only compatible goals, but are also two sides of the same strategy to achieve sustainable development on a global scale (Ruggiero, 1998a). This insistence on a denial of a conflict is also seen in the area of the relationship between the multilateral trade system and the multilateral environmental agreements, though, as we will see below, there are more problems in this case.

Use of trade measures to secure international environmental objectives

The multilateral environmental regime has been developing simultaneously with the multilateral trading system to regulate transboundary environmental concerns and also to co-ordinate efforts aimed at solving environmental problems, the solution of which requires action at the international level. There are about 185 extant multilateral environmental agreements, about 20 of which can be identified as including trade measures in pursuit of their objectives.[7] The provisions of these agreements are well known and in most cases could come into conflict with the provisions of the multilateral trading system under the aegis of the WTO. If the trade provisions of these agreements have not come in open conflict with the multilateral trade regime it is not because there are no inconsistencies between the two in law, but because of restraint exercised at the political level. Thus, Hutton and Chitsike (1998) show how the provision of 'Stricter Domestic Measures' under CITES can be an ideal candidate for a future flashpoint between the CITES and the WTO and how, in the past, Zimbabwe and the US were on the brink of a WTO dispute on the issue of crocodile leather exports:

> The Nile crocodile population of Zimbabwe was transferred to CITES Appendix II in 1983 in recognition of a conservation programme of sustainable use that was leading to real conservation gains for the species [which should have enabled restricted exports of crocodile leather products], but despite the best efforts of the Zimbabwe Government, producer associations and conservation groups such as the IUCN/SSC Crocodile Specialist Group, it took an additional 13 years for the US government to allow commercial shipments made from Zimbabwe's crocodile leather to enter its markets. It may be relevant that US action on this issue followed shortly after producers requested that the Zimbabwe Government refer the matter to the WTO/GATT dispute settlement mechanism.

Yet, in the WTO, much is made of the fact there has to date not been a single case of conflict between the multilateral environmental agreements and the WTO/GATT agreements that have been brought to the dispute settlement process. The WTO Director-General says: Several of these multilateral environmental agreements also contain trade measures, and despite concerns from some in the environmental community, no legal dispute has ever arisen between the WTO and an MEA on this count (Ruggiero, 1998).

National environmental regulations and product-related standards

There has however been no dearth of such legal disputes when countries have sought unilaterally to enforce environmental regulations or environment-related product standards and not under the provisions of some multilateral environmental agreement. As we will see below, there has been a tendency in such cases to uphold, through the dispute settlement process, the requirements of the trading system as against those of the environmental agendas of national governments.

A recent WTO document lists seven such cases of the so-called environmental disputes that have been brought to the GATT/WTO dispute settlement process.[8] The cases have been identified on the basis of the fact that they invoked 'environmental' exceptions under Paragraphs (b), (d) and (g) of Article XX (General Exceptions) of GATT.[9]

The case histories are replete with examples of the intricacies of international law; but the broad picture that emerges from a perusal of these cases is that, under the current practice of dispute settlement, most environmental measures are bound to contradict with one or other of the above-mentioned GATT Articles I, III and XI; and that it would be difficult, though not impossible, to claim exceptions under Article XX for measures intended to regulate the environment or to specify environment-related product standards.

Process and production methods

Thus Article III requires that 'like products' from external sources must be treated the same as products of national origin. The issue then hinges around the definition of 'like products'. In the context of measures for environmental protection this definition is linked to the concept of 'process and production methods (PPMs)'. Two kinds of PPMs can be distinguished, product-related PPMs and non-product-related PPMs. Product-related PPMs are those processes and production methods which transform the final product, e.g., by leaving a trace beyond acceptable levels, in the final product, of a hazardous substance used in the production process; whereas non-product-related PPMs do not affect the characteristics of the finished good – marine shrimp harvested by using turtle-excluding devices cannot be distinguished in terms of its characteristics from shrimp harvested by using traditional mechanical nets.

The definition of 'like products' that has been adopted in the practice of dispute settlement does not allow for distinguishing between products based on non-product-related PPMs and yet many of the environmental regulations brought to WTO dispute settlement would have required precisely such a distinction between products if these measures were to stand the scrutiny of the panels and appellate bodies. Thus, in terms of the concept of PPM, 'dolphin-safe' tuna and tuna harvested with methods which are not 'dolphin-safe' turn out to be 'like products' and any restriction on the importation of the so-called 'dolphin-unsafe' tuna will inevitably conflict with relevant GATT provisions.

Article XX as a limited and conditional exception

That, however, is not the end of the matter. As noted above, the defendant has the right to invoke Article XX exceptions to uphold environmental measures which are otherwise GATT-inconsistent. The important question then turns out to be whether Article XX can be recognised as an unconditional exception from obligations under other provisions of the General Agreement. Dispute settlement practice has clearly determined that Article XX is a limited and conditional exception and not an unconditional one.

As has been admitted in the Secretariat Note referred to above,

1   Panels have interpreted Article XX narrowly – in a manner that preserves the basic objectives and principles of the General Agreement.
2   Panels have traditionally considered that, since Article XX is an exception, it is up to the party invoking it to demonstrate that the measure at issue meets the requirements laid down in that provision. Practically, the party must demonstrate that the measure (a) falls under at least one of the exceptions listed under Article XX, and (b) satisfies the requirements of the preamble to that article, i.e., it is not applied in a manner which would constitute 'a means of arbitrary or unjustifiable discrimination between countries where the same conditions prevail' and is not 'a disguised restriction on international trade'. The burden of proof thus lies with the party invoking the article.

The dispute settlement practice, therefore, is such that national environmental measures have consistently been shown to be against GATT provisions and have been difficult to uphold as exceptions. We examine below the implications of this to the conception of global regulation that emerges in the WTO.

WTO and the global regulation

The relationship between trade and environment as it is being worked out in the MTS fits in clearly with the singular objective of neo-liberal agenda which emphasises increased efficiency in the allocation of global resources through the creation of a world market for goods, services and investment. The global structures that are visualised under this agenda are those which facilitate the creation of such a market through dismantling of all barriers to trade and investment flows.

This is clearest in attempts to bring a comprehensive investment agreement under the WTO. The Agreement on TRIMS has been explicitly referred to as an 'incomplete agenda' of the WTO and we have made a reference to the missing Annex 1 D to the WTO Agreement for a multilateral investment agreement (MIA). The multilateral agreement on investment (MAI) that is being negotiated at the Organisation for Economic Co-operation and Development is hailed as an attempt to write 'the constitution of a single global economy'. Gone are the days when the discussion in UN bodies was about regulating transnational corporations and foreign investment. The MAI aims at facilitating investment. It is, of course, being negotiated with the explicit purpose of ultimately bringing it under the aegis of the WTO.

It is recognised that the WTO will increasingly interact with other policy areas, though not necessarily in a conflicting relationship; but the WTO seems to be explicitly rejecting a wider role in dealing with issues that arise through such interactions especially in the non-economic areas. The WTO Director-General is explicit in this matter (Ruggiero, 1998):

> The trading system will continue to grow in global relevance as trade policy continues to move beyond simple border tariffs, to involve deeper issues inside national boundaries like investment policy, competition policy . . . But this is not an argument for turning the WTO into an environmental watch-dog, human rights body, or a development agency. Such a policy would firstly, harm the trading system itself with all the collateral effects this would have for a sustainable global economy; and secondly, it would fail to solve any of the other problems . . .
>
> The WTO is not – and has no intentions of becoming – a supranational body with unilateral powers. It is not a world policeman that can enforce compliance upon unwilling governments.

III The northern NGO perspective on global regulation: governance through the WTO

If the WTO itself is reluctant to take on the role of a world policeman, the northern NGOs[10] and trade union organisations want it to assume precisely that role in the environmental and social spheres. We consider these positions again in the environmental sphere.

Environmental effects of trade liberalisation

The northern NGO position on the role of trade liberalisation in promoting growth and that of growth in alleviating poverty in the developing countries is consistent with the mainstream position.[11] Thus one of the Points of Departure for IISD's Principles for Trade and Sustainable Development states:

> Barriers to trade can create impediments to the achievement of sustainable development, particularly for developing countries, and trade liberalisation is an important component of progress toward sustainable development for all countries.

The difference arises in postulating the link between trade liberalisation and environmental protection. The WTO position in the matter, elaborated on in section II, is that trade liberalisation will enhance environmental protection through the removal of price distortions and through growth. The NGO position, on the other hand, is that trade liberalisation does not necessarily create conditions conducive to environmental protection unless appropriate environmental management policies are adapted at the domestic level.

The differences arise over the issue of whether market prices reflect scarcity of resources. The WTO position is that they do, unless subsidies drive in a wedge. The environmental NGOs, of course, accept that subsidies create a problem[12] but they maintain that the existence of subsidies is not the whole problem. There is a more fundamental Pigouvian divergence between private and social costs especially in regard to natural resources and that, in the absence of market mechanisms for the internalisation of social costs, there is a need for regulatory mechanisms. The WTO is visualised as a problem precisely because obligations to the MTS come in the way of domestic regulations in the interest of environmental protection.

Trade measures for environmental protection

WTO becomes important to the environmental NGOs in two ways:

1   There is the concern that obligations to the WTO can stand in the way of national environmental regulations leading globally to a 'race to the bottom' on environmental standards.
2   There is, on the other hand, a possibility of using trade sanctions through the WTO to further international environmental objectives.

Article XX of GATT becomes important in both cases. The contention of the NGOs is that there exists enough scope in the provisions of this article not only to defend national regulations but also to protect the trade provisions of the multilateral environmental agreements. As we have seen in section II, the WTO interprets Article XX as 'a limited and conditional exception' from obligations under other provisions of GATT. Some of the NGOs, basing their reasoning on the very language in which the article has been framed, think otherwise. It is contended that the drafting history of this article, including that of its antecedents in some earlier documents, makes it clear that the article was intended to strike a balance between domestic autonomy in non-economic policy matters and trade liberalisation.[13] It is further contended that this balance has been undermined by interpretations of the GATT dispute settlement panels. A large body of work has been done by these NGOs and others to suggest ways in which the original balance can be set right. Suggestions vary from an amendment of Article XX to signing an understanding among the WTO contracting parties that exception under Article XX will always be available if an action is taken pursuant to the provisions of a multilateral environmental agreement.

Governance through the WTO

Given their recognition of the role of trade liberalisation, the NGO position is not one of an outright rejection of the MTS. It should be noted that such an outright rejection has been propounded by various grassroots peoples' movements in different parts of the world. An attempt has been made recently to bring these movements on a common platform through the 'Peoples' Global Action against "Free" Trade and the WTO'. Their manifesto brings out the adverse effects of free trade on various sections of the population and gives a call for a complete rejection of neo-liberal ideology and the principle of free trade.[14]

That, however, cannot be the NGO approach. On the contrary, the NGO approach relies on making use of the MTS in the furtherance of their objectives in the environmental and social spheres. In the MTS, under the aegis of the WTO, the NGOs have discovered a potent instrument for the protection of environment and propagation of other social values. Thus, WWF considers trade measures as an important component in the success of a multilateral environmental agreement like the Montreal Protocol:

> The Montreal Protocol's Trade Measures appear to have been crucial to its success. The key conclusion of a major recent study is that the discriminatory restrictions on trade between parties and non-parties to the agreement were a vital component in (a) building the wide international coverage the treaty has achieved, and (b) preventing industrial migration to non-parties to escape the controls on ozone depleting substances.

The attempt, therefore, has been to develop further mechanisms within the MTS to enable trade sanctions in the pursuit of environmental and social objectives. These efforts are most evident in the case of the social clauses that are to be used for the implementation of core labour standards. These standards have been developed in the ILO through a long process of consensus formation. The ILO mechanisms for securing the ratification and implementation of these core labour standards essentially relies on moral suasion. The ILO is thus considered as lacking the necessary teeth for implementing these standards and there are proposals to establish links between the ILO and the WTO which will enable the enforcement of these standards through trade sanctions in the WTO. The WTO is supposed to provide the necessary teeth in the matter.[15]

In the NGO way of thinking, therefore, the WTO is thus considered to be ideally suited for playing the role of a supranational regulatory authority to take care of problems arising in the social and environmental areas. Social and environmental clauses inserted in the WTO agreement can be a potent instrument not only for safeguarding the ozone layer and for providing basic human rights to labour, but also for protecting turtles, dolphins and children from the ravages of those seeking profits in the international trade of shrimp, tuna and carpets.

Reference has been made to Cottier (1998) explicitly conceiving the WTO in 'constitutional' terms as an instrument for balancing a variety of equally legitimate interests and policies. According to Cottier, 'from a point of view of democratic legitimisation, global integration may eventually require the establishment of a WTO Parliament representing a wide range of interests, including those representing global commons'.[16] The WTO is thus clearly conceived as the seed for a world government. In the following section we attempt a critique of the idea that the WTO itself should be endowed with power to regulate social and environmental areas.

IV Toward a critique of the governance through the WTO approach

The problems that arise, in the present context, with the regulation-through-the-WTO approach have to do with two questions:

1   What are the standards that are sought to be enforced?
2   Is the WTO the best forum for developing and enforcing those standards?

What standards?

Mechanisms for the enforcement of standards assume the existence of commonly accepted criteria. Do such standards exist in the environmental and social spheres? We see below that such standards perhaps exist to some extent in the social sphere, but are more difficult to come by in the environmental sphere.

Labour standards

In the case of labour standards, a distinction can be made between human rights and conditions surrounding work. The former includes, for example, abolition of forced labour; whereas the latter would concern matters like safety measures and hours of work. There is an emerging consensus in the world community around the former; but, in the very nature of things, universally acceptable and enforceable standards are difficult to establish around the latter.

Thus, there is emerging in the ILO a clear definition of fundamental labour rights in the form of core labour standards. From the considerable list of 180 International Labour Conventions, it is now commonly agreed that the core ILO conventions are those concerning abolition of forced labour (Nos 29 and 105), freedom of association and the right to organise and bargain collectively (Nos 87 and 98), equal remuneration for men and women for work of equal value and non-discrimination in employment (Nos 100 and 111), and abolition of child labour (No. 138 to be supplemented by a new convention on the most exploitative form of child labour in 1998–99). These are basic human rights and it is now generally accepted that these rights should be available in all countries *irrespective of their level of development*. Efforts are hence being made in the ILO, with some success, to secure an accelerated rate of ratification and stricter enforcement of these basic conventions.

It is also commonly understood that standards concerning conditions surrounding work belong to a different category in so far as they are essentially *related to the level of development* attained in a country. The heterogeneity in these levels precludes the emergence of meaningful common standards in matters like hours of work. It becomes important, nevertheless, to emphasise this aspect because there are, even today, demands in some quarters in the northern trade union organisations that social clauses should be used to enforce minimum wage standards.

Environmental standards

Commonly accepted standards are even more difficult to obtain in the broader area of environment. There is a large number of multilateral environmental agreements dealing with individual aspects of environment like the ozone-layer depletion and trade in endangered species; and standards are set in these individual areas through a long process of negotiations and consensus building. Such standards are easier to arrive at in the case of problems threatening on a global scale like the ozone layer; though the experience of negotiating the Kyoto Climate Change Convention clearly shows that there can be difficulties even in cases where the consequences of not initiating timely corrective action are grave indeed.

In the absence of commonly accepted criteria, any attempt to enforce environmental standards through trade measures would, perhaps, involve extra-jurisdictional application of national sovereignty and, ironically enough, what the WTO Director-General has to say in the matter becomes relevant:

> it would be a profound mistake to assume that the challenges of our global age can be met by imposing our policies and our values on others. Whose environmental standards, cultural traditions, political systems represent a universal norm? When is it right to impose our values and standards on other countries and peoples? And do we really want to invest the WTO – or any other international organisation – with powers to define our environmental, social and ethical values?

Such standards can only be defined if they emerge in the relevant forums through a process of protracted negotiations and consensus building and it would be premature to think in terms of trade measures before such clear standards emerge.

Which structures?

The issue can also be discussed by examining whether trade measures are the right kind of instrument and WTO the right structure to implement social and environmental standards. There are, at least, two broad problems with using the MTS to enforce social and environmental standards, one having to do with protectionist interests and the other with the question of relative power of the developing and developed countries. It would be impossible to devise a system of implementing trade measures that would not be misused by individual protectionist interests. Moreover, trade measures would be an asymmetric international instrument –

effective when imposed by developed countries against the developing countries, but not in the other direction.

More importantly, however, the WTO is not a suitable institution for tackling those environmental and social problems in the developing countries that are at the root of the demand for social and environmental clauses in trade agreements. Two examples would suffice to show this. In the environmental area, a reference has been made above to the role of trade measures in the success of the Montreal Protocol. There are, however, other aspects of the Montreal Protocol which have contributed perhaps more to its success than its trade provisions, e.g., the principle of common but differentiated responsibility and the global facility for financing the transfer of relevant technology to the developing countries. In the social area, the clearest example is provided by the problem of child labour in the carpet industry. Mechanisms for putting children out of work by banning the import of carpets produced by child labour would be of use only if institutional mechanisms exist to provide resources to put those children in schools. The WTO can do the former; but not the latter.[17]

The WTO can never be a suitable forum for performing the so-called constitutional function of balancing a variety of legitimate interests and policies at the global level.

Notes

1 All but one of the six codes negotiated at the Tokyo Round were included in Annex 1 A of the WTO Agreement and, in many cases, with much stronger obligations than in their original form under the Tokyo Round. The Agreement on Government Procurement is the only Tokyo Round Code which forms a part of the WTO Annex 4 plurilateral agreements and in the matter of joining which therefore the governments have an option.

2 The TRIMS Agreement is in Annex 1 A of the WTO Agreement along with GATT and other agreements on trade in goods. A multilateral agreement on investment would have secured its own independent annex, perhaps Annex 1 D in continuation with Annex 1 B of GATS and Annex 1 C of the Agreement on TRIPS. Annex 1 D can, hence, be referred to as the missing annex of the WTO Agreement denoting its incomplete agenda on investment! (As we will see in section III, the northern NGOs too are talking in terms of missing clauses in the WTO Agreement – the social and environmental clauses.)

3 The discussion on illicit payments is a part of the discussion on the Agreement on Government Procurement which is currently one of the plurilateral agreements and not a multilateral one.

4 These distinctions become important in the tuna-dolphin disputes and the current shrimp–turtle disputes. The ban on imports of goods produced by child labour also is an example of extra-territorial enforcement of values.

5 The case of 'battery' eggs and 'free-range' eggs brings this out very clearly, as does the child labour issue.

6 Pearson (1993) and Esty (1994).

7 The Basle Convention on the Control of Transboundary Movements of Hazardous Wastes and Their Disposal, the Convention on International Trade in Endangered Species of Wild Fauna and Flora (CITES), and the Montreal Protocol on Substances that Deplete the Ozone Layer.

8 GATT/WTO Dispute Settlement Practice Relating to Article XX, Paragraphs (b), (d), and (g) of GATT.

9 The Articles of GATT which go against environmental protection measures and which have generally been invoked by the complainants are Article I (General Most-Favoured-Nation Treatment), Article III (National Treatment on Internal Taxation and Regulation) and Article XI (General Elimination of Quantitative Restrictions). The defendant can invoke the environmental exceptions referred to above.

10 The northern NGOs do not, of course, have a commonly articulated position on social and environmental issues. The term is used to denote large environmental organisations like the World Wildlife Fund (WWF), Friends of the Earth, Greenpeace; and the International Institute for Sustainable Development (IISD). In the matter of social clauses, the position is more homogenous among the large trade union organisations in the north including the International Confederation of Free Trade Unions.

11 This is also the position found in the Rio Declaration and in Agenda 21.

12 This is clearly brought out by a WWF statement on fisheries subsidies. Such subsidies are said to lead to over-exploitation of global fishery resources.

13 The earlier GATT-related documents are the 1927 'International Convention for the Abolition of Import and Export Prohibitions' of the League of Nations and the 'International Trade Organisation Charter' of the United Nations. Though neither of these documents took effect, their provisions formed the basis for the drafting of Article XX.

14 The manifesto is available at the website (www.agp.pga).

15 One such proposal is from the International Confederation of Free Trade Unions.

16 Cottier recognises that this may be far fetched, but that does not stop him from making a concrete suggestion that the idea of parliamentary participation could build on the existing models of regional economic integration.

17 A global regulatory authority to take care of social and environmental problems would be ineffective unless it plays, in effect, a minimal redistributive function. Proposals like the Tobin tax could play an important role in facilitating such a function of a global regulatory authority.

References

Cottier, Thomas, 1998. 'The WTO and Environmental Law: Some Issues and Ideas', Paper presented at the WTO Symposium on Trade Environment and Sustainable Development, Geneva, 17–18 March.

Esty, Daniel C., 1994. *Greening the GATT: Trade, Environment and the Future, Institute for International Economics*, Washington, DC.

Hoekman, Bernard and Michel Kosteki, 1995. *The Political Economy of the World Trading System: From GATT to WTO*, Oxford University Press, Oxford.

Hutton, John and Langford Chitsike, 1998. 'Stricter Domestic Measures: A Future Flashpoint Between CITES and the WTO?', *Bridges*, vol. 2, no. 2.

Pearson, Charles S., 1993. 'The Trade and Environment Nexus: What is New Since "72"', in *Trade and the Environment: Law, Economics and Policy*, Island Press, Washington, DC.

Ruggiero, Renato, 1998a. 'The Coming Challenge: Global Sustainable Development for the 21st Century', Address by WTO Director-General at the WTO Symposium on Trade Environment and Sustainable Development, Geneva, 17–18 March.

Ruggiero, Renato, 1998b. 'A New Partnership for a New Century: Sustainable Global Development in a Global Age', *Policing the Global Economy*, ed. Prince Sadruddin Aga Khan, Cameron May, London.

7 What role for the Tobin tax in world economic governance?

Philip Arestis and Malcolm Sawyer

Introduction

The purpose of this chapter is to discuss the contribution which a tax on foreign exchange dealings (often called a Tobin tax) could make to world economic governance. The Tobin tax, at least in its modern formulation,[1] began with Tobin's 1972 Janeway lecture at Princeton (Tobin, 1974; see also 1966, 1978; and Eichengreen, Tobin and Wyplosz, 1995) in which he specifically proposed a tax on foreign exchange transactions as a way of limiting speculation, enhancing the efficacy of macroeconomic policy in the process and raising some tax as a by-product.[2] Some official interest in a transactions tax has been expressed by the United Nations Development Programme (1994) and UNCTAD (1995) who have seen its possibilities for raising large amounts of money which could be used to finance development – Tobin suggests that 'the revenue potential is immense, over $1.5 trillion a year for the 0.5% tax' (in UNDP, 1994, p. 70) (see also Michalos, 1997, pp. 23–4).

Volatility, speculation and the efficiency of foreign exchange markets

Much of the reasoning which lies behind the advocacy of a transactions tax arises from the observation of the growing volume of foreign exchange trading.[3] The volume of foreign exchange transactions worldwide reached $1,300 billion a day in 1995 (with the corresponding figure in the early 1970s being $18 billion), equivalent to $312 trillion in a year of 240 business days (Tobin, 1996, p. xvi). By comparison, the annual global turnover in equity markets in 1995 was $21 trillion, the annual global trade in goods and services was $5 trillion (and total reserves of Central Banks around $1.5 trillion at the end of 1995). A tax on foreign exchange dealings would clearly be expected to reduce the volume of those dealings. But more significant than this growth in the volume of foreign exchange dealings is the perception that the exchange markets are not operating in an overall beneficial manner. The defenders of the exchange markets would view them as efficient – using the term efficient in a number of ways. Efficiency here would include the notion of 'efficient markets' in which information is rapidly absorbed into the price (and hence that prices follow a random walk), and also the idea that there are (social) benefits (e.g. of risk spreading) from trading in the exchange markets which match the (social) costs. An alternative view, on which we would see much of the case for the Tobin tax resting, starts from a different analysis of competitive markets (which we take the exchange markets to be) associated with Keynes and others.[4] This emphasises the role of expectations, conventions and perceptions of the views of others ('we devote our intelligences to anticipating what average opinion expects the average opinion to be', (Keynes, 1936, p. 156)), the instability which arose from speculation and the suggestion that long term commitment should be encouraged. Market operators are more concerned with the rate of change of price than with the price level. This has variously been described as, for example, 'noise' trading and trading motivated by price dynamics. This approach would suggest that exchange rates are rather volatile, that there are periods of substantial overvaluation (relative to some norm such as purchasing power parity or consistency with trade balance) and others of substantial undervaluation, and that the resources devoted to exchange dealings may be excessive.

In so far as foreign exchange dealing (for speculative purposes) is a zero-sum game, undertaken because of different expectations on interest rate and exchange rate movements, then a lower volume of transactions does not entail any costs (though there would be a redistribution of benefits and costs). It is argued that arbitrage through foreign exchange dealings brings about an equalisation of interest rates (adjusted for expected exchange rate movements), and that a 'thicker' market would encourage a speedier return to equilibrium and to such an equalisation of interest rates across countries. Assuming that such equalisation brings a benefit, even then we do not know what volume of transactions would be required to bring it about: indeed the theory of efficient markets would suggest that very few, if any, transactions would be required for any such equalisation. Thus, if the foreign exchange market has elements which could be seen as efficient (with respect to use of information), then the current volumes of transactions would not be required in order for the exchange rate to be in line with 'fundamentals'. In order to establish the optimal amount of trading it would be necessary to establish the extent of foreign exchange required for international trade, direct and portfolio investment.

There is now an extensive literature which indicates that financial market prices can be over- or under-valued for substantial periods of time (and casual observation of the movements in the exchange rates in the past twenty-five years, reflected to some degree in Tables 7.1 and 7.2, would be supportive of that view), and in that sense suffer from medium-term volatility. The work of Shiller (e.g. Shiller, 1981, 1984, 1990, and the papers in Shiller, 1989) has strongly suggested that there is excessive (medium term) volatility in the stock and bond markets. Further, there are theoretical literatures (surveyed by, for example, Camerer, 1989) which show that behaviour which could be termed as rational or 'near rational' at the level of the individual can generate 'bubbles'.[5] Indeed, bubbles can be an intertemporal manifestation of markets having 'multiple' equilibria. Under these circumstances bubbles 'need never break' (Stiglitz, 1990, p. 14). Also under the assumptions of uncertainty and of investors being short-lived and risk averse, again 'bubbles need not be completely eliminated' (Shleifer and Summers, 1990). Even if there are *some* risk-averse and *some* risk-loving speculators, to the extent to which they have limited access to capital, they are likely to have only a limited impact on markets – a result which is consistent with the Stiglitz and Weiss (1981) analysis of capital markets under asymmetric information. In a world of uncertainty where knowledge of the economic fundamentals is given to few it is perhaps inevitable that asset prices will fluctuate and follow fads and fashions.

Most economists today believe 'foreign exchange markets behave more like the unstable and irrational asset markets described by Keynes than the efficient markets described by modern finance theory' (Krugman, 1989). Isard (1995) suggests that 'few [economists] still believe that the behavior of flexible exchange rates can be accurately described by a model based on the hypothesis that market participants are both fully rational and completely informed about the structure of the model and the behavior of relevant macroeconomic fundamentals' (p. 182).

The term volatility suggests an instability on a short term basis, e.g. variance of price or price change measured on a daily basis. It can, of course, be the case that there is considerable volatility on this basis and yet the market be deemed efficient (in the sense that there is a lack of correlation between daily price movements). But this volatility may be inconvenient for those involved in international trade because of the uncertainty which it engenders, though the use of forward contracts can reduce the uncertainty. Volatility which involved minor fluctuations around the 'fundamental' equilibrium exchange rate would be little more than a nuisance. The aspect of exchange rate movements since the early 1970s which is of more significance is the year (or longer) to year volatility which has generated substantial periods when exchange rates are substantially over- or under-valued. This medium and long term volatility cannot be escaped through the use of forward contracts (which generally do not extend more than 12 months into the future), and is likely to have a much more significant impact on international trade than short term volatility.

There can be little doubt that the era of flexible exchange rates since 1971 has been associated with a considerable degree of volatility of exchange rates. Some crude indicators show that since 1980 on average the standard deviation relative to the mean of the sterling/DM rate was 3.9 per cent on a monthly basis, and the ratio of the maximum to minimum during a year varied from 5 per cent (in 1991 the only full year for which sterling was a member of the ERM) and 22 per cent. There is also considerable variation in the month to month changes with an average standard deviation of 2.33 per cent. Comparable figures for the dollar/yen rate were 5.2 per cent for the standard deviation relative to the mean, a ratio of maximum to minimum up to 30 per cent and a standard deviation of monthly changes of 2.83 per cent. These figures suggest significant volatility within a year, as well as suggesting considerable variation in the real value of the exchange rates.

Mussa (1986) calculates the changes in the logarithm of ratio of price levels in the two countries concerned, of the nominal exchange rate and of the real exchange rate. He concludes that under floating exchange rates, 'there is a strong correlation between short-term movements in the real exchange rate and short-term movements in the nominal exchange rate' (p. 131). Further, 'short-term changes in nominal exchange rates and in real exchange rates show substantial persistence during subperiods when the nominal exchange rate is floating' (p. 132). He makes many cross-currency comparisons, and not surprisingly there is a wide variation in the degree of variability in bilateral exchange rates. Variances of up to 25 per cent per quarter are found, implying a standard deviation of 5 per cent per quarter: this would of course mean that in approximately one-third of quarters the rate of change deviated by more than 5 per cent from the average. Further evidence is provided in Rose (1994) (cited by Eichengreen *et al.*, 1995). Rogoff (1996) poses what he terms the purchasing power parity puzzle, which is 'How can one reconcile the enormous short-term volatility of real exchange rates with the extremely slow rate at which shocks appear to damp out? . . . Consensus estimates for the rate at which PPP deviations damp . . . suggest a half-life of three to five years, seemingly too long to be explained by nominal rigidities' (pp. 647–8).

The possible costs of volatility are well-known even if they are difficult to quantify and are subject to some debate. Volatility engenders a degree of price uncertainty, making effective decision-making more difficult. The price (of currency) uncertainty may lead firms to be reluctant to engage in international trade and thereby reduce the volume of international trade. Others (e.g. Krugman, 1989) suggest that uncertainty over exchange rates generates incentives for firms to postpone investment in export (or import substitution) capacity that would be difficult to reverse. In the context of exchange rate volatility, there may be asymmetric responses to the upward and downward movements of the exchange rate. An over-valued exchange rate reduces export demand, leading to a decline in the domestic tradable goods sector and a reduction of capacity (or a failure to invest) in that sector, and this may not be fully compensated by the stimulus of export demand coming from an under-valued exchange rate in terms of the opening of new capacity. The effect of volatility on policy-makers can be a further concern in so far as volatility generates uncertainty and deflationary responses. If say a fall in the exchange rate (arising from the volatility of the exchange rate and unconnected with real variables) generates a deflationary response (e.g. increase domestic interest rates) there are detrimental effects on the domestic economy. This may, of course, be offset by a reflationary response to a rising exchange rate, and if the policy responses are symmetrical there would appear to be no net damage. Even so, there may still be some harm in so far as sudden and frequent changes in exchange rate movements generate changes in the economic policy stance, and thereby a more uncertain economic environment. However, Frankel (1996), drawing on the survey of Goldstein (1995), argues that 'Most studies have concluded that short-term volatility has little effect on trade' (p. 52). But a study by Frankel and Wei (1995) on bilateral trade 'shows statistically significant effects of bilateral volatility in the 1960s and 1970s' (Frankel, 1996, p. 52). Isard (1995) similarly concludes that 'empirical studies have failed to uncover statistical evidence that exchange rate variability has had much of a depressing effect on international trade volumes' (p. 196). However, we can note the conclusions of Gagnon (1993) based on a theoretical approach that 'under a very extreme combination of assumptions, the breakdown of Bretton Woods is estimated to reduce the level of trade by about 3 percent. This effect is shown to be too small to detect statistically. A further increase in exchange rate variability would lower the volume of trade by a statistically significant 9 percent, but this latter scenario requires a degree of exchange rate variability much larger than has been observed historically' (p. 287).

One advantage of such a reduction would be to reduce the relative influence of financial and short term factors on the exchange rate and to increase the relative influence of real factors. Harcourt (1995) argues that 'if we want exchange rates to reflect real economic forces – trading prospects, real investment opportunities – we need greatly to reduce speculation and thereby its effects on the determination of exchange rates in both the short and longer term. For neither in the short term nor on average over longer periods do exchange rates at the moment reflect these economic activities' (p. 34).

It would be usually assumed that very short term foreign exchange transactions (say those involving a round trip of less than one week) would be largely undertaken in pursuit of gains from movements in the exchange rate, and not for gains from interest rate differentials. Even if transactions costs were as low as 0.1 per cent, then on a round trip of one week the anticipated interest rate differential would need to be 5.3 per cent expressed on an annual basis (with no expected compensating movement in the exchange rate) in order for a switch between currencies to appear profitable. In contrast, long term foreign exchange transactions could be expected to be more geared towards differentials in the rates of return, and small differences in the annual rate of return may be sufficient to generate capital flows.

However the short term and the long term flows are similar in that capital flows proceed if the anticipated (presumably risk adjusted) return is greater than the transaction costs involved. Thus, for any given expected change in market price that exceeds the total tax imposed, speculation is profitable regardless of whether the expected change is of one day, one week, or one year, or even longer. From that angle, a transactions tax may have a similar relative effect on short term and on long term transactions. In both cases (and the intermediate ones as well), the effect of the transactions tax would depend on the frequency of returns lying between the current transactions costs, and those costs plus a transactions tax, where the returns are calculated over the expected holding period. Hence a transactions tax would have a greater effect on short term transactions than on long term transactions if the frequency distribution of the former (around the current cost) is denser than the corresponding distribution for the latter. We could expect this to be the case from the following illustration. Over say a week the frequency distribution across individuals as to their expectations of the change in the exchange rate may well cluster between say +1 per cent and –1 per cent, whereas the distribution of expectations on interest rate differentials could cluster between say +3 per cent and − 3 per cent per annum, and hence a wider distribution over say five years is more likely. With those illustrative numbers, a 0.1 per cent transactions tax is likely to eliminate for active consideration a higher proportion of the short term exchanges than the long term ones. We would have to stress that these numbers are only illustrative but may catch the flavour of the case that a transactions tax would have more effect on short term transactions than on those designed to be long term ones. On that basis, a transactions tax may have more impact on short term volatility than on medium or long term volatility (if there is a link between the volume transactions and volatility), though it is the medium or long term volatility which is the more costly.

Attempts at fixed exchange rates are made much more difficult by the volume of transactions. This is reflected in: 'Modest uncertainty about whether national monetary authorities are inclined to make use of their theoretical independence can lead to significant financial market volatility. If currencies are floating, they can fluctuate widely. If the authorities attempt to peg them, the costs of doing so, measured by reserve losses or interest-rate increases, can be extremely high. Even a government otherwise prepared to maintain a pegged exchange rate may be unwilling or unable to do so when attacked by the markets and forced to raise interest rates to astronomical heights' (Eichengreen, Tobin and Wyplosz, 1995, p. 162).

Foreign exchange dealings absorb resources, and a reduction in the volume of dealing would reduce the resources devoted to dealing. Frankel (1996, p. 61) suggests 'a typical transaction cost for foreign exchange might be 0.1 per cent' though much smaller for interdealer trading. Felix and Sau (1996) use the much higher figures of 0.5 per cent and 1.0 per cent for the transaction costs. But they also report that 'the quoted bid-ask spreads on trades of major currencies in the "wholesale" foreign exchange market (trades less [sic] than $50 million) over the electronic network are usually less than 0.1% . . . The spreads are doubled for "retail" trades (less than $5 million) and can rise to more than 1.0% for small retail transactions' (p. 231). However, other figures on the bid-ask spread are much lower (noting that transaction costs are broader than the bid-ask spread): Kenen (1996) states that 'spreads in the wholesale market are well below 10 basis points [i.e. 0.1 per cent] for the major currencies' (p. 110).

On the basis of the estimates given above on the volume of transactions, a figure of 0.05 per cent for transaction costs would suggest a total cost of $150 billion *per annum* (in 1995). This may suggest that if a transactions tax halved the volume of transactions, and assuming that the transaction costs reflect resource costs, then annual savings of the order of $75 billion (£50 billion) could be involved (i.e. more than 6 per cent of UK GDP, and nearly 0.4 per cent of OECD GDP). This figure may be an over-estimate if there are economies of scale in foreign exchange transactions and to the extent that the foreign exchange transactions which are reduced are concentrated amongst those which attract lower transaction costs (e.g. in the wholesale market).

Tax-raising potential

The second line of reasoning for a transactions tax is simply its tax-raising potential. Tobin (1978) suggested this possibility as a by-product of a transactions tax, not as the main aim of his proposal, but others (e.g. United Nations Development Programme, 1994) put more emphasis on the revenue aspects. The revenue aspects may be linked with the view that the financial sector is relatively under-taxed in the sense that financial transactions do not usually bear general sales or value-added taxes nor are they usually subject to specific taxes in the way in which, for example, tobacco and alcohol are. Calculations for OECD (1995) for OECD countries indicates that on average such taxes account for 1.3 per cent of tax revenue. However, most countries do have such taxes (see Campbell and Froot, 1994, summarised in Frankel, 1996, for an indication that there are only a few industrialised countries without any transactions taxes; and Spahn, 1995, pp. 51–4). It could also be added that a Tobin tax 'would tend to be progressive because relatively low income people would not be involved in the capital transactions captured by the tax' (Michalos, 1997, p. 31).

The tax-raising potential of a transactions tax is considerable. The most widely cited figures on turnover on the foreign exchange markets are summarised in Tables 7.1 and 7.2. In April 1992, the gross daily turnover was estimated at over $1.3 trillion, which comes down to around $1.08 trillion when local double-counting is eliminated. This represented a growth of 50 per cent in three years. For April 1995, the figure had grown again by nearly 50 per cent to $1.57 trillion. After adjustments for cross-border double-counting and for gaps in data, the net daily turnover was estimated at $880 billion in 1992 and $1.25 trillion in 1995. The latter figure generates, on the basis of 240 business days, an annual turnover of $300 trillion. World trade for 1995 is a little over $5 trillion[6] suggesting a multiple of financial transactions relative to world trade of around 60.

Table 7.1 Countries with the largest volume of trading in foreign currency, 1992 and 1995

	Daily average foreign exchange turnover 1992 (US$ billion)	% share	Daily average foreign exchange turnover 1995 (US$ billion)	% share
United Kingdom	290.5	27	464.5	30
United States	166.9	16	244.4	16
Japan	120.2	11	161.3	10
Singapore	73.6	7	105.4	7
Switzerland	65.5	6	86.5	5
Hong Kong	60.3	6	90.2	6
Germany	55.0	5	76.2	5
France	33.3	3	58.0	4
Australia	29.0	3	39.5	3
All others	181.9	16	246.2	14
Total of above	1,076.2	100	1,572.2	100

Source: BIS estimates as reported in Felix (1996).

Note: Net of local double-counting, but not adjusted for cross-border double-counting.

Table 7.2 Market segments, April 1992

Market segment	Gross turnover (US$ billion)	% share
Total	1,353.7	100
of which		
Spot market	659.5	49
Forwards	626.4	46
of which		
Outright	77.6	6
Swaps	547.1	40
Futures	9.5	1
Options	51.6	4

Source: BIS (1993) Table IV, as reported in Mendez (1996).

Notes: Gross of both local and cross-border double-counting. Totals do not sum because of incomplete reporting of market segment breakdowns. The number of countries reporting disaggregated data varies from component to component: total 21, spot 20, outright forwards and swaps 12, futures 12, and options 17. No adjustment for double-counting in futures and exchange-traded options.

The estimation of potential tax yield would clearly require estimates of the price-elasticity of the volume of foreign exchange transactions, and of the degree of tax avoidance and evasion which could be expected to be involved with some shift to untaxed transactions (e.g. to countries which do not impose the tax) and also to non-reporting of transactions which should be subject to tax. The proportional significance of a transactions tax will vary greatly between different types of purchaser. For the tourist buying foreign exchange with a buy–sell spread of say 7 per cent and a transaction fee of 2 per cent, a 0.5 per cent tax would be of little significance. For the long term investor, a 0.5 per cent tax (1 per cent on a round trip transaction) represents an annualised cost of 0.1 per cent over 10 years. In contrast, for the short term such a tax represents nearly 4,000 per cent per annum on a one-day shift, and for those transacting large volumes the buy–sell spread and the current transactions costs are likely to be small. Mendez (1996) suggests a spread of 10 basis points for the publicly quoted markets and 3 to 4 basis points on the interbank market (basis point being one digit in the fourth decimal place of a foreign exchange price quotation). We would assume that the vast bulk of foreign exchange transactions fall into the latter rather than the former categories, and hence a transactions tax would have a substantial impact. If we take the 'price' of a round trip foreign exchange transaction to be the spread, then the imposition of a 0.5 per cent tax (equal to 1 per cent on the round trip) would amount to a very substantial price increase: on the basis of a 0.1 per cent spread, a tenfold increase. For example, on the basis of the 1992 figures of $300 billion daily turnover in the UK, the tax yield on the basis of a 0.5 per cent tax on transactions in the UK and unchanged volume would yield around £1 billion per day, that is £240 billion per annum which is comparable to the total tax yield (cf. Kelly, 1994, p. 230).

But the tax may have considerable effect on the volume of transactions, and obviously the tax yield is much reduced (and in that case the tax would have achieved its objective of reducing the volume of transactions). It would, though, seem quite possible that a 0.5 per cent tax could reduce financial flows to say one-tenth of their present volume (a unit elasticity in face of a ten-fold increase in the cost as indicated above) which still put the worldwide yield at $150 billion (in 1995). However a realisation of the relative size of say a 0.5 per cent tax and the spreads has led to suggestions of a tax more of the order of 0.1 per cent.

D'Orville and Najman (1995) estimated the revenue from a transactions tax for 1992 at $140.1 billion for a tax of 0.25 per cent and $56.32 billion for a 0.1 per cent tax (as reported in Frankel, 1996, p. 60). However, Frankel (1996) argues that they have made a major mistake in these calculations. 'They have assumed, incorrectly, that only a portion of transactions carried out through foreign exchange brokers would be subject to the tax – about one-third of the total. The mistake probably arose from assuming that the term "brokers" applies to all foreign exchange dealers or traders. In reality, the other two-thirds of transactions are handled directly by foreign exchange dealers at private banks, who would be subject to a Tobin tax every bit as much as brokers' (p. 60). D'Orville and Najman estimate a fall in volume of 20 per cent as a result of the imposition of a transactions tax.

Frankel (1996) suggests that an elasticity of 0.32 for transactions initiated by financial customers 'might not be a bad guess' (p. 62), but with no change in orders from exporters and importers. With an assumed doubling of transaction costs through the imposition of a 0.1 per cent tax, he suggests a fall in transactions from $376 billion to $346 billion *per diem* for transactions by financial customers. Further, it is assumed that the customer-to-transaction ratio rises from the current 0.31 to 0.5. The new volume of transactions would be $346/0.5 billion *per diem* (i.e. $692 billion) which yields an annual revenue of $166 billion. Felix and Sau (1996) provide a range of estimates though starting with an assumption of considerably higher transaction costs (0.5 per cent and 1 per cent are used): their central estimates range between $205.5 billion and $267.6 billion for a 0.25 per cent tax in 1995. We may conclude that revenue of the order of $200 billion a year could be generated through a modest transactions tax.

The application of an international tax raises the question of the allocation of the proceeds of the tax. A number of proposals have been put forward on the way to distribute the tax proceeds. To the extent that it is the IMF or World Bank who are the intermediate recipients, a further proposal may be to enhance the lending capabilities of these institutions especially to third world counties which could embrace development and anti-pollution projects. Kaul and Langmore (1996) focus on three: the 'Agenda 21' action programme emanating from the 1992 UN Conference on Environment and Development which would cost $125 billion per annum in terms of external concessional financing alone; a poverty eradication programme as formulated at the World Summit for Social Development, 1995, at an additional external cost of $40 billion per annum; and infrastructure and other needs which according to World Bank estimates would involve external concessional funding of around $20 billion per annum. These total $185 billion per annum, which is the same order of magnitude as many of the estimates of the revenue from the transactions tax as discussed above.

The workings of the tax could be reinforced by making the administration of a transactions tax a condition of membership of the IMF and the BIS though that may not be sufficient to prevent the growth of off-shore dealing since a small country would have so little to gain from membership of the IMF as compared with the potential revenue for the location of off-shore financial markets (though if the off-shore locations are competing on the basis of low or no tax, there is the question of how much revenue would be generated). It can also be asked whether the tax could be levied on the participants based on their location rather than on the basis of the location of the transaction. Thus a UK bank (for this purpose being one which is regulated by the Bank of England) would be subject to a tax on its foreign exchange transactions, wherever they are made.

There is widespread agreement that the tax would have to be implemented on a co-ordinated international basis. 'The Tobin tax would be introduced through an international agreement, giving it its global characteristic. But revenue collection would be a national responsibility. Tax yields would accrue on a country-by-country basis, raising the question of how much revenue each country would be likely to collect' (Kaul and Langmore, 1996, p. 257). It may not be necessary for there to be full agreement over the tax rate, though there would be strong pressures towards a degree of uniformity (and probably a requirement for a minimum rate to avoid competitive undercutting of the tax rate between countries). It is clear that there would be very considerable differences in the amount of tax collected in each country. Based on the current composition of foreign exchange dealings (cf. Table 7.1), the UK would collect near to 30 per cent of the total, USA 15.5 per cent, Japan 10 per cent, Singapore 6.6 per cent and Hong Kong 5.7 per cent. Part of the international agreement could clearly be that a proportion of the tax collected is paid over to an international body and/or used for agreed development and environmental purposes (in one way this would be comparable to the collection of value-added tax in EU member countries with the equivalent of 1 per cent of turnover being handed on to the European Commission). Kaul and Langmore (1996, pp. 260–1) point out that a modest transactions tax would have a large impact on the national budgets in a few countries (notably UK, USA and Japan) if the tax revenue collected within the country were largely or wholly retained by that country (and in the case of the UK would be sufficient to eliminate the current £30 billion deficit). Kaul and Langmore (1996, pp. 266–7) make some suggestions on how the revenues might be shared (e.g. the percentage of tax raised by a country retained would vary between 80 and 100 per cent, depending on their level of income. The obvious difficulty which arises here is obtaining international agreement over the introduction and the rate of the tax when the revenue from the tax would be so unequally distributed across countries (and to the extent to which countries fear that their financial centres would be reduced in size, the costs also unequally distributed). Further, a substantial retention of revenue at the national level obviously reduces the funds available for international development and environmental purposes.

National economic policy autonomy

The Tobin tax is also seen as possibly enhancing the autonomy of national economic policy, and reducing the constraints on such policy imposed by the financial markets. This runs counter to the widely held view since financial markets 'know best' (and that exchange rates and stock market prices reflect 'fundamentals'), they exert a healthy discipline on central banks and governments. Adverse capital movements is the usual example cited to support this view: these should be read as a sober judgement that macroeconomic policies are unsound, and as such should be abandoned. A further argument in this context is that a transactions tax can potentially tackle these problems more flexibly which previously required the introduction of financial controls, especially quantitative exchange controls which are normally viewed as rigid. A related argument is that a transactions tax by reducing foreign exchange rate volatility increases the independence of policy-makers. The famous 'impossible trinity' may be invoked to make this point. This is that out of the three attributes of financial openness, currency stability and monetary independence, a country can only have two. Thus, for a country seeking currency stability, a transactions tax might help to restore some measure of monetary independence, and widen the scope in, for example, the determination of domestic interest rates.

Some have argued that a transactions tax would enhance the autonomy of national economic policies. We would cast some doubt on the extent of any increase in national autonomy. It is clear that a tax of the order of 0.1 per cent would make little difference in the degree to which domestic interest rates can diverge from (risk adjusted) international interest rates. If a transactions tax were successfully implemented, that could be a signal that the economic and political power of the financial markets has been reduced, and that governments do not subscribe to the doctrine that the financial markets 'know best'. A reduction in the volume of transactions would mean that the reserves of central banks would be greater relative to the volume of transactions and hence may make central bank intervention in foreign exchange markets somewhat more effective.

Distortions and feasibility

There are a range of objections which have been raised against the Tobin tax either in terms of desirability or of feasibility. We have discussed these at length elsewhere (Arestis and Sawyer, 1997b) and summarise the arguments here.

One common argument raised against the transactions tax relates to its distortionary effects. The argument is straightforward with a tax which leads in a competitive market to an equilibrium being established which involves lower quantity and fewer resources being allocated to that particular market. It should first be noted that the financial sector may be lightly taxed. Second, the distortionary nature of a tax arises from the discouragement of some potentially beneficial trades which would have otherwise taken place. But it may be zero-sum game transactions which are discouraged, and some would argue that the Tobin tax 'penalizes and thus restricts socially undesirable behavior' (Felix, 1995, p. 39).

Third, the analysis of distortions is an equilibrium one and it is equilibrium trades which are discouraged. But there is a sense in which much of the trading in currency markets is disequilibrium trading in terms of seeking to take advantage of price changes. Thus the conventional analysis of distortions does not apply to this situation, and if it is argued that the amount of 'noise trading' is excessive, then a tax is beneficial rather than distortionary.

A second line of argument is that proposals for a transactions tax 'could inhibit international financial investment or trade finance' (Holtham, 1995, p. 237). The imposition of a transactions tax in itself would add to the costs of conducting international trade, and the likelihood is that trade would thereby be diminished. With some allowance for multiple foreign exchange transactions lying behind each international trade (as argued by Davidson, 1997), a transactions tax of say 0.1 per cent might raise the cost of international trade by the order of 0.5 per cent. This would need to be balanced against the benefits for international trade from any reduction in exchange rate volatility.

Most advocates of a transactions tax recognise that it would have to be 'universal and uniform: it would have to apply to all jurisdictions, and the rate would have to be equalised across markets' (Eichengreen, Tobin and Wyplosz, 1995, p. 165). The tax 'would be an internationally agreed uniform tax, administered by each government over its own jurisdiction. Britain, for example, would be responsible for taxing all inter-currency transactions in Eurocurrency banks and brokers located in London, even when sterling was not involved. The tax proceeds could appropriately be paid into the IMF or World Bank' (Tobin, 1978, p. 158).

While it is accepted that the tax could not be implemented in one country, the question does arise as to whether it would have to be universal in order to be effective. As Table 7.1 indicates, at present nine countries account for 84 per cent of foreign exchange transactions. A tax introduced in those nine countries plus a few others might be sufficient to provide a workable tax regime since, at least initially, this tax would capture the bulk of foreign exchange transactions. There may be ways of avoiding a shift of transactions to 'tax havens'. One possibility is to consider the transfer of funds to or from such location as taxable transactions at penalty rates. Thus the movement of say £1 million in sterling from the UK (assumed to be applying the tax) to a 'tax haven' (not applying the tax) would be subject to tax at a multiple of the transactions tax. Another possibility would be to tax at the site where the deal is made rather than at the site where the transaction occurs (cf. Tobin, 1996).

The widely recognised requirement that any transactions tax on foreign exchange dealing would have to be virtually universal may well be the most important practical obstacle to the implementation of a transactions tax. It would clearly require the co-operation of all countries with significant foreign exchange dealings within their borders (and, one might add, those with the potential to develop foreign exchange dealing centres), although there would be incentives (comparable with any cartel) for countries to apply a lower tax rate within their jurisdiction. One partial solution to this runs as follows: 'Enforcement of the universal tax would depend principally on major banks and on the jurisdictions that regulate them. The surveillance of national regulatory authorities could be the responsibility of a multilateral agency like the Bank of International Settlements or the International Monetary Fund' (Eichengreen, Tobin and Wyplosz, 1995, p. 165). We would suggest that given the IMF's considerable expertise in international financial markets it should be in a good position to undertake such a task. Furthermore, the fact that the IMF's central objectives of promoting international monetary co-operation, and maintaining exchange rate stability and orderly exchange arrangements amongst its members, are objectives which the Tobin transactions tax shares, strengthens the argument substantially that the IMF should play a central role in its implementation.

Garber and Taylor (1995) start from the view that 'a well-known feature of financial markets [is] that attempts to regulate them are frequently thwarted as market participants formulate sophisticated ways of avoiding the regulation' (Garber and Taylor, 1995, p. 173). They, then, argue that there are problems in defining the nature of the transactions to be taxed. 'The overall effect on gross volume, however, depends on how a foreign exchange transaction is defined by the regulators. If foreign exchange is defined as an exchange of one bank deposit for another in a different currency, gross trading in these claims will be effectively eliminated in favour of T-bill swaps in currencies with liquid (same day) T-bill markets. The swapped T-bills will be immediately sold for deposits. The foreign exchange market will shift to this form, no tax will be paid, and position taking will be unaffected' (p. 179).

Our view here would be that the appropriate definition of the transaction would be any transaction which involved the exchange of a financial asset denominated in one currency for a financial asset denominated in another currency. This was Tobin's initial suggestion when he wrote that 'the tax would apply to all purchases of financial instruments denominated in another currency – from currency and coin to equity securities. It would have to apply, I think, to all payments in one currency for goods, services, and real assets sold by a resident of another currency area. I don't intend to add even a small barrier to trade. But I see offhand no other way to prevent financial transactions disguised as trade' (Tobin, 1978, p. 159). However, 'while the implementation of the tax may appear complex, it is not any more complicated, probably much less so, than the detailed provisions of many existing taxes . . . Indeed if the standards of what is feasible employed here had been used before imposing income tax or VAT they would never have been introduced! The dominant feature in the introduction of new taxation has always been the political will rather than administrative feasibility' (Grieve Smith, 1997).

The introduction of a transactions tax would be a major economic and political development but at the same time it would have to be introduced on a 'big bang' basis for otherwise foreign exchange dealings would quickly move to those countries which were not applying the tax. A transactions tax would have a significant impact on worldwide aggregate demand. At this point we can do little more than speculate on the likely effects. The aggregate demand effects will depend on the use to which the tax revenue is put and on which, if any, other taxes are abolished. However, it is quite reasonable to think that a transactions tax would be levied on those with a low propensity to spend, and the re-distribution would be towards those with a much higher propensity to spend. Hence aggregate demand may well increase. This would be added to by the effect of the enhanced capability of national governments to pursue economic policies which stimulate a higher level of demand.

Some concluding remarks

The obstacles at a political level to the introduction of a transactions tax are well summarised in the following. 'The institution of a [transactions] tax would be vig-orously opposed by many as an interference in the market mechanism, one that would make it more inefficient and dampen capital investment. It could be argued that volatility is not a result of speculation but rather of balance-of-payments problems and uncoordinated national monetary policies, and that so-called spec-ulators actually include companies changing currencies to protect themselves against losses from a depreciation of their currency holdings. It could also be asserted that the market is now too large for any single private or public party to sway, and that the activities of speculators actually contribute to the liquidity of the market. In view of the above, it is probable that the proposed tax, in political and practical terms, would be a "non-starter"' (Mendez, 1996, p. 500). Two politi-cal obstacles stand out: namely the international co-ordination which would be required, and the political power of the financial sector.

A Tobin transactions tax is a feasible tax for raising substantial sums of taxation, and 'the feasibility issues raised by the Tobin tax are more political than technical' (Kaul, Grunberg and Haq, 1996, p. 7). It would substantially reduce the volume of currency transactions, with significant resource savings and the hope that it may diminish the volatility of exchange markets. Its introduction would face formida-ble political problems and its implementation would need to be carefully arranged. In this sense, we should conclude by suggesting that the Tobin tax by itself cannot perform miracles. It would seem more appropriate to use the tax as one of several policy instruments that could be deployed to discourage speculation or unsustainable short term capital flows. The contribution of a Tobin tax in creat-ing a new economic order may come particularly from its potential as a source of revenue, generated at the international level, from which development pro-grammes could be financed.

Notes

1   The origins of the Tobin tax idea can be traced to Keynes's argument in the *Treatise on Money* that it may be necessary to tax foreign lending to contain speculative capital movements (1980, chap. 36). In 1936, Keynes wrote that '[t]he introduction of a sub-stantial government transfer tax on all transactions might prove the most serviceable reform available, with a view to mitigating the predominance of speculation over enter-prise in the United States' (Keynes, 1936, p. 160) though that was more related to domestic financial transactions.

2 Following the Stock Market crashes of 1987, Summers and Summers (1989) updated the argument and proposed new taxes on securities transactions (see also, Stiglitz, 1989). Harcourt (1995) and Kelly (1994) have advanced variants of a tax on foreign exchange dealings: this concern has emerged in view of the severe speculative attacks on the European Exchange Rate Mechanism (ERM) (see also, Neuburger and Sawyer, 1990, p. 116). A recent proposal along Tobin's line of argument is Spahn's (1995) suggestion for a two-tier system. This would impose additionally a penal tax on transactions outside a specified band. For example, the penal rate could be imposed on the difference between the exchange rate in the transaction and the specified outer limit of the band.

3 See Michalos (1997, pp. 23–38) for a list of 19 arguments in favour of a Tobin tax.

4 See Arestis and Sawyer (1997a) for further discussion.

5 There are many formal definitions of what a 'bubble' is, and an example of the variety can be found in the *Journal of Economic Perspectives*, vol. 4, no. 2. In the same issue, though, Stiglitz (1990) offers an intuitive definition which suggests that 'if the reason the price is high today is *only* because investors believe that the selling price will be high tomorrow – when 'fundamental' factors do not seem to justify such a price – then a bubble exists. At least in the short run, the high price of an asset is merited, because it yields a return (capital gain plus dividend) equal to that on alternative assets' (p. 13).

6 The figures are $5,239.4 billion for exports but only $5,124.3 billion for imports (source: *International Financial Statistics*, June 1996).

References

Arestis, P. and Sawyer, M. (1997a), 'How many cheers for the Tobin tax?', *Cambridge Journal of Economics*, vol. 21, pp. 753–768

Arestis, P. and Sawyer, M. (1997b), 'The Tobin financial transactions tax: its potential and feasibility', *International Papers in Political Economy*, vol. 3, pp. 1–32

Bank for International Settlements (1993), *Central Bank Survey of Foreign Exchange Market Activity in April 1992*, Basle: BIS Monetary and Economic Department

Camerer, C. (1989), 'Bubbles and fads in asset prices', *Journal of Economic Surveys*, vol. 3, pp. 3–43

Campbell, J.Y. and Froot, K. (1994), 'International experiences with security transaction taxes' in J. Frankel (ed.) *The Internationalization of Equity Markets*, Chicago: University of Chicago Press

Davidson, P. (1997), 'Are grains of sand in the wheels of international finance sufficient to do the job when boulders are often required', *Economic Journal*, vol. 107, pp. 671–686

D'Orville, H. and Najman, D. (1995), *Towards a New Multilateralism: Funding Global Priorities*, New York: United Nations

Eichengreen, B. and Wyplosz, C. (1996), 'Taxing international financial transactions to enhance the operation of the international monetary system' in Haq *et al.* (1996)

Eichengreen, B., Tobin, J. and Wyplosz, G. (1995), 'Two cases for sand in the wheels of international finance', *Economic Journal*, vol. 105, pp. 162–172

Felix, D. (1995), *Financial Globalization versus Free Trade: the Case for the Tobin Tax*, Discussion Paper No. 108, Geneva: United Nations Conference on Trade and Development

Felix, D. (1996), Statistical appendix to Haq *et al.* (1996)

Felix, D. and Sau, R. (1996), 'On the revenue potential and phasing in of the Tobin tax' in Haq *et al.* (1996)

Frankel, J. (1996), 'How well do foreign exchange markets work: might a Tobin tax help?' in Haq *et al.* (1996)

Frankel, J. and Wei, S.-J. (1995), 'Regionalization of world trade and currencies: economics and politics' in J. Frankel (ed.) *The Regionalization of the World Economy*, Chicago: University of Chicago Press

Gagnon, J.E. (1993), 'Exchange rate variability and the level of international trade', *Journal of International Economics*, vol. 34, pp. 269–287

Garber, P. and Taylor, M.P. (1995), 'Sands in the wheels of foreign exchange markets: a skeptical note', *Economic Journal*, vol. 105, pp. 173–180

Goldstein, M. (1995), *The Exchange Rate System and the IMF: A Modest Agenda*, Policy Analyses in International Economics No. 39. Washington, DC: Institute for International Economics

Goodhart, C.A. (1996), 'Discussant to Professor J. Tobin', *Economic Systems with Journal of International and Comparative Economics*, vol. 20, pp. 91–95

Grieve Smith, J. (1997), 'Exchange rate instability and the Tobin tax: review article', *Cambridge Journal of Economics*, vol. 21, pp. 745–752

Haq, M.U., Kaul, I. and Grunberg, I. (eds) (1996), *The Tobin Tax: Coping with Financial Volatility*, Oxford: Oxford University Press

Harcourt, G.C. (1995), 'A "modest proposal" for taming speculators and putting the world on course to prosperity' in G.C. Harcourt, *Capitalism, Socialism and Post-Keynesianism*, Aldershot: Edward Elgar, chapter 3 (originally published in *Economic and Political Weekly*, vol. 29 (28), September 1994, pp. 2490–2492)

Holtham, G. (1995), 'Managing the exchange rate system' in J. Michie and J. Grieve Smith (eds) *Managing the Global Economy*, Oxford, Oxford University Press

International Monetary Fund (IMF) (1995a), *International Capital Markets: Developments, Prospects and Policy Issues*, Washington, DC: IMF Publications

International Monetary Fund (IMF) (1995b), *World Economic Outlook,* May, Washington, DC: IMF Publications

Isard, P. (1995), *Exchange Rate Economics*, Cambridge: Cambridge University Press

Kaul, I. and Langmore, J. (1996), 'Potential uses of the revenue from a Tobin tax' in Haq *et al.* (1996)

Kaul, I., Grunberg, I. and ul Haq, M. (1996), 'Overview' in Haq *et al.* (1996), pp. 1–12

Kelly, R. (1994), 'A framework for European exchange rates in the 1990s', in J. Michie and J. Grieve Smith (eds), *Unemployment in Europe*, London: Academic Press

Kenen, P.B. (1996), 'The feasibility of taxing foreign exchange transactions' in Haq *et al.* (1996)

Keynes, J.M. (1936), *The General Theory of Employment, Interest and Money*, London: Macmillan

Keynes, J.M. (1980), *The Collected Writings of John Maynard Keynes, vol. VI, A Treatise on Money, 2 The Applied Theory of Money*, London: Macmillan

Krugman, P. (1989), 'The case for stabilizing exchange rates', *Oxford Review of Economic Policy*, vol. 5, pp. 61–72

Mendez, R.P. (1996), 'Harnessing the global foreign currency market: proposal for a foreign currency exchange (FXE)', *Review of International Political Economy*, vol. 3, pp. 498–512

Michalos, A.C. (1997), *Good Taxes*, Toronto: Dundurn Press

Mussa, M. (1986), 'Nominal exchange rate regimes and the behavior of real exchange rates: evidence and implications', *Carnegie-Rochester Conference Series on Public Policy*, vol. 25, pp. 117–214

Neuburger, H. and Sawyer, M. (1990), 'Macroeconomic policies and inflation' in K. Cowling and R. Sugden (eds) *A New Economic Policy for Britain: Essays on the Development of Industry*, Manchester: Manchester University Press

Organisation for Economic Co-operation and Development (1995), *Revenue Statistics 1995*, Paris: OECD

Rogoff, K. (1996), 'The purchasing power parity puzzle', *Journal of Economic Literature*, vol. 34 (2), pp. 647–668

Rose, A. (1994), 'Are exchange rates macroeconomic phenomena?', *Federal Reserve Bank of San Francisco Review*, vol. 1, pp. 19–30

Shiller, R.J. (1981), 'Do stock prices move too much to be justified by subsequent changes in dividends?', *American Economic Review*, vol. 71, pp. 421–435

Shiller, R.J. (1984), 'Stock prices and social dynamics', *Brookings Papers on Economic Activity*, no. 2, pp. 457–498

Shiller, R.J. (1989), *Market Volatility*, Cambridge, Mass.: MIT Press

Shiller, R.J. (1990), 'Speculative prices and popular models', *Journal of Economic Perspectives*, vol. 4, no. 2, pp. 55–66

Shleifer, A. and Summers, L. (1990), 'The noise trader approach to finance', *Journal of Economic Perspectives*, vol. 4, no. 2, pp. 19–33

Spahn, P.B. (1995), *International Financial Flows and Transactions Taxes: Surveys and Options*, Washington, DC: International Monetary Fund

Stiglitz, J. (1989), 'Using tax policy to curb speculative short-term trading', *Journal of Financial Services Research*, vol. 3, pp. 101–115

Stiglitz, J. (1990), 'Symposium on bubbles', *Journal of Economic Perspectives*, vol. 4, no. 2, spring, pp. 13–17

Stiglitz, J. and Weiss, A. (1981), 'Credit rationing in markets with imperfect information', *American Economic Review*, vol. 71, June, pp. 393–410

Summers, L. and Summers, V.P. (1989), 'When financial markets work too well: a cautious case for a securities transactions tax', *Journal of Financial Services Research*, vol. 3, pp. 163–188

Tobin, J. (1966), 'Adjustment responsibilities of surplus and deficit countries', in W. Fellner, F. Machlup and R. Triffin (eds) *Maintaining and Restoring Balance in International Payments*, Princeton: Princeton University Press

Tobin, J. (1974), 'The new economics one decade older', *The Eliot Janeway Lectures on Historical Economics in Honour of Joseph Schumpeter, 1972*, Princeton: Princeton University Press

Tobin, J. (1978), 'A proposal for international monetary reform', *Eastern Economic Journal*, vol. 4, nos 3–4, pp. 153–159 (reprinted in J. Tobin, *Essays in Economics: Theory and Policy*, Cambridge, Mass.: MIT Press)

Tobin, J. (1996), 'Prologue' in Haq *et al.* (1996)

United Nations Conference on Trade and Development (UNCTAD) (1995), *Trade and Development Report, 1995*, New York and Geneva: United Nations

United Nations Development Programme (1994), *Human Development Report 1994*, New York and Oxford: Oxford University Press

Part III

A new structure for international payments

8 Transnational rules for transnational corporations

What next?

Paz Estrella Tolentino

Introduction

The Bretton Woods system did not provide institutions to deal with international capital movements, transnational corporations (TNCs), nor the internationalization of production.[1] And yet, the importance of foreign direct investment (FDI) has grown dramatically since World War II, and much of it has been stimulated by the liberalization of trade and financial flows promoted by the Bretton Woods system and technological innovations. The worldwide foreign capital stock – an estimate of the total value of real assets attributable to foreign ownership or TNCs – has increased from $67 billion in 1960 to $2.7 trillion in 1995.[2] The average annual growth of global FDI flows during the second half of the 1980s was almost three times faster than world economic output and twice that of international trade.[3] Even with the FDI recession that prevailed in 1991 and 1992, global FDI flows from 1991 to 1994 grew at a rate three times faster than both international trade and world economic output. Global sales generated by foreign affiliates of TNCs – the closest measure of the value of the international production of TNCs – amounted to $6.0 trillion in 1993, exceeding worldwide exports of goods and non-factor services of $4.7 trillion (UNCTAD, 1996). The increasing significance of TNCs consisting of some 40,000 parent firms and some 250,000 foreign affiliates and the totality of their cross-border transactions in the world economy has made TNCs the new instrument of international economic integration.[4]

The increased significance of TNC activities in general and FDI in particular has led most national governments to adopt legislation to deal with the control, treatment and protection of TNCs within their jurisdiction. But national laws are inadequate for the effective control of TNCs that transcend traditional legal and territorial borders, particularly where national bargaining powers are weak. The transnational structure and scope of firms therefore demand a transnational regime to supplement national regimes (Asante, 1989). Indeed, adverse economic factors or adverse changes in regulations have led TNCs to shift activities and resources from one location to another to take advantage of differences in investment standards among countries by engaging in a practice of 'shopping' for the most favourable policies, particularly prevalent in the provision of investment incentives thus placing governments and host countries eager to attract foreign investment projects in competition with one another in incentive bidding wars (Graham, 1994). The current trend towards liberalization of FDI policies at the national level has necessitated more than ever before a transnational legislative response that embodies internationally agreed principles and standards on the regulation and treatment of foreign investors. This would ensure an investment climate of stability, predictability and transparency within which TNCs and countries can benefit (Sauvant and Aranda, 1994; Graham, 1994).

Unlike with international trade and international monetary issues where the Bretton Woods system established both a set of rules and dedicated international institutional structures in the form of GATT and the IMF/IBRD, there are no dedicated international institutional structures to deal with TNCs and a truly comprehensive set of rules at the global level has yet to emerge despite a long process of international rule building since 1948. The plethora of international frameworks dealing with TNCs differ considerably from one another in terms of the particular issues they address, the forums in which they were negotiated, the level of their country coverage (multilateral or regional), legal form (voluntary or binding), regulatory approach (control or protection/facilitation) and status (adopted, not adopted, impasse in negotiations, under negotiation or pending). They nevertheless coexist and interact significantly with one another. The next section deals with the development of the main international instruments dealing with TNCs over the past fifty years, and draws possible routes that may lead to the emergence of a comprehensive set of rules at the global level and an international institutional structure to implement those rules. It argues that the development of international rules and an institutional structure in the area of TNCs and FDI have evolved in a radically different way from that in the area of international trade or international finance. The design of international instruments has been by inter-governmental organizations and non-governmental organizations that were either limited in focus in terms of issues or that addressed the needs of countries of a region (e.g. Andean Pact) or a particular group of countries (e.g. OECD, APEC). Previous attempts to negotiate a comprehensive set of rules at the global level through the United Nations led to deadlock because far from having a political determination to bring the negotiations to a fruitful conclusion bearing in mind mutuality of interests, the issue drove a wedge between developed and developing countries and sometimes between developed and socialist countries thus carving North–South and East–West divisions.[5]

The evolution of an international legal framework dealing with TNCs: the post-World War II period to 1998

The emergence of international rules dealing with TNCs has proceeded through the elaboration of instruments at the multilateral and regional levels (see Table 8.1). In the main, the regulatory approach of the international instruments that have been adopted or negotiated have aimed to either *control* the behaviour of TNCs in the interest of host countries or *protect* TNCs or international investment by assuring a facilitating investment environment (Sauvant and Aranda, 1994; Salacuse, 1987).[6] Sauvant and Aranda (1994) identify three phases in the evolutionary pattern of international instruments: the era of competition between control, protection and facilitation in the period from the mid-1940s to the 1960s, the era of control of TNC conduct in the 1970s, and the era of promotion and protection in the 1980s and 1990s.

From the mid-1940s to the 1960s: the era of competing regulatory approaches – control, protection and promotion

The post-World War II period saw the emergence and growth of two major actors in the world economy that were not considered in the organization of the postwar international economic order fashioned at Bretton Woods. These actors are the 'new' countries (Japan, oil-producing countries and the newly independent countries from the Third World) and TNCs (Bergsten, Keohane and Nye, 1975). Indeed, initial attempts at establishing international rules on foreign investment arose from a consideration of the needs and interests of the newly independent countries from the Third World to increase their bargaining power *vis-à-vis* TNCs.

The draft Havana Charter in 1948 represented the first major effort to establish an international framework governing foreign investment in the post-World War II period. Apart from proposing the establishment of an International Trade Organization to handle a comprehensive range of issues concerning world trade, the charter contained provisions that aimed to balance 'investor protection' against 'decent conduct', but to some quarters the provisions on the protection of investments was rendered too weak owing to the greater emphasis placed on the rights of capital-importing developing countries. This controversial feature of the FDI provisions of the charter explains its ultimate non-ratification by the United States and other signatory states.

The Havana Charter heralded the dawn of adversarial North–South relations. The attainment of newly independent status by former colonial territories in Africa, Asia and, to a lesser extent, Latin America associated with the decolonization process and the realization that political and legal sovereignty is separate from economic sovereignty and economic development (Dell, 1990) led to several initiatives by the new nations to develop international frameworks that addressed their aspirations to establish a new and more equitable world economic order.[7] In particular, many of the newly independent countries sought to elaborate new customary rules given that the traditional legal doctrine of state responsibility for injuries to aliens and their property – regarded as the international minimum standard by Western governments and jurists – had been developed without their participation and had led to the use of force based on the principle of diplomatic protection by home countries of foreign persons.[8] This led to the elaboration of the modern international law doctrine – the Calvo Doctrine and the Calvo Clause – which formed the basis of the treatment of foreign investors in many Latin American countries (Bunge, 1987).[9] In their quest for economic independence as political and legal sovereign states, the newly independent countries

Table 8.1 Main international intergovernmental instruments concerning transnational corporations, 1948–1998

Year	Title	Setting	Level	Form	Approach	Status
1948	Draft Havana Charter	International conference	M	B	Facilitation	Not adopted
1952	General Assembly resolution 626 (VII)	United Nations (UN)	M	V	Control	Adopted
1961	Code of Liberalization of Capital Movements	Organization for Economic Cooperation and Development (OECD)	M	B	Facilitation	Adopted
1961	Code of Liberalization of Invisible Operations	OECD	M	B	Facilitation	Adopted
1962	General Assembly resolution 1803 (XVII)	UN	M	V	Control	Adopted
1965	International Convention for Settlement of Investment Disputes	World Bank	M	B	Facilitation	Adopted
1966	Draft Convention on Protection of Foreign Property	OECD	M	B	Protection	Not adopted
1970	Decision 24	Andean Pact	R	V	Control	Adopted
1974	General Assembly resolution 3201 (S-VI)	UN	M	V	Control	Adopted
1975	Draft Statute for the Treatment of Foreign Investment, Transnational Corporations and the Transfer of Technology	Non-aligned countries	R	V	Control	Adopted
1975	Guidelines of Behaviour that could be Observed by Transnational Enterprises	Organization of American States	R	V	Control	Not adopted
1976	Declaration on Multinational Enterprises	OECD	M	B/V	Control/ facilitation	Adopted
1976	Draft Code on Transfer of Technology	United Nations Conference on Trade and Development (UNCTAD)	M	V	Control	Impasse in the negotiations
1977	Tripartite Declaration	International Labour Organization	M	V	Control	Adopted
1979	Draft Agreement on Illicit Practices	UN	M	B	Control	Pending
1990	Draft Code on Transnational Corporations	UN	M	V	Control/ facilitation	Impasse in the negotiations
1980	International Set of Rules on Restrictive Business Practices	UNCTAD	M	V	Control	Adopted
1981	International Code of Marketing of Breast-milk Substitutes	World Health Organization (WHO)	M	V	Control	Adopted

Table 8.1 cont.

Year	Title	Setting	Level	Form	Approach	Status
1981	Action Programme on Essential Drugs and Vaccines	WHO	M	V	Control	Adopted
1984	Third ACP–EEC Convention	European Community (EC)/African, Caribbean and Pacific (ACP) States	M	B	Facilitation	Adopted
1984	Euro-Arab Convention	EC/Arab League	M	B	Facilitation	Pending
1984	Right of Establishment	OECD	M	B	Facilitation	Adopted
1985	Guidelines for Consumer Protection	UN	M	V	Control	Adopted
1985	International Code on Distribution of Pesticides	UN	M	V	Control	Adopted
1985	Convention Establishing the Multilateral Investment Guarantee Agency	World Bank	M	B	Facilitation	Adopted
1987	Decision 220	Andean Pact	R	V	Facilitation	Adopted
1990	Decision 291	Andean Pact	R	V	Facilitation	Adopted
1990	Fourth ACP–EC Convention	EC/ACP	M	B	Facilitation	Adopted
1990	Criteria for Sustainable Development	UN	M	V	Control	Adopted
1994	Agreement on Trade-Related Investment Measures	Uruguay Round of GATT	M	B	Facilitation	Adopted
1994	General Agreement on Trade in Services	Uruguay Round of GATT	M	B	Facilitation	Adopted
1994	Asia-Pacific Investment Code	Asia–Pacific Economic Cooperation	M	V	Facilitation	Adopted
1994	North America Free Trade Agreement	North America Free Trade Area (Canada, Mexico and United States)	R	B	Facilitation	Adopted
1994	Energy Charter Treaty	Central and Eastern Europe	R	B	Facilitation	Adopted
1998	Multilateral Agreement on Investment	OECD	M	B	Facilitation	Under negotiation

Source: Sauvant and Aranda (1994) supplemented by Hamilton (1984), Graham (1994), Witherell (1995), Brewer and Young (1996), and other sources.

Notes: M: multilateral; R: regional; V: voluntary; B: binding.

found in the United Nations a forum to pursue the principle of 'respect for the principle of equal rights and self-determination of peoples' set out in the first article of the UN Charter. Their priorities lay in control over their own resources in the face of the dominant role of TNCs and the developed countries in their economies and in such strategic areas as technology, investments and trade. The control of TNCs was therefore regarded as key to regaining control over their resources, to reassert their national sovereignty and to ensure their full and equal participation in the world economy.

It was against this background that two General Assembly resolutions were adopted to reaffirm the permanent sovereignty of a state over its natural resources. Resolution 626 (VII), adopted in 1952, proclaimed *inter alia* the principle of state sovereignty, i.e. the right of states to exercise sovereignty and enact and implement laws affecting persons, goods and economic activity within its territory. Perhaps of most concern to TNCs was the proclamation in this resolution as inherent in sovereignty the right of peoples to use and exploit freely their natural resources. This principle was strengthened by Resolution 1803 (XVII) adopted by consensus in 1962 which proclaimed the right of peoples and nations to permanent sovereignty over their wealth, natural resources and economic activities, and which established on grounds of public utility the legitimacy of nationalization with appropriate compensation. These two UN General Assembly resolutions although of voluntary form had an important impact on relations between TNCs and resource-rich developing countries. These principles were reaffirmed or restated in the norms of the UN Draft Code of Conduct on TNCs.

In response, the priorities of the capital-exporting countries was to protect foreign property, particularly from nationalization by the host country. Attempts at the multilateral level to elaborate international standards through the adoption of the Draft Convention on Protection of Foreign Property of the OECD in the mid-1960s failed.[10] So did attempts to establish multilateral insurance schemes against political risks in foreign investment by the World Bank, the Council of Europe, the OECD, the Inter-American Development Bank and the European Community (Sauvant and Aranda, 1994).[11] What proved rather more successful owing to its efforts to address the concerns of developing and developed countries as well as TNCs was the World Bank-sponsored International Convention on the Settlement of Investment Disputes (ICSID) adopted in 1965. This Convention established a multilateral forum for the conciliation, binding arbitration and resolution of disputes between foreign investors and their host countries. At the time of its adoption, most major capital-importing countries including some developed countries that preferred to retain sole domestic jurisdiction over investment activities within its borders did not sign the Convention. This included Latin American countries, socialist states (with the exception of Yugoslavia), Australia, Canada, India, Iran and Saudi Arabia (Keohane and Ooms, 1975).[12]

The difficulty in obtaining multilateral agreement on international standards and insurance schemes against expropriation and other non-commercial risks and the need to overcome the limitations of national laws or contractual agreements with private investors led to the use of binding inter-governmental agreements particularly between home and host developing countries in the form of bilateral investment treaties for the promotion and protection of foreign direct investment. These treaties first emerged around the late 1950s and grew rapidly in importance (UNCTC and ICC, 1992; Salacuse, 1987).[13] They were initiated by the Federal Republic of Germany and other major Western European capital-exporting countries mainly with developing countries that saw in these treaties an important instrument to attract FDI.[14] Apart from being subject to international law, the bilateral investment treaties had the advantage of providing a stable basis for investment relations between countries as they could not be modified or repudiated unilaterally. These treaties which numbered more than 80 in the 1960s prescribe on a reciprocal basis general standards of treatment (i.e., fair and equitable treatment, non-discrimination, national treatment and most-favoured-nation treatment) as well as specific standards on such key issues as expropriation, compensation for losses due to armed conflict or internal disorder, transfer of payments and settlement of disputes – important elements of concern to capital-exporting countries to ensure the protection of investments.

An important limitation of bilateral and multilateral treaties during this period was the exclusion of rules governing entry and establishment for investors. These remained essentially in the domain of national laws. However, these issues started to emerge as a multilateral concern in the Organization for Economic Co-operation and Development (OECD) in its efforts to progressively liberalize capital movements.[15] Towards this end, the OECD adopted in 1961 two significant instruments of a binding nature – the Code of Liberalization of Capital Movements and the Code of Liberalization of Current Invisible Operations – to facilitate FDI and other types of transnational economic activities.

In sum, during the period from the 1940s to the 1960s the elaboration of international frameworks governing TNCs took varying regulatory approaches. In the control of TNCs there was the elaboration of new principles of international law to address the aspirations of newly independent countries. These new principles embodied the right of peoples and nations to permanent sovereignty over their wealth, natural resources and economic activities, and established on grounds of public utility the legitimacy of nationalization with appropriate compensation. The elaboration of these principles precipitated attempts by capital-exporting countries to elaborate international standards to protect foreign investment against the risks of nationalization.

The 1970s: the era of control of TNC conduct

In the 1970s, concern grew over the growing economic power and influence of TNCs, particularly in developing countries. This led to efforts to advance international standards at various forums at the multilateral level (ILO, UN, UNCTAD) and in non-governmental organizations. A plethora of standards was elaborated to define the responsibilities of TNCs to host countries regarding employment and industrial relations, restrictive business practices, illicit payments and transfer of technology. The control of the conduct of TNCs was the objective for the 1970s (Sauvant and Aranda, 1994). Given the pioneering role of Andean Pact countries in elaborating international codes for TNC conduct in 1970, the analysis of the evolving international norms during this decade begins with those advanced by developing countries, followed by those of developed countries, the multilateral forums and, finally, those of the non-governmental organizations.

International standards advanced by developing countries

The dependence of many developing countries on foreign capital and technology and their concern over notorious instances of TNCs' intervention in their internal political affairs led to further attempts by these countries to deal with foreign investors effectively.[16] This provided popular support for Marxist and radical views, that large TNCs dominate society and the state, leading to dependent development, exploitation of labour and imperialism. It also fuelled the trend towards nationalization of foreign property starting from the 1960s which reached a peak in the mid-1970s (UNCTC, 1988) and the demands of developing countries for international regulation of TNCs. With increased awareness of their strengths and needs, including their possession of many key primary products, the commodity price boom and the increased clout of oil-rich developing countries through OPEC, developing countries had gained international bargaining power (Sauvant, 1981).

The Latin American countries played a key role in elaborating international codes for TNC conduct (Sauvant and Aranda, 1994). The first successful intergovernmental attempt to control TNCs was in the context of a sub-regional integration agreement between five Latin American countries (Bolivia, Chile, Colombia, Ecuador and Peru) codified in the Cartagena Agreement or the Andean Pact of 1969.[17] In 1970 the Andean member states adopted Decision 24 – the most comprehensive and rigorous attempt to control TNC conduct, to render them consistent with the development needs and objectives of host countries (Black, Blank and Hanson, 1978). It was a framework that governed for the Andean Pact area industrial development, foreign exchange management, technology transfer and, in the case of FDI, the screening and selective entry as well as eventual liquidation of investments by TNCs to reduce foreign control over a period of 15–20 years.[18]

International standards advanced by developed countries

The elaboration of standards for TNCs by the OECD sought to fulfil two major objectives. The first was to establish a framework for the rights and duties of TNCs and governments that addresses concerns about low levels of investment, weak economic growth, persistent excess capacity in many industries and growing unemployment on the one hand and the need to regulate some of the negative impacts of TNCs on the other. The second objective was to strengthen the OECD's negotiating position and thereby influence significantly other international standards on TNCs, and in particular the United Nations Code of

Conduct on TNCs (Lévy, 1984; Sauvant and Aranda, 1994).[19] The OECD Declaration on International Investment and Multinational Enterprises was adopted in 1976. The concerns of countries such as Canada, Holland and the Scandinavian states, to regulate to the largest extent possible the activities of TNCs, had to be reconciled with that of the United States and West Germany to advance the liberalization and protection of FDI. The inclusion of the principles governing national treatment and international incentives and disincentives in the section dealing with the treatment of TNCs by governments was clearly the *sine qua non* for the United States government to agree to the whole instrument (Hamilton, 1984).

The first element of the Declaration – the Guidelines for Multinational Enterprises – represents the second attempt after the Andean Pact Investment Code to elaborate general standards of TNC conduct, but the first attempt by a group of major countries. The Guidelines were not legally enforceable but embodied in a joint recommendation of OECD member states to TNCs operating in their territories (Lévy, 1984). Its aim 'is to encourage the positive contribution which TNCs can make to economic and social progress and to minimize and resolve the difficulties to which their various operations may give rise' (OECD, 1976). Global political shifts led to greater emphasis on the protection and liberalization aspects of the Declaration since the early 1980s.

International standards advanced at multilateral forums

During the 1970s, developing countries persisted in their endeavours at the United Nations. There were the efforts of the Andean Pact countries, Brazil and Mexico to internationalize the Andean Pact investment code. And building on the permanent sovereignty principle, the Declaration and the Programme of Action on the Establishment of a New International Economic Order was enshrined in the United Nations General Assembly Resolution 3201 (S-VI) adopted in 1974. With a similar nationalist rhetoric to the Andean Pact Code, Section V of the resolution called for the regulation and control of the activities of TNCs in the interest of the national economies where such TNCs operate, and to formulate, adopt and implement an international code of conduct for TNCs.

There were parallel efforts around the mid-1970s to conclude international standards at the multilateral level to address specific aspects of TNC activities that were at that time of pressing concern to both developing and developed countries. These were employment and labour relations, restrictive business practices, illicit payments and transfer of technology. The elaboration of international standards in each of these areas were pioneering attempts to formulate multilaterally agreed rules to encourage the positive contribution which TNCs can make and to minimize and resolve the difficulties to which their various operations may give rise – an objective shared by the OECD Guidelines on Multinational Enterprises being discussed around the same time. The negotiations on international standards on employment and labour relations and restrictive business practices were concluded successfully while those on illicit payments and transfer of technology were not.

Concern over the ability of TNCs to shift production across national boundaries causing loss of jobs and trade union bargaining power, and the need to advance standards on labour relations in host countries led to the 1977 adoption of the Tripartite Declaration of Principles Concerning Multinational Enterprises and Social Policy (the Tripartite Declaration) by the Governing Body of the ILO. The Tripartite Declaration, concluded on the basis of negotiations between representatives of governments, employers and workers, contained recommended principles of a non-mandatory nature to TNCs, governments and organizations of employers and workers on employment, training, conditions of work and life and industrial relations.[20] The Tripartite Multinational Committee was established in 1980 consisting of 16 members from each of the three ILO constituent groups to organize government reporting, to promote the Declaration at the national level and to establish a procedure for raising disputes in individual cases. The procedures, which only allowed cases to be raised that were not covered by prevailing national law and practice nor by ILO convention or procedures, were regarded to be too restrictive and prevented the effective implementation of the Tripartite Declaration (Hamilton, 1984).

The advancement of international rules to control 'restrictive business practices' arose partly from the need to harmonize national antitrust regimes where these existed among developed countries and to assist in the formulation of competition laws in developing countries where these did not exist or were unsophisticated; and partly from the objectives of developed countries to secure a more liberal world order.[21] Towards this end, the Set of Multilaterally Agreed Equitable Rules and Principles for the Control of Restrictive Business Practices (the 'Set') was adopted by consensus in 1980 by the UN General Assembly after ten years of negotiations in the UNCTAD forum.

Apart from efforts to conclude international standards at the multilateral level to address other specific issues of concern to TNCs such as bribery and extortion and transfer of technology, there were also efforts to formulate a more general Code of Conduct for TNCs in the United Nations that would be both comprehensive in scope (unlike the issue-specific codes that have been or are being elaborated) and universal in its geographical application. This would share a common goal with the OECD Declaration, the Tripartite Declaration of the ILO, and other issue-specific codes to enhance the positive contributions that TNCs can make while minimizing the difficulties to which their various operations may give rise. By tacit consensus the draft Code when adopted will take the form of a UN Resolution or other international declaration establishing broad fair and equitable guidelines and norms of a voluntary nature, with the exception of those norms that reaffirm or restate well-established principles of international law (Asante, 1989; Baade, 1980).

In common with the OECD Declaration, the original intention of the UN Code of Conduct of TNCs was to elaborate standards for the regulation of TNCs conduct in host countries and not to establish rules on their treatment. The Intergovernmental Working Group created by the UN Commission on TNCs in 1976 thus began work on January 1977 on the formulation of a regulatory code and by 1981 most of the provisions particularly on the legal, economic, political and social aspects of TNC conduct had been drafted. It had always been an objective of the developed countries to expand the draft Code of Conduct to include *quid pro quo* complementary provisions to provide basic guarantees to protect foreign investment particularly against nationalization and to provide fair and equitable treatment for TNCs.

The Code suffered the same fate as the negotiations on the UN Draft Code of Transfer of Technology where the wide divergence of interests along the North–South divide and in some instances along the East–West divide meant that no consensus could be reached on the adoption of a final text. The lesson that can be drawn is that codes do not lead to the reconciliation of deep and important differences, particularly where these reflect conflicts in the interests between states (Keohane and Ooms, 1975).

International standards advanced by non-governmental organizations

The need to regulate TNCs in the 1970s was also manifested in the initiatives of non-governmental organizations and in particular the International Chamber of Commerce (ICC) and the International Confederation of Free Trade Unions (ICFTU). Their efforts to formulate their own codes derived partly from their dissatisfaction with the codes produced elsewhere and partly from their need to influence the negotiation of certain codes particularly the OECD Declaration of 1976 and the UN Code of Conduct on TNCs.

The International Chamber of Commerce adopted the Guidelines on International Investment in 1972 and the Code on Illicit Payments in 1977. These complemented the many corporate codes of conduct adopted by individual firms, particularly those of the United States. The most well known of these corporate codes are those of Caterpillar and Coca-Cola (Hamilton, 1984). While limited in scope and objectives (usually dealing with accounting standards, antitrust, employment and conflicts of interest), the corporate codes reflected an attempt at self-regulation in an era of adverse reaction against TNCs with the business community wanting to be regarded as responsible corporate citizens (Kline, 1985).

The ability of TNCs to relocate production to lower-cost developing countries causing production and job displacement in the home countries precipitated efforts by the ICFTU to curb the power of TNCs. These fell short of the formation of an international industrial organization of workers to which TNCs would be accountable, but did lead to the creation of an international code to provide a political countervailing force to TNCs. Towards this end, the Charter of Trade Union Demands for the Legislative Control of Multinational Enterprises otherwise known as the Multinational Charter was adopted by the IX Congress of the ICFTU in 1975. The charter describes the public accountability and social obligations of TNCs and called for international conventions on the control of FDI. It proposed a general multinational treaty for the control of TNCs in the UN forum, with a UN agency that has direct trade union participation to be responsible for implementation (ICFTU, 1975).

These non-governmental actors have access to intergovernmental forums through advisory committees (OECD), and observer status and representation (UN), and consequently have been able to exert considerable influence in the elaboration of international standards on FDI and in the case of the OECD Declaration also in implementation.

The 1980s and 1990s: the era of promotion and protection

With the international frameworks to regulate TNCs set in place in the 1970s, the dominant agenda in the 1980s was the pursuit of international norms to promote or facilitate FDI expansion, complemented by continuing efforts to formulate rules to address the pressing issues of the time that have a bearing on TNC conduct: the marketing of infant formula, pharmaceutical products and pesticides; consumer protection; and the environment. Unlike in the previous decades where of the non-governmental organizations the international trade union movement, corporate groups and individual firms constituted the active force behind the adoption of issue-specific standards, in the 1980s the main force was the International Consumer Organization (ICO).[22] In 1981, the Governing Body of the World Health Organization (WHO) adopted the International Code of Marketing of Breast Milk Substitutes, recommending voluntary restrictions on the marketing of infant formula through advertising and promotion particularly where these discouraged the practice of breast feeding.[23] In the same year, the WHO adopted its Action Programme on Essential Drugs and Vaccines which aimed to ensure the availability of essential drugs that are safe, effective and of acceptable quality at the lowest possible cost.[24] This in turn encouraged the International Federation of Pharmaceutical Manufacturers Association's Code of Pharmaceutical Marketing Practices to be seen as good corporate citizens in their compliance with WHO guidelines, and to pre-empt the adoption of binding and more hostile instruments in other forums. Relating to pesticides, the International Code of Conduct on the Distribution and Use of Pesticides was adopted by the Food and Agriculture Organization (FAO) in 1985, while a more general framework for consumer protection was adopted in the same year by the United Nations General Assembly in its set of Guidelines for Consumer Protection. While these voluntary guidelines are not solely addressed to TNCs – but apply equally to domestic firms – it is assumed that TNCs are the dominant providers of products on sale in the world market.

Similar calls for voluntary guidelines to encourage TNCs to consider the environment have been embodied in the Criteria for Sustainable Development Management endorsed by the United Nations Economic and Social Council in 1990, and also in the 1991 review of the OECD Guidelines on Multinational Enterprises which had been expanded to include a chapter containing detailed provisions dealing with environmental protection (Sauvant and Aranda, 1994).

Despite the adoption of these voluntary guidelines to influence TNC behaviour, the dominant approach regarding international rules relating to TNCs over the past two decades has been the promotion or facilitation of FDI expansion by defining the responsibilities of countries towards foreign investors.[25] The shift was manifested in a marked tendency towards liberalization at the national level of host government policies towards TNCs since the early 1980s.[26]

This emphasis on facilitating foreign investment flows was reflected at the regional, multilateral and global levels. The liberalization of regional frameworks was evident in the new investment codes of the Andean Pact and the establishment of new regional cooperative and integration schemes that facilitated international trade and production activities within the cooperating area through informal cooperation, complemention agreements, the removal of tariff barriers and, in some cases, also non-tariff barriers. Some of these schemes and the year of their establishment are the Australia–New Zealand Closer Economic Relations Trade Agreement (1983), Latin American Integration Association (previously LAFTA) (1980), MERCOSUR (1992), Southern and East African Preferential Trade Area (1982) and the Union de Maghreb Arabe (1989). There was also the adoption in 1994 by the economies of Central and Eastern Europe of the Energy Charter Treaty – a regionally oriented and sector-specific agreement to liberalize energy trade and investment. But the most far-reaching changes in intra-regional economic relations are seen in the free trade areas established in the context of the Canada–US Free Trade Agreement (1989) and its extension to the North America Free Trade Agreement (1994).

At the multilateral level there has been the facilitation of closer trade and international links between developed and developing countries in the context of the EC–ACP Lomé Convention, the Asia–Pacific Investment Code and the Free Trade Area for the Americas initiative in which cooperation in the area of investment policy is under study. There was also the further elaboration of rules on the rights of establishment in the OECD in 1984, and negotiations aimed at reaching a Multilateral Agreement on Investment have been ongoing since 1995.

At the global level there was the adoption of the convention establishing the Multilateral Investment Guarantee Agency but the most notable of all was the successful conclusion in 1994 of the Agreements on Trade in Services and the Trade-Related Investment Measures within the Uruguay Round of GATT. The latter set the stage for more ambitious initiatives envisaged for the future with the WTO.

Developments at the regional level

Among the most remarkable turnarounds in policy stance was the case of the Andean Pact countries. Individual member countries gradually began to detach themselves from the restrictive foreign investment regime embodied in Decision 24 in their quest to attract increasing amounts of FDI. As a result, Decision 220 and Decision 291 adopted in 1987 and 1990 respectively superseded Decision 24 and abolished most of the principal restrictions on foreign investment, and allowed individual member states to deal with FDI on their own terms (Sauvant and Aranda, 1994).

The trend towards liberalization was most significant in the case of the North

America Free Trade Agreement (1994) which had important repercussions on trade and production between the United States, Canada and Mexico. Mexico had to depart from its previously restrictive stance towards foreign investment and to adopt some of the most liberalized policies yet announced, including the *de facto* abandonment of the Calvo Doctrine (Hufbauer and Schott, 1993).[27] The regional trade and investment agreement contains liberal provisions on FDI not quite seen in other agreements before (Graham, 1994; Graham and Wilkie, 1994). Key aspects of the investment regime include a considerable broadening of the definition of investment; the right of establishment and commercial presence on a non-discriminatory basis and of temporary entry for executive staff; national treatment and most-favoured nation principles for TNC operations; the abolition of main performance requirements on TNCs as well as nationality restrictions of the senior management of NAFTA investments; the freedom to make all transfers of payments without delay; guarantees for the protection of FDI against non-commercial risks (notably expropriation and state contracts); and the elaboration of a fair dispute settlement mechanism between TNCs and NAFTA member countries (UNCTAD, 1993).[28] Some of its most important effects on FDI include substantial restructuring and reorganization of TNC activity both within the region and between the region and other countries and increased opportunities for firms from the rest of the world to expand their FDI in the North American free trade area (Dunning, 1992).

Developments at the multilateral level

The promotion of trade and FDI in developing countries was also evident in the Third and Fourth EC–ACP Lomé Conventions adopted in 1984 and 1990 between the European Community (EC) and a group of Asian, Caribbean and Pacific (ACP) states. The Conventions sought to continue the preferential treatment accorded the ACP states in their trade with the EC, including measures for the protection and promotion of investments. The legally binding Conventions contain provisions for the accordance of fair and equitable treatment to foreign investors and the maintenance of a secure and predictable investment climate. Similar arrangements on reciprocal protection and promotion of investments have been envisaged in the Euro-Arab Convention between the EC and the Arab League, currently still at a pending stage.

Another multilateral instrument for the promotion and protection of investment between developed and developing countries is the Asia–Pacific Investment Code endorsed in 1994 by ministers of the Asia–Pacific Economic Cooperation (APEC) organization created in 1989 as a forum for regular discussions on regional trade issues and economic cooperation between 17 member states.[29] The code is a set of non-binding principles whose goal is to facilitate FDI within the APEC member states through a series of commitments to create and maintain a favourable investment climate. A similar voluntary code applies to the member states of the Pacific Economic Cooperation Conference (PECC) (Graham, 1994).[30]

In the OECD, FDI frameworks were further liberalized in the 1980s. A binding agreement on The Right of Establishment was adopted in 1984 strengthening the two OECD Codes of Liberalization to cover most aspects of the right of establishment on inward capital movements.

Taken together with other OECD investment instruments – the Codes of Liberalization of Capital Movements and Invisible Transactions, and the Declaration on Multinational Enterprises – the Right of Establishment provides for multilateral investment rules covering national treatment both pre- and post-establishment; repatriation of profits, dividends, rents and the proceeds of liquidated investments; transparency of regulations; a dispute-settlement mechanism and a peer review to promote rollback of remaining restrictions. But these instruments do not constitute a comprehensive and fully binding multilateral agreement on investment as foreign investors continue to encounter investment barriers, discriminatory treatment and legal and regulatory uncertainties that act as barriers to market access. With the GATT Agreements on TRIMs, TRIPs and GATS (see below) addressing only FDI in services, the absence of multilateral disciplines has resulted in a plethora of bilateral, regional and sectoral agreements that lack an overall cohesive structure, have conflicting rules and lay open the danger of spreading individualistic solutions by countries and regions (Witherell, 1995). It is against this background that a broader and more comprehensive multilateral framework for foreign direct investment in the form of a Multilateral Agreement on Investment (MAI) has been under negotiation since 1995, aiming at binding investment rules for the treatment of FDI across all sectors, reinforced with effective dispute-settlement procedures. It seeks to widen the scope of existing liberalization, covering both the establishment and post-establishment phase as well as improving market access. These liberalization obligations would be complemented by similar obligations for legal security for international investors. Although negotiated in the OECD forum, the MAI is to be understood as a free-standing international treaty open for adoption by all OECD member states and the European Union, and to accession by non-OECD member states which are being consulted as negotiations progress (OECD, 1995).

Developments at the global level

The shifting regulatory approach towards protection and promotion was also evident at the global level in the World Bank and GATT.

After unsuccessful attempts by the World Bank to establish a multilateral insurance scheme in previous decades, a Convention establishing the Multilateral Investment Guarantee Agency (MIGA) was adopted in 1985. Over 120 countries have signed the MIGA Convention, many of which are developing countries; and a substantial number have ratified the Convention. MIGA is an international insurance mechanism which supplements the insurance mechanisms established in most of the major capital-exporting countries. As with the national insurance mechanisms, MIGA is intended to promote investment flows among its member countries and in particular flows from developed countries to developing countries as well as among developing countries by issuing investment guarantees against four broad areas of non-commercial risks: transfer risk resulting from host government restrictions on currency conversion and transfer; risks of loss resulting from legislative or administrative actions and omissions of the host government which deprive the foreign investor of ownership or control of, or a substantial benefit from, investment; repudiation of government contracts in cases where the investor has no access to a competent forum, faces unreasonable delays or is unable to enforce a final judicial or arbitral decision; and armed conflict and civil unrest risk (Shihata, 1994).

The most significant step towards a global framework for FDI was initiated in the Uruguay Round of Multilateral Trade Negotiations launched in 1986 by GATT. As with the previous rounds, the goal of the Uruguay Round was to expand and strengthen the open international trading system with the adoption of instruments on trade liberalization that would be legally binding upon states. The negotiations reached a successful conclusion in 1993, with all the instruments contained in the Final Act of the Uruguay Round of Multilateral Trade Negotiations adopted formally in 1994 and being implemented by the World Trade Organization (WTO).[31] Although FDI was not part of the explicit negotiations in the Uruguay Round, a number of the Agreements covered by the Final Act are directly relevant to FDI and TNCs, namely the General Agreement on Trade in Services (GATS), the Agreement on Trade-Related Investment Measures (TRIMs) and the Agreement on Trade-Related Aspects of Intellectual Property Rights, including Trade in Counterfeit Goods (TRIPs). These Agreements have the objective of binding GATT member states to facilitate the growth of trade and FDI (the latter confined to services) by specifying the responsibilities of countries towards foreign investors.

In the GATS, FDI constitutes one of four modes of delivery of services to foreign markets, with commercial presence being the mode most directly linked with FDI. The Agreement constitutes a global investment framework governing FDI in services which currently accounts for 50 per cent of the global FDI stock (UNCTAD, 1996).

The Agreement on TRIMs prohibits local content and trade-balancing requirements imposed by governments on TNCs. While considered useful instruments to promote development by countries that impose them, these requirements are regarded by the business community as obstacles to investment (UNCTC and UNCTAD, 1991; OECD, 1982). Other forms of TRIMs such as export-performance requirements were not covered in the Final Act as these would have been an addition to existing GATT rules, as would technology-transfer requirements, local equity requirements, remittance restrictions and investment incentives.

Although the TRIPs Agreement does not deal directly with investment issues, it influences the legal environment affecting FDI and TNCs in knowledge-intensive industries, namely the protection of intellectual property. The Agreement covers the main areas of intellectual property rights: copyright and related rights, trademarks, geographical indications, industrial designs, patents, lay-out designs of integrated circuits and undisclosed information or trade secrets. The Agreement contains two sets of substantive obligations: first, it lays down minimum standards of substantive protection of each category of rights that must be available in the national law of each country; and second, the Agreement for the first time in international law requires member countries to provide within their national law effective procedures and remedies for the enforcement of intellectual property rights.

Prospects for the further evolution of a global framework dealing with FDI and TNCs

The above discussion of the evolution of international legal frameworks concerning TNCs and FDI over the last fifty years indicates the slow rule-building in this area which has not yet resulted in a balanced and comprehensive universal instrument that could prove to be a durable framework that preserves the trend towards a more open economic system and at the same time fills the void in global investment standards to achieve balance and stability in the world economy (Kline, 1993). Clearly the process of legal and institutional change in this area remains in a state of flux and will remain so for the considerable future. The ongoing negotiations on the MAI at the OECD on what is essentially an instrument solely of investment promotion and protection provide evidence of the difficulties of moving forward to advance more comprehensive and binding multilateral rules even among countries that have long experience in the development of international investment rules, are broadly like-minded and have every interest in the conclusion of such an instrument, being the major home and host countries for FDI.

Although the seeds for a multilateral instrument have been planted in the 1990s with the GATT Agreements currently implemented by the WTO and the MAI still being negotiated at the OECD, the attainment of a global and truly comprehensive instrument requires a consideration of broader issues that deals with FDI in all sectors of economic activity and one that addresses policies on the protection of FDI as well as regulation of aspects of TNC conduct that have been and will continue to cause concern.[32] Any international agreement or treaty that fails to provide that balance could hardly be able to form the basis of a durable global instrument in the long term.[33] What is required is an acceptance by TNCs and capital-exporting countries of rules to protect capital-importing nations from the negative aspects of behaviour by TNCs. This final part of the chapter analyses the possible routes for developing such a global and comprehensive framework for investment and TNCs, including the institutional context and broad outlines of the substantial issues desirable in a meaningful framework.

The routes for the development of a global and comprehensive regime for FDI and TNCs

As pressures mount to conclude a universal and comprehensive agreement and significant progress beyond the existing fragmented international regime is envisaged, the path ahead can be described in three routes.[34] Routes 1 and 2 consider building on existing international institutional structures in the OECD and the WTO, while the third envisages the establishment of a new international institutional machinery dealing specifically with TNC and FDI issues.

The first two routes envisage a larger role for the GATT/WTO which differ in many respects from the OECD in terms of their relative inexperience with FDI issues and international rule building in this area; their formal approach to negotiation through many rounds compared with the more informal approach of analysis and discussion of issues in the OECD; and the larger size and universal nature of WTO membership compared to the smaller size and developed country membership of the latter (Brewer and Young, 1995). It is this third aspect of the differences between the WTO and OECD and the binding nature of its agreements that suggest that any truly universal instrument on investment and TNC issues must emerge from the WTO. But there are other fundamental reasons that favour the WTO as a forum for the elaboration of a global instrument. First, the fact that through GATS and the Agreement on TRIMs and TRIPs, GATT/WTO has embarked on the road of establishing at least partially a global investment framework governing FDI. Second, the close interlinkages between trade, FDI, international production and related issues require an integrated forum for the discussion of these issues, including in the elaboration of rules. Indeed, there are complex inter-relationships of FDI issues to trade policy and other policy areas (Brewer and Young, 1995; UNCTAD, 1996).[35] Third, the diplomatic feasibility of the WTO forum given that the United States has worked for FDI agreements in the GATT during the Uruguay Round, the European interest in making negotiations on FDI issues a central item on the WTO agenda to facilitate and protect its investments in developing countries, and the public endorsement of Japan, Australia and Sweden on further WTO action on FDI issues (Brewer and Young, 1995).

Route 1: successful conclusion of the MAI at the OECD and adoption at the WTO

This is the route envisaged when MAI negotiations were launched in 1995 as a treaty negotiated at the OECD forum with non-member countries involved in a consultative process but when concluded open for adoption also to non-member states. This route is beset with problems even for unilateral adoption by non-member countries. The MAI would be a *fait accompli* by the developed countries in which developing countries resent their non-participation in the consensus-forming process in an area that has important repercussions on their potential for growth and development. This problem of the absence of 'inclusiveness of the process' (Brewer and Young, 1995) which leaves a large scope for friction and discord cannot be overlooked given the historical resentments displayed by developing countries against acceptance of customary principles of international law that were formulated without their participation. This problem would need to be overcome if the MAI is to be adopted as a global instrument in a global forum such as the WTO. Besides, one has to bear in mind that even if MAI is adopted as a global instrument it would be an instrument of investment promotion and protection which leaves it wanting in the area of control of TNC conduct.

Route 2: the initiation of negotiations for an entirely new legal framework at the WTO regardless of the fate of the MAI at the OECD

This route is more diplomatically feasible and allows the possibility of a more global framework favoured by the inclusiveness of the process brought about by the large size and universal membership of the WTO and the opportunity to fashion a balanced and comprehensive instrument that takes into account the purposes of investment promotion and protection as well as the need for control of TNCs. It envisages the gradual buildup of experience of the WTO in FDI issues with its implementation of GATS and the Agreement on TRIMs and TRIPs combined with the augmentation of its expertise in this area.

Route 3: the initiation of negotiations for an entirely new legal framework at a new international institutional structure regardless of the fate of the MAI at the OECD

This new structure could be along the lines of a General Agreement on International Corporations envisaged some thirty years ago by Goldberg and Kindleberger (1970) or a General Agreement on International Investment (Salacuse, 1987) or an International Investment Organization (Wallace, 1976). In all cases, it was regarded that an international regulatory body drawing on the principle of international law or international social controls would assist in the resolution of some of the cross-border conflicts arising from TNC activity through the promulgation of rules and the establishment of institutions to implement those rules. Although on a different level and serving a different purpose, it has also been suggested that an inter-regional Third World Organization be established that is parallel to the OECD that would act for the collective interest of developing countries for effective regulatory control of TNCs (Acquaah, 1986). The problems with this route stem from the large costs and the difficulties associated with concluding a treaty establishing a new international institutional machinery, including the risks of the further politicization of FDI and TNC issues (Keohane and Ooms, 1975).

Given the pragmatism of using existing international institutional structures the route most likely to succeed is the second one in terms of inclusiveness of the process and multilateral forum for negotiations – two criteria considered important by Brewer and Young (1995) as elements of success. However, this route still begs the question of what this entirely new global and comprehensive legal framework might be if it were to be a meaningful one.

Desirable elements in a global framework for FDI and TNCs

In the development of a global and comprehensive framework for FDI and TNCs, lessons need to be drawn from existing bilateral, regional and multilateral investment agreements. This would require the identification and adoption of 'best practice' or 'state of the art' investment rules while minimizing their deficiencies. Existing regional and multilateral agreements vary both in terms of the width and the depth of coverage of investment rules and although the more specific agreements such as NAFTA and the European Energy Charter have tended to have a greater width and depth of coverage than others, their application to a broader forum may prove difficult (Brewer and Young, 1996).

The broad outline of substantive issues of a meaningful global and comprehensive framework dealing with TNCs is shown in Table 8.2. Many of the substantive issues listed are considered standard items in bilateral, regional and multilateral investment agreements. The list of issues should be understood as suggestive of the types of issues that are considered crucial; the possibility exists for other issues to be included, or some issues listed to be excluded.

One final note. The Asian financial crisis has once again highlighted the recurrent question of the regulation of short-term capital movements that are regarded to be sometimes associated with TNCs and in particular their potential ability to shift large amounts of liquid funds between countries using methods and procedures of international financial management (including evasion via transfer pricing or the use of tax havens, etc.) with adverse repercussions on exchange rates and the balance of payments. In this view, TNCs are generally believed to maximize profits from currency fluctuations, or to protect themselves from its consequences because of the high manoeuvrability of foreign exchange generated by intracompany payments. TNCs act as agents either to take risks (to maximize profits or minimize losses through outright speculation) or avert risks (to hedge in order to protect assets and to cover liabilities at the global level). However, studies on the determinants of capital flows financing FDI show little support for this view except in unusually unstable circumstances (see Gilman, 1981). This is because TNCs are essentially non-financial enterprises whose financial resources are primarily devoted to the functions of production, sales and investment both at home and abroad and therefore uncommitted financial assets are not a normal feature of these companies. While under the fixed exchange rate system, TNCs engaged in short-term capital movements to a degree in order to protect their positions, this practice is pursued more actively by banks, governments, central banks, and other institutions (Wallace, 1976).

Conclusion

Unlike with international trade and international monetary issues where the Bretton Woods system established both a set of rules and dedicated international institutional structures in the form of GATT and the IMF/IBRD, there are no dedicated international institutional structures to deal with TNCs and FDI, and a truly comprehensive set of rules at the global level has yet to emerge despite a long process of international rule building since 1948. The evolution of the main international instruments dealing with TNCs over the past fifty years has been analysed above in the context of three phases: the era of competition between

Table 8.2 Crucial elements of a global and comprehensive multilateral agreement concerning transnational corporations

---

I Treatment of transnational corporations

A. Right of establishment
    Industry restrictions
    Ownership-share restrictions
    Screening on the basis of economic or other criteria

B. Equitable treatment
    National treatment
    Non-Discrimination or Most-Favoured Nation treatment
    Regional arrangements and international commitments

C. Protection
    Nationalization and expropriation
    Compensation
    Property damage due to war (or other armed conflict), revolution, state of emergency, insurrection, civil disturbances or similar events
    Legislative or administrative actions and omissions of the host government which deprive the foreign investor of his ownership or control of, or a substantial benefit from, his investment
    Loss resulting from repudiation of government contracts
    Currency convertibility and funds transfer
    Repatriation of profits, earnings and other payments

D. Incentives
    Taxes
    Export subsidies

E. Performance requirements
    Domestic content
    Trade balancing
    Provision for coverage of other types: export performance, technology-transfer requirements, etc.

F. Personnel restrictions
    Nationality of directors and other officers
    Visa requirements for employers

G. Transparency

H. Sub-national governmental units' obligations in federal political systems (United States, Canada, Australia)

I. Government procurement

J. Exceptions: reservations and derogations
    Public order
    National security
    Balance of payments
    Stage of development

K. Standstill on new reservations (long-term exceptions) and derogations (temporary exceptions)

L. Rollback to reduce overtime exceptions with a view to their eventual elimination

---

II Guidelines of transnational corporations

A. Transfer pricing and taxation

B. Competition and restrictive business practices

C. Employment and industrial relations

D. Environmental protection

E. Accounting standards

III Enforcement and dispute settlement

A. Procedures
    Notification
    Examination
    Consultation and negotiation
    Binding obligations
    Sanctions
    Review of Reservations and Derogations

B. Dispute settlement mechanisms
    Government–government disputes
    Government–firm disputes
    Firm–firm disputes

Source: Adapted from Brewer and Young (1995).

control, protection and facilitation in the period from the mid-1940s to the 1960s, the era of control of TNC conduct in the 1970s, and the era of promotion and protection of FDI in the 1980s and 1990s. The prospect for the further evolution of a comprehensive and balanced global framework on TNCs and FDI (possibly through WTO) would need to strike a balance between the rights of TNCs and the rights of governments to exercise some degree of control over the behaviour of TNCs.

Notes

1 In this chapter, the term transnational corporation is used as opposed to multinational enterprise as it provides a more accurate description of the manner in which these firms operate in a transnational economic space that transcends traditional legal and territorial borders (Fatouros, 1984).

2 In assessing the role played by the productive activities of TNCs, economists most frequently use data on FDI as a proxy or second-best measure. This is because FDI is but one means by which the production of TNCs outside their home countries is financed, i.e. the foreign financing of international production. It does not normally include the investments of TNC affiliates financed by local borrowing or depreciation allowances nor of finance by other international borrowing that is not the responsibility of the parent company. For these reasons, data on FDI do not provide the total value of real assets engaged in international production (Cantwell, 1992).

3 While foreign capital stock provides an estimate of the total value of assets attributable to foreign ownership at a given point in time, the flows of FDI on an annual basis although tending to be volatile provides an indication of more recent changes in the level of FDI and therefore of the direction of evolution of international production (UNCTAD, 1995).

4 A similar but more limited view is given by Julius (1990) who refers to a new level of international economic integration through FDI. But although TNCs are the agents behind international production financed by FDI, they also play a key role in international trade, international finance as well as in a variety of non-equity relationships such as turnkey contracts, management and service contracts, co-production agreements, subcontracting agreements, licensing and franchising agreements, arrangements concerning the transfer of technology and know-how, and other forms of collaborative arrangements with entities and enterprises in all parts of the world.

5 The North–South divisions also explain the failure of the UN Draft Code on the Transfer of Technology.

6 There were only two main international instruments that fulfilled both functions: the OECD Declaration on Multinational Enterprises adopted in 1976 and the Draft Code on Transnational Corporations of the United Nations which negotiations failed to conclude successfully.

7 Until the end of the 1960s, developing countries regarded economic development as 'low politics' to be relegated to the technical ministries of planning, economics, commerce, finance and development. This attitude did not prevail in the 1970s in the face of the widespread poverty of many less developed countries and the economic crisis of the early 1970s brought about by the breakdown of the fixed exchange rate regime, inflation, rising protectionism and the food and oil crises (Sauvant, 1981).

8 For further discussion on the use and effectiveness of force for intervention and deterrence by the superpowers and other developed countries, see Bergsten, Keohane and Nye (1975).

9 On the premise of the principle of equality of states, the Calvo Doctrine denies that foreign nationals are entitled to special rights and privileges and emphasized that disputes

related to the claims of foreign nationals against host states are to be settled exclusively under domestic law and by domestic tribunals. The intervention of foreign states in these disputes was seen as a violation of the territorial jurisdiction of the host states. While the Doctrine attempted to formulate rules applicable to the relations among states, the Calvo Clause was devised to formulate rules applicable to the relations between a host country and foreign investors. The different principles of international law invoked by developed and developing countries on the treatment of TNCs contributed greatly to the impasse in the negotiations over the UN Draft Code of Conduct of Transnational Corporations as well as the UN Draft Code on the Transfer of Technology.

10 Some member states felt that such a convention offered too few rights to developing countries ('Controlling the multinationals', *The Economist,* 24 January 1976, pp. 68–69). Although it was not adopted, the OECD Draft Convention on the Protection of Foreign Property became the model for bilateral investment treaties (Witherell, 1995).

11 This favoured the establishment by most developed countries of national insurance schemes under which TNCs could insure their investments in developing countries against a number of risks. For examples of some of these guarantee schemes established by capital-exporting countries, see OECD (1972).

12 The abandonment of the Calvo Doctrine led Ecuador, Honduras and Paraguay to sign and ratify the ICSID Convention in the 1980s and Argentina, Bolivia, Brazil, Chile, Costa Rica and Peru followed suit in the 1990s (Shihata, 1994).

13 Bilateral treaties of friendship, commerce and navigation (FCN) provided the ground rules governing economic relations between the United States, Canada, Japan and other developed countries. However, it was not until after World War II that these treaties began to include explicit investment protection provisions, however broadly defined. The treaties provide for the protection of natural and juridical persons and their property; national treatment in the application of local laws; equal tax treatment and the right to compete with local monopolies (Sauvant and Aranda, 1994).

14 This was complemented in some cases by bilateral investment guarantee agreements developed during the 1950s and 1960s. Their main objective was to settle any disputes between the investor and a host government through international arbitration. There were also specific bilateral agreements for the avoidance of double taxation through the harmonization of tax policies on the treatment of income and capital flowing between the two contracting countries. These treaties have been concluded by many countries from all regions and are perhaps one of the most successful examples of intergovernmental bilateral cooperation (Sauvant and Aranda, 1994).

15 The OECD evolved in 1960 from the Organization for European Economic Cooperation. It is an association of the developed market economies. There are 26 member states at the present time: Australia, Austria, Belgium, Canada, Denmark, Finland, France, Germany, Greece, Iceland, Ireland, Italy, Japan, Luxembourg, Mexico, Netherlands, New Zealand, Norway, Portugal, Republic of Korea, Spain, Sweden, Switzerland, Turkey, the United Kingdom and the United States.

16 The events surrounding the *coup d'état* in Chile in September 1973 in which the regime of Salvador Allende was overthrown by the Chilean armed forces with the support of ITT provided a trigger for the demands of developing countries for international control of these companies (UNCTC, 1990).

17 Venezuela joined the Pact in 1973 (Grosse, 1983).

18 In the area of industrial development, the member countries agreed to a rationalization of investment on a sectoral basis to encourage industrial specialization and increased economic efficiency. In the area of foreign exchange management, there were limitations on profit remittances and repatriation of invested capital through tight controls and in the area of technology transfer, there were prohibitions on price fixing and output and export restrictions in licensing contracts, limits on the use of patents and trademarks by foreign investors to protect industrial technology and prohibitions on payment of royalties to the parent firm for technology transfer (Grosse, 1983).

19 In the view of Hamilton (1984), the elaboration of a code of conduct on TNCs applicable to the developed countries – the most important home and host countries of FDI – was an attempt to forestall the developing country-inspired United Nations Code of Conduct which was expected to be more restrictive in its control of TNCs.

20 Employers were initially uncomfortable with their participation in the ILO negotiations particularly because of the hostile atmosphere in which discussions on advancing international rules to control their conduct were taking place and also because at the same time discussions regarding employment and industrial relations were being deliberated in the context of the Guidelines for Multinational Enterprises in the OECD forum. Despite this, there was a realization that their cooperation in the ILO negotiations would lead to the prevention of government hostility which might lead to unproductive regulations; and second, their participation at the ILO forum gave them their only chance to influence the code-making process at the multilateral level. This would enable them to influence the code-making process in other multilateral forums such as the UN (Coates, 1981).

21 The United States originally proposed the UN antitrust code while the EEC has favoured international antitrust competition rules since 1950 (Hamilton, 1984).

22 This led the Heritage Foundation, a Washington business group, to comment that a growing and potentially dangerous international consumer movement was helping to set the agenda at various UN agencies in controlling TNCs (*Multinational Monitor*, January 1983).

23 Although 118 countries had supported this WHO Code with only the United States voting against it, only a handful of governments had taken steps to implement the Code. By contrast, companies such as Nestlé implemented the Code within its company – a successful strategy that led to the weakening and eventual suspension of the boycott of the company's products in 1984. At its height, the boycott of Nestlé's products involved some 100 groups in 65 countries. The WHO Code therefore played an important role in the legitimization of a TNC (Hamilton, 1984).

24 This programme of action resulted in the promulgation and regular review of a list of essential drugs by a WHO expert committee. This list was adopted by many governments of developing countries (Hamilton, 1984).

25 In an analogous fashion, Brewer and Young (1995) refer to the shift in emphasis from firms' obligations and governments' rights, to firms' rights and governments' obligations.

26 See annual issues of the *World Investment Report* of the United Nations for updates and analysis of the trend towards the liberalization of national laws and policies regarding FDI since the early 1980s.

27 The reversal of Mexico's policy stance is not solely related to NAFTA. Its investment liberalization is enshrined in Mexican law and even in the event that NAFTA failed, Mexico committed itself to a multilateralization of the most-favoured-nation clause consistent with the idea of open regionalism (Graham, 1994).

28 For a more comprehensive analysis of the NAFTA provisions on FDI, see Gestrin and Rugman (1993) and UNCTAD (1993).

29 The member states of APEC are Australia, Brunei, Darussalam, Canada, China, Hong Kong, Indonesia, Japan, Republic of Korea, Malaysia, Mexico, New Zealand, Papua New Guinea, Philippines, Singapore, Taiwan, Thailand and the United States.

30 The member states of the PECC are common with APEC with the exception of Papua New Guinea and the inclusion of Chile, Peru and Russia.

31 The Final Act of the Uruguay Round of Multilateral Trade Negotiations contains a package of economic reforms involving key economic transactions in the global economy, and notably trade. Part of the Final Act is the Agreement establishing the World Trade Organization, the latter being an implementing body for a number of agreements on trade in goods, trade in services and trade-related aspects of intellectual property rights (GATT, 1994).

32 The present regime of bilateral, multilateral and some global frameworks also suffers from coherence. Thus, to determine the specific international rules that apply to a particular transaction involving a TNC one has to scan through a large number of materials, select the relevant instruments, determine the kinds of obligations and rights they impose for either countries or TNCs and determine their status *vis-à-vis* other national and international instruments (Sauvant and Aranda, 1994). This is a cumbersome process that contributes to instability in world economic governance.

33 The unbalanced nature of bilateral investment treaties that solely emphasizes the obligations of governments to TNCs is unlikely to be the basis of a durable regime (as noted by Salacuse, 1987, and Vernon, 1987).

34 Scenarios for a global multilateral framework have also been drawn by Brewer and Young (1995), some elements of which were considered here.

35 The relationships between FDI and these other policy areas work through two clusters: first, with policies concerning environment, labour and trade policy and, second, with policies concerning competition, industry targeting, technology and trade policy (Brewer and Young, 1995).

References

Acquaah, K. (1986), *International Regulation of Transnational Corporations,* New York: Praeger.

Asante, S. K. B. (1989), 'The Concept of the Good Corporate Citizen in International Business', *ICSID Review – Foreign Investment Law Journal,* 4: 1–38.

Baade, H. W. (1980), 'The Legal Effects of Codes of Conduct for MNEs', in Horn, N. (ed.), *Legal Problems of Codes of Conduct for Multinational Enterprises,* Deventer: Kluwer.

Bergsten, C. F., Keohane, R. O. and Nye, J. S. (1975), 'International Economics and International Politics: A Framework for Analysis', in Bergsten, C. F. and Krause, L. B. (eds), *World Politics and International Economics,* Washington, DC: The Brookings Institution.

Black, R., Blank, S. and Hanson, E. C. (1978), *Multinationals in Contention,* New York: The Conference Board.

Brewer, T. L. and Young, S. (1995), 'Towards a Multilateral Framework for Foreign Direct Investment: Issues and Scenarios', *Transnational Corporations,* 4: 69–83.

Brewer, T. L. and Young, S. (1996), 'Investment Policies in Multilateral and Regional Agreements: A Comparative Analysis', *Transnational Corporations,* 5: 9–35.

Bunge, C. A. (1987), 'The Calvo Doctrine and the Codes of Conduct for Transnational Corporations', Ch. 9 of Norton, J. J. (ed.), *Public International Law and the Future World Order,* Littleton: Rothman & Co.

Cantwell, J. A. (1992), 'The Methodological Problems Raised by the Collection of Foreign Direct Investment Data', *Scandinavian International Business Review,* 1: 86–102.

Coates, J. (1981), 'ILO Tripartite Declaration concerning Multinational Enterprises and Social Policy', in *International Codes of Conduct,* London: CBI.

Dell, S. (1990), *The United Nations and International Business,* Durham and London: Duke University Press.

Dunning, J. H. (1992), *Multinational Enterprises and the Global Economy,* Wokingham: Addison-Wesley.

Fatouros, A. A. (1984), 'The UN Code of Conduct on Transnational Corporations: Problems of Interpretation and Implementation', Ch. 6 of Rubin, S. J. and Hufbauer, G. C. (eds.), *Emerging Standards of International Trade and Investment,* Totowa: Rowman & Allanheld.

GATT (1994), *The Final Act Embodying the Results of the Uruguay Round of Multilateral Trade Negotiations,* Geneva: GATT.

Gestrin, M. and Rugman, A. M. (1993), 'The NAFTA's Impact on the North American Investment Regime', *C. D. Howe Institute Commentary,* 42: 1–19.

Gilman, M. G. (1981), *The Financing of Foreign Direct Investment,* London: Frances Pinter.

Goldberg, P. M. and Kindleberger, C. P. (1970), 'Toward a GATT for Investment: A Proposal for Supervision of the International Corporation', *Law and Policy in International Business,* 2: 295–325.

Graham, E. M. (1994), 'Towards an Asia–Pacific Investment Code', *Transnational Corporations,* 3: 1–27.

Graham, E. M. and Wilkie, C. (1994), 'Multinationals and the Investment Provisions of the NAFTA', *The International Trade Journal,* 8: 9–38.

Grosse, R. (1983), 'The Andean Foreign Investment Code's Impact on Multinational Enterprises', *Journal of International Business Studies,* 14: 121–133.

Hamilton, G. (1984), 'The Control of Multinationals: What Future for International Codes of Conduct in the 1980s?', *IRM Multinational Reports,* No. 2, October–December.

Hufbauer, G. C. and Schott, J. J. (1993), *NAFTA: An Assessment,* Washington, DC: Institute for International Economics.

ICFTU (1975), *Multinational Charter,* Mexico.

Julius, D. (1990), *Global Companies and Public Policy,* London: Frances Pinter.

Keohane, R. O. and Ooms, V. D. (1975), 'The Multinational Firm and International Regulation', in Bergsten, C. F. and Krause, L. B. (eds), *World Politics and International Economics,* Washington, DC: The Brookings Institution.

Kline, J. M. (1985), *International Codes and Multinational Business,* Westport: Quorum Books.

Kline, J. M. (1993), 'International Regulation of Transnational Business: Providing the Missing Leg of Global Investment Standards', *Transnational Corporations,* 2: 153–164.

Lévy, P. (1984), 'The OECD Declaration on International Investment and Multinational Enterprises', Ch. 4 of Rubin, S. J. and Hufbauer, G. C. (eds.), *Emerging Standards of International Trade and Investment,* Totowa: Rowman & Allanheld.

OECD (1972), *Investment in Developing Countries,* Paris: OECD.

OECD (1976), *International Investment and Multinational Enterprises: Declaration by the Governments of the OECD Member Countries,* Paris: OECD.

OECD (1982), *Investment Incentives and Disincentives and the International Investment Process,* Paris: OECD.

OECD (1995), 'Communiqué of the Meeting of the OECD Council at Ministerial Level', May, mimeo, Paris: OECD.

Salacuse, J. W. (1987), 'Toward a New Treaty Framework for Direct Foreign Investment', Ch. 17 of Norton, J. J. (ed.), *Public International Law and the Future World Order,* Littleton: Rothman & Co.

Sauvant, K. P. (1981), 'The Role of TNCs in the Establishment of the NIEO: A Critical View', in Lozoya, J. and Green, R. (eds), *International Trade, Industrialization and the New International Economic Order,* Oxford: Pergamon.

Sauvant, K. P. and Aranda, V. (1994), 'The International Legal Framework for Transnational Corporations', Ch. 3 of Fatouros, A. A. (ed.), *Transnational Corporations: The International Legal Framework,* vol. 20, United Nations Library on Transnational Corporations, London and New York: Routledge.

Shihata, I. F. I. (1994), 'Towards a Greater Depoliticization of Investment Disputes: The Roles of ICSID and MIGA', Ch. 15 of Fatouros, A. A. (ed.), *Transnational Corporations: The International Legal Framework,* vol. 20, United Nations Library on Transnational Corporations, London and New York: Routledge.

UNCTAD (1993), *World Investment Report 1993: Transnational Corporations and Integrated International Production,* New York: United Nations.

UNCTAD (1995), *World Investment Report 1995: Transnational Corporations and Competitiveness,* Geneva: United Nations.

UNCTAD (1996), *World Investment Report 1996: Investment, Trade and International Policy Arrangements,* New York: United Nations.

UNCTC (1988), *Transnational Corporations in World Development: Trends and Prospects,* New York: United Nations.

UNCTC (1990), *The New Code Environment,* Current Studies, Series A, no. 16, New York: United Nations.

UNCTC and ICC (1992), *Bilateral Investment Treaties 1959–1991,* New York: United Nations.

UNCTC and UNCTAD (1991), *The Impact of Trade-Related Investment Measures on Trade and Development: Theory, Evidence and Policy Implications,* New York: United Nations.

Vernon, R. (1987), 'Codes on Transnationals: Ingredients for an Effective International Regime', in Dunning, J. H. and Usui, M. (eds), *Structural Change, Economic Interdependence and World Development,* vol. 4, New York: St Martin's Press.

Wallace, D. Jr (1976), *International Regulation of Multinational Corporations,* New York: Praeger.

Witherell, W. H. (1995), 'The OECD Multilateral Agreement on Investment', *Transnational Corporations,* 4: 1–14.

9   Will the real IMF please stand up

What does the Fund do and what should it do?

Laurence Harris

1

In the midst of a war that dominated the economies of all participants and destroyed or severely damaged all their economies except the United States' – a war that ended normal international trade and investment – Keynes and Harry Dexter White began to plan the construction of a new, post-war world. Bretton Woods came later, the climax of a long period of discussion and negotiation, and its most remarkable, ingenious product was the International Monetary Fund (IMF). While the International Bank for Reconstruction and Development provided a foundation both for financing reconstruction's capital projects and for rebuilding international bond markets, the IMF was the true innovation.

Both Keynes and White saw their designs as foundations for achieving social democratic ideals, enabling national governments to pursue full employment objectives through fiscal and monetary policy. If, as they believed, the disasters of pre-war policy – mass unemployment – were due, in many countries, to balance of payments constraints that led governments into beggar-my-neighbour devaluations and deflationary policies, how could that threat from a 'faulty' system of international finance be overcome? The trick was to create a system of rules for national management of currencies – fixed, but adjustable, par values with the US dollar, which itself had a commodity anchor in the form of a guarantee of the dollar's value in terms of gold – and an international institution, the IMF, that would have two tasks: it would enforce the rules and it would provide the short-term finance to assist governments in dealing with the problems that would arise from temporary shocks. It was an ingenious design that brought order to international finance, in chaos since the collapse of the gold standard and the end of the dominance of sterling.

Today the IMF has many critics. A feature of most criticisms is the absence of a definition of what the Fund is, and, hence, of a standard against which to judge its performance. In this chapter I argue that the lack of definition stems from the accumulation of distinct functions in the evolution of the Fund.

The IMF has become very different from the institution Keynes and White envisaged. Not only did those men envisage full employment as the principal goal, which, in turn, would underpin rising living standards, they also saw it as an instrument enabling governments, rather than financiers, to control countries' external financial position. Moreover, far from the IMF imposing itself on individual governments by lending to them with tight conditions, Keynes at least had initially seen it as a cooperative fund in which member countries pooled currencies and from which they could borrow as of right. The institution that emerged at Bretton Woods already had a different shape from that envisaged by its two founding fathers. Negotiations were dominated by the US government pursuing its agenda of breaking the hegemony of European imperial economic blocs, partly by enshrining the principle of multilateralism and partly by ensuring its dominance in the funding and voting structure of the IMF. That agenda effectively ruled out the idea that the IMF could operate as a cooperative fund with automatic borrowing rights and non-interference in national policies. Although the principle continues to exist formally, the countervailing principle that all except the lower tranches of loans and some special funds are subject to strict conditionality was established as Fund practice and rule in a number of developments in the one and a half decades following 1946.

Conditionality is the fulcrum for the Fund's relations with the governments to which it lends. Its standard form is a set of quantitative conditions on macroeconomic variables attached to a stand-by agreement: the country is required to define satisfactory objectives on variables such as domestic credit expansion (domestically generated money supply increases) as a condition for obtaining a loan and to meet those objectives as a condition for later disbursement of the loan. There is much to be said about conditionality, and, indeed, within the World Bank, International Monetary Fund and United Nations, there has been an active debate over alternative forms of conditionality (not least in the Special Programme for Africa forums). But this chapter is not concerned with the general debate over conditionality. Instead, it focuses on three problems:

- the evaluation of the Fund's role in the 1997 Asian crises;
- the extension of the Fund's responsibilities for surveillance; and
- the problem of determining the Fund's role in view of the number of distinct roles it has accumulated.

2

Let us begin with some history. How did the IMF get from the post-war hopes for a rationally ordered system of international economic relations to its present role?

The changes in the IMF's role since its foundation have been driven by fundamental changes in the world economy. It is common to see the IMF from the angle of an individual member country – its ability to support desirable forms of adjustment that are consistent with growth – which would suggest that changes in the IMF's practice are driven by that objective. But the alternative view, that the IMF's fundamental position is essentially concerned with the world economy rather than any individual country's, would lead us to seek the source of the Fund's evolution in changes in the world economy.

In the founding negotiations the centrality of multilateralism as the Fund's objective was not only an instrument enabling the US to break into formerly protected markets. Coming after three decades of an increasingly fragmented world economy, in which war, US protectionism, the (self-)exclusion of the Soviet Union from world markets, and currency breakdown were superimposed on old imperial blocs, enshrining multilateralism as the principle underlying Bretton Woods meant that the IMF's fundamental responsibility was the creation of a new world order. In that, the IMF's task was to support trade multilateralism by promoting both full current account convertibility of currencies and currency stability in the face of temporary shocks.

The Fund's implementation of this task was based upon a particular structure of the world economy; in the view of Banuri and Schor[1] it was one in which national economic policies, along broadly Keynesian lines, could be followed. That structure existed in the context of limited international capital markets, a fracturing that the IMF's Articles reflected by permitting countries to retain controls over capital movements.[2] Its greatest achievement was current account convertibility among the major industrial countries although the full mechanism of the Bretton Woods system never worked with the smoothness its designers intended; adjustments of par values and symmetric actions by surplus and deficit countries were not fully achieved.

The events of 1973 were a turning point. The failure of the IMF to address fundamental imbalances in the world economy in previous decades, as it was supposed to do by enabling negotiated adjustment of par value exchange rates, meant that when the exchange rate of the US dollar became unsustainable the only way forward was to break the fixed dollar price of gold – the dollar-exchange standard, upon which the Bretton Woods system of par values and reserves was founded. By 1973 the system of adjustable peg exchange rates was abandoned and the world entered an era of high volatility in exchange rates, interest rates, and commodity prices.

The oil price shock of that year contributed to the creation of a world in which volatility is the norm and it had further effects that were to transform the IMF from being the overseer of the Bretton Woods system to being a key player in poor countries' development. The first was that the oil shock greatly boosted the growth of Euro-currency markets and Euro-credit markets, whose key characteristic is that they are outside the control of national governments. Thus, the possibility of a return to the IMF's original primary function, supervision of major powers' currencies based on national governments' control, was eradicated. Second, the price rise created major imbalances in developing countries, contributing to large surpluses in oil exporting countries and large deficits in non-oil exporters. For some – both oil exporters such as Nigeria, Venezuela, and Mexico and oil importers such as Argentina – these imbalances were the foundation for large scale bank borrowing of euro currencies which was the origin of the developing countries' sovereign debt crisis that broke in 1982. For others, such as non-oil sub-saharan African countries, the imbalances moved them onto a low growth or stationary path with accumulating current account deficits requiring official financing.

The post-1973 trajectories of both types of developing countries led to new roles for the IMF, giving the Fund a centrality in the third world and the third world's problems a centrality in the Fund. The large scale borrowers of bank credit which had to negotiate debt crises and rescheduling in the 1980s required IMF monitoring of their reform programmes as a precondition for rescheduling. While that IMF role could be seen as time-limited and, hence, an evolution from the original concept of the Fund advising a member on adjustment to overcome a fundamental disequilibrium, the IMF's involvement in the 1980s with the second group, typically sub-saharan African countries, was as permanent monitor. Sub-saharan African countries, on low growth paths and heavily aid dependent with notable exceptions such as South Africa, Zimbabwe, and Botswana, became numerically significant borrowers from the IMF as they accumulated official debt in the 1980s. For such countries, the experience has been one of a succession of IMF monitored adjustment programmes with no prospect of becoming free from such oversight. If we ask the question 'on whose behalf was the IMF acting as monitor?' a first answer might be that in the case of countries that had borrowed euro currencies heavily and experienced the debt crisis of 1982, the IMF was monitoring on behalf of creditor banks while in the case of countries accumulating debt to official lenders in the 1980s the IMF explicitly acts as monitor on behalf of the official lenders ('the "donor" community').

From 1990, changed conditions of international financing led to the growth of portfolio investment in Latin America and the former Soviet bloc and greatly increased portfolio investment in the fast growing developing countries of Asia.[3] Two quite different crises in that process have forced the IMF to address new types of problem. The 1994 Mexican peso crisis, accompanied by contagion across Latin American markets, arose from failure of confidence in the US-dollar guarantee the Mexican government had given on short term government paper (*tesorbons*) when a previously-hidden decline in foreign exchange reserves became evident.

The 1997 Asian crisis was quite new for it centred on the international debt of local corporations and banks rather than government debt and it affected countries with relatively strong current account and fiscal positions. The following section will consider the assessments that have been made of the IMF's role there, suggesting that their underlying approach largely misses an important aspect of crisis – the distribution of rewards and losses for risk taking – and discussing the new roles the IMF acquired in the crisis.

3

The 1997 Asian crisis was both unexpected and unlike other financial crises in which the Fund had to take a leading role. One unusual characteristic was that the countries at its centre, facing severe exchange rate depreciation, had sound fiscal positions in terms of standard measures, a continuation of the fiscal prudence that had historically accompanied their high growth. Elsewhere, countries requiring Fund-supported stabilization programmes usually had both fiscal deficits and balance of payments deficits. A second unusual aspect is that, whereas in most previous crises where Fund-supervised stabilization programmes have been adopted the cost of external government debt has been a major problem, in the Asian crisis the external debt of the highly leveraged private sector has fuelled the crisis by multiplying the contractionary effects of exchange rate depreciation.

The standard Fund prescriptions, developed and widely applied over many years, gave a central role to fiscal tightening in order to overcome fiscal and external deficits and stabilize external public debt. Since the Asian crises had different features the application of such policies in the Asian crisis prompted critics, especially Sachs,[4] Wade and Veneroso,[5] and, from a related angle, Stiglitz,[6] to argue that the Fund made things worse by inflexibly repeating policies that might have been appropriate in countries with more common macroeconomic problems. According to those critics the Fund was mistaken to apply a 'one size fits all' policy requiring both fiscal discipline and tightening of monetary policy. But, at the same time, the Fund has been criticized for going beyond its traditional macroeconomic role and prescribing wholesale reform of the countries' financial institutions and structure.[7]

The IMF's policies in the Asian crisis were not immediately successful if the measure is the attainment of currency stability and renewed economic growth, although it is important to note that one year after the crisis was sparked by the initial devaluation of the Thai bhat, the Thai and Korean currencies have stabilized and since the end of 1997 overnight interest rates have declined from 30 per cent to 15 per cent in Korea and from 25 per cent to 17 per cent in Thailand. It may be that the Fund's prescriptions, intended to bolster confidence, did initially contribute to weakening market confidence. There can be no doubt that at crucial times such as the Korean crisis in December 1997, the Fund did see its task as underpinning financial confidence by acting as a 'traditional lender of last resort', and, although it required high local interest rate policies to be adopted, they were seen as standard confidence-boosting measures to stimulate demand for the countries' currencies. But, as Stiglitz argues, in a world of imperfect information such confidence-boosting measures can have perverse effects if they signal weakness and severe reversals of previous growth trends.

The critics' rapidly evolved 'conventional wisdom' is, however, limited by its concentration on the Fund's actual response to the crisis. The underlying assumption is that the crisis was avoidable, or, at least, that a disturbance in financial markets need not have been allowed to generate such large real shocks. After all Korea, Malaysia, Indonesia, and even Thailand had experienced consistently high growth rates for years, had macroeconomic indicators that were conventionally sound – low inflation, high saving, conservative fiscal positions, and low current account deficits – and had high credit ratings. Why should financial markets' sentiment cause them to change direction? Underlying the critics' view is the idea that if the Fund had adopted appropriate policies, respecting the specific character of Asian capitalism, the initial disturbance on foreign exchange markets would have been contained without serious disruption to economic growth.

An alternative view is that a break in growth was inevitable; from that starting point, the evaluation of the crisis and the IMF's policies look different from the critics' view, for risk and the distribution of the costs of the crisis take centre stage. Since the mid-nineteenth century it has been recognized that capitalist economies grow unevenly, with high growth periods ending temporarily in downturns, and economic theory analyses this pattern in business cycle models of many types. Arguably, current developments in the Asian crisis countries conform to a Marx–Schumpeter model of creative destruction in which crises in the real economy have their roots in the growth of the real economy itself and involve a restructuring that lays the conditions for potential future growth.

It is not difficult to identify reasons for thinking that the Asian economies' growth could not continue uninterrupted on the same basis as previously. For advanced economies such as South Korea, core industries such as automobile manufacturing and computer hardware were showing signs of overinvestment with falling margins and oversupplied world markets, the conditions that have historically accompanied Marx–Schumpeter-type crises. Even though other countries in the region had different growth paths and economic structures, all were affected by the stagnation of Japan's economy. The dominant regional economy itself had ended its period of fast growth several years before the 1997 crisis, and by 1997 Japan's decline in profitable investment projects, high personal savings ratios, and high liquidity preference had acquired the characteristics Keynes ascribed to major slumps – albeit at lower rates of unemployment than seen since the 1930s. From a Marx–Schumpeter perspective, Japan had entered a crisis of overinvestment and was facing the prospect of renewal of its productive base through creative destruction. And the economies of the newly industrializing countries of Asia, whose growth had been linked to Japan's, now faced the prospect of being linked in the downturn.

The view that the Asian economies' growth was interrupted in 1997 due to underlying real factors does not deny that the volatility of financial markets contributed to the crisis and accentuated it, for financial panics have been a general feature accompanying real crises in growing capitalist economies. But it does imply that financial instability was not the only or most fundamental force at work. Most relevant to this chapter is that such a view implies that even if the IMF had been able to implement policies that restored financial market 'confidence', the underlying causes of crisis would have produced a reversal of growth nevertheless.

The notion that economies are inherently subject to cycles of various types, including cycles which involve major real crises, gives us a new perspective on how to evaluate the IMF. Assuming that turning points cannot be perfectly foreseen, cycles introduce an element of undiversifiable risk to households', non-financial firms', banks' and governments' decision-making. All intertemporal positions taken during the boom, as at other times, are risky, whether they are a firm's real investment decisions, households' saving and consumption decisions, banks' and firms' financing decisions, or a household's irreversible decision to move from agriculture to industrial employment, from countryside to town. The policies adopted when the downturn comes determine the distribution of costs and rewards or who, ex post, suffers losses on the risky positions taken during the boom, and the IMF inevitably has an impact on those outcomes.

A simple benchmark case illustrates the effect IMF policies can have on risk bearing. A small country with an undemocratic ruling elite borrows externally, using public or government-guaranteed debt, to finance a public sector and external current account deficit while the elite invests its private rents abroad. A combination of nominal exchange rate rigidity and a long-cycle decline in the world market price for the country's principal commodity export leads to an external crisis and an agreement with the IMF. The conditions agreed with the Fund require a devaluation and a cut in the fiscal deficit, achievable only through cuts in current expenditure and net transfers.

In those circumstances who bears the costs of adjustment? Clearly the country's labour force bears costs both because a devaluation, if it is to work, reduces the real value of wages and because fiscal cuts normally reduce the real disposable income of sections of the labour force. The elite is unlikely to bear significant costs because their assets are held abroad and denominated in foreign currencies. Foreign portfolio investors do not normally bear the costs because interest payments are privileged items in the government budget. In other words, in the years before the crisis, all forward-looking decisions were taken, knowingly or not, in an environment of risk because of the probability of cyclical decline in world markets, but agents do not bear the costs of that cyclical decline equally. Labour does bear the costs, although the assumptions in this model make it plausible that they did not have full information about the risks and had no influence over national policies that could have mitigated them. The elite does not bear significant costs although it was in a position to be aware of the risks facing the economy and did have effective policy choices. Foreign investors do not bear the costs although they were able to access full information and make decisions based on risk assessment. A standard IMF agreement, determining the structure of the macroeconomic adjustment, would have been instrumental in ensuring that pattern of payoffs. In other words the IMF programme would have helped to distribute payoffs in a manner that distorts the rewards to risk taking, for the highest payoffs go to agents who are protected from risk while those who have not chosen a risky path suffer negative payoffs. Whether that conclusion is valid depends on an assessment of the argument that there could have been no alternative – the IMF would simply have been promoting policies that followed from inescapable macroeconomic principles; indeed, by lending credibility to the government's pursuit of those policies the IMF could be judged to have reduced the total costs of adjustment.[8]

Such considerations have become increasingly strongly articulated by some critics of the IMF loans to Thailand, Korea, and Indonesia who have argued that the IMF is effectively 'bailing out' US and other foreign banks, thereby creating moral hazard in international banking. But the Asian crisis economies differ from the simple benchmark economy in several respects, particularly the facts that their macroeconomic fundamentals were not in a comparable severe disequilibrium and their financial systems were both more developed and had richer links with international markets.

The financial system, and particularly the role of the banking system, significantly affects the allocation of burdens and the rewards of risk taking. Foreign savings have financed expansion by being invested in the liabilities of the banking system and through investment in the emerging market stock markets. The returns expected by foreign investors included a low risk premium for currency depreciation, for it was believed that governments, backed by strong macroeconomic fundamentals, were able to guarantee exchange rates pegged to the dollar. But the collapse of that belief, following the mid-1997 devaluation of the Thai baht, led to a reversal of foreign investment flows. And the failure of that imputed guarantee drove local banks into effective insolvency for two reasons; first, their dollar-denominated debt liabilities increased in value while locally denominated assets did not, and, second, the collapse of stock market and other asset values undermined the value of collateral held by banks.

In those circumstances, the measures taken to solve the crisis produce a particular pattern of rewards and costs. The prescription of high interest rates was designed to restore foreign exchange market confidence and prevent excessive exchange rate depreciation. Coinciding with the foreign exchange shock and asset value shock to a fragile banking system – together with the banks' obligation to adhere to Basle capital adequacy requirements – the sharp rise in overnight interest rates made a credit crunch less avoidable. That credit crunch has real effects, contributing to negative feedbacks within the stabilization programme; the expansionary effect of exchange rate depreciation, through its effect on the relative costs of exports and imports, is undermined by the inability of firms to obtain bank finance for expansion. In terms of the pattern of rewards and losses it means that owners of domestic banks would bear losses as would depositors and creditors of banks whose insolvency is precipitated by the crisis, but those losses will be transferred to the government, or ultimately taxpayers, if it implements an implicit guarantee of the monetary system by buying insolvent banks.

The IMF's role in the Asian crisis included an attempt to address the special circumstances of bank fragility, although it may not have been well designed. For example, the Fund justified the prescription of current account fiscal tightening in Korea on the grounds that it was necessary to offset, to some extent, the upward pressure on government borrowing created by the need to inject funds into the banking system. More fundamentally the IMF has promoted fundamental restructuring of the crisis countries' financial sectors. The logic behind that reform is partly that since the banking systems were inherently weak, reform and restructuring were necessary to reduce the risk of further economic disruption through a second wave of banking crises; after all, one lesson of the 1930s for the United States was that the effects of the 1929 stock market crash were compounded by (or even less important than) the secondary shocks produced by bank collapses in the following years. The promotion of banking sector reforms has prompted criticism that it is beyond the IMF's responsibility for short term macroeconomic adjustment, and that it is inconsistent with the IMF's crisis-calming measures since it amounts to shouting 'Fire' instead of announcing 'Keep calm, it's business as usual'. Those criticisms are considered in later sections.

The high level of foreign capital in financing the Asian countries' growth and their asset price expansion, through both the local banking system and equity market portfolios, also makes the international sharing of the costs and rewards of the crisis a central matter. The IMF's role in trying to achieve stability and orderly adjustment, which is inherent in its responsibility for an orderly global system, does offer some protection to international finance houses from the costs of the crisis. Therefore, it does carry the possibility of creating moral hazard, for international investors' high expected (and, between 1990 and 1997, realized) rewards for emerging market investment was the price of high risk, a risk that is mitigated if, in fact, the IMF provides an implicit guarantee against downside risk. In fact, however, concerns over moral hazard arising from the IMF programmes have little practical significance, for such is the severity of the crisis that any stability achieved in the medium term is at a low level and international investors have suffered significant losses.

In the following section I consider wider surveillance as an alternative route for the IMF to follow in order to reduce macroeconomic risks and financial market volatility.

4

Monitoring members' economies is an established, major function of the Fund. In the case of countries that have borrowed, it is a necessary part of conditionality, for if conditions are to be effective Fund staff have to evaluate whether the benchmarks laid down in the conditions have been met. But Fund staff also monitor all other member countries; under Article IV of the Fund's basic document, regular visiting missions evaluate individual member countries' macroeconomic prospects and their policy stance. In recent years the concept of monitoring has been enlarged as the Fund has been given additional responsibility for 'surveillance'. From the point of view of financial markets, the Mexican crisis of 1994 and the Asian crises of 1997 were judged to have arisen from, or at least been magnified by, information failures, therefore a remedy appeared to be to give the Fund a special responsibility for improving information by increased and widened surveillance.[9] What does surveillance mean? And can it be successful?

The idea of greater IMF surveillance promoted by the G7 at its Halifax meeting after the 1994 Mexican crisis was an extension and intensification of the IMF's traditional monitoring of national governments' policies. That crisis was initiated by the Mexican government's failure to publish timely and full information on its external accounts, and subsequent discovery of the weakness of its foreign exchange reserves. Giving the Fund responsibility for surveillance has been envisaged as a way of monitoring national and government accounts more fully, and in that sense is merely a strengthening of Article IV reporting and of the monitoring that takes place to enforce the conditionality of countries that have borrowed from the Fund. But there is a crucial difference, for one interpretation of such surveillance is that it should improve the flow of information to investors, whereas traditional monitoring associated with conditionality has normally been subject to confidentiality.

The Asian crisis has led to further calls for improved IMF surveillance. But the concept has broadened beyond a country's macroeconomic position or foreign exchange reserves to calls for surveillance of its financial structure, the debt ratio and foreign debt ratio of its major companies and banks. In some Asian countries, such as South Korea, the currency crisis of 1997 was worsened by lack of published information on the government's foreign exchange reserves and contingent foreign exchange liabilities – the type of problem that post-Mexico surveillance would cover – but a consensus that an underlying problem is the fragility of those countries' financial systems has led to a belief that better information on general financial conditions is required. In Korea, at least, the IMF saw its role as being similar to that of a classic 'lender of last resort', and it might be argued that such a role requires a complementary surveillance of the financial systems that are being supported.

The new concepts of surveillance would move the IMF beyond the monitoring traditionally associated with conditionality. Conditionality has required quantitative monitoring of macroeconomic variables amenable to being targeted by government policy[10] implemented when the country borrows from the Fund, but the post-Asia idea of surveillance requires continual evaluation of financial systems. The logic of such a development can be located in the world economy's changes. In the age that has been called 'global neoclassicism' the financing of economies increasingly revolves around the links between local banks and firms and global financial markets, in contrast to the heyday of Keynesianism when local financial conditions were dominated by national governments' financing. Since lending to local banks and firms involves both flows of new saving and reallocation of international portfolios, the latter, especially, occurring with a high degree of volatility, the system contains the possibility of great instability. Thus, it can be argued, achieving macroeconomic stability requires surveillance of those financial systems.

But the concept of surveillance is confused and not able satisfactorily to define a new role for the IMF; consequently the IMF's future is very unclear. The problem can be seen in several ways. First, it can be argued there is no reason to expect that the IMF has a comparative advantage over banks and investors themselves in monitoring financial systems. The theory of financial intermediaries ascribes to them a role as delegated monitors, such that savers are able to gain cost advantages by delegating to them the responsibility of monitoring the ultimate borrowers (either pre- or post-delinquency). In practice they may carry out that role more or less satisfactorily, but it is not certain that the IMF can do it better. It would have to be the case that the IMF can monitor risks in individual countries' financial systems better, at less cost, than the banks who are themselves lending into those local institutions. That is implausible. In practical terms it is implausible that, for example, the IMF could have better knowledge than the international banks operating in Korea that South Korea's corporate governance and ownership structures involved lack of financial transparency and that the system depended upon heavily geared financing with high exposure to currency risk.

The IMF suffers from the disadvantage that its operations do not integrally deliver contact with the local banking system in contrast to a national central bank whose daily operations are integral to its country's banking system and, unlike national bank supervisors, the Fund has neither the experience nor the legal instruments to back its surveillance. Nevertheless, the Fund does have a potential source of strength. To the extent that countries' governments and local banks benefit from the market credibility that IMF backing can offer, member states have an incentive to provide information required by the Fund, thus the Fund has a power to force disclosure that individual financial intermediaries do not.

The Fund's comparative advantage in surveillance can be judged by using as a benchmark the credit ratings given by financial intermediaries themselves and independent monitors. Studies by ul Haque and colleagues[11] indicate that the assessments of developing countries by rating agencies have reflected key 'macro-economic fundamentals' variables well, especially the ratio of non-gold foreign exchange reserves to imports, the ratio of current account balance to GDP, the country's rate of growth, and inflation. Can the IMF do better? If it can, it will be for the following reasons. The studies' data series are from 1980 to 1993, but it is likely that the fit between credit ratings and fundamentals will have deteriorated in a sample that includes 1997; if the IMF's surveillance is to be superior the Fund will have to overcome its own failure to identify advance signs of the 1997 crisis better than the agencies overcome theirs. Moreover, since the econometric results suggest that the significant relation between credit ratings and fundamentals is accompanied by a high degree of persistence in credit ratings, it may be that the Fund is able to identify changes in fundamentals more quickly and clearly. But there are no obvious reasons for assuming that the Fund will have such a comparative advantage.[12]

A final reservation about the ability of the Fund to improve stability through improved surveillance is that there is no reason to think that even superior information gained or published through increased surveillance of financial systems and markets would avert crises. Models of rational bubbles show that speculative bubbles (and, hence financial crises) can occur in economies with costless full information freely available and rational expectations,[13] and the existence of bubbles and crashes in financial systems such as the United States' demonstrates that near full information does not guarantee stability or efficient allocation. The difficulty is accentuated by the announcement problem. If the IMF obtains superior negative information through surveillance, an announcement might cause a crash either because it comes after a speculative bubble based on poor information has begun or because the announcement leads to excess adjustments of investors' expectations. But on the other hand, the Fund's own credibility would be compromised by non-announcement. If, for example, it found that official reserves were unexpectedly low, or that the country's authorities had unrecognized contingent foreign exchange liabilities, or that local banks had unduly exposed real balance sheets, but did not announce that, such facts would eventually become evident. Thus, critics who argue that in 1997 the Fund failed in its lender of last resort role because it did not disguise its discovery that local financial systems were weak identify one side of the announcement problem, but ignore the negative consequences that would follow from the Fund trying to bluff.

5

The IMF's role in today's world is confused and not sustainable in its present form, consequently it is subject to criticism of both right and left wing types; from the right the criticism is that the Fund 'gives' money to profligate governments, from the left it is that Fund conditionality penalizes the poor and is unremittingly and excessively contractionary, and from both directions the Fund is criticized for bailing out international banks and financiers who should themselves bear the cost arising from loans to high-return high-risk borrowers. One reason for the IMF's current lack of direction is that it has developed in response to world changes that are not of its own making and that has led to an uneasy bifurcation of responsibility.

Today, discussion of the Fund's role concerns responsibility for prevention of Asian-type crises, and, hence, the interface between local finance, corporate governance, and global financial markets. The Fund was designed to work with national governments in relation to macroeconomic policy and targets, and its skills, methods of analysis, operations and policy prescriptions are rooted in simple macroeconomic stabilization models, not in corporate finance or international markets. But the Asian crisis has shown that in such countries the Fund does precisely need to address corporate finance issues (such as the corporate debt rescheduling that enabled Korea's financial markets to stabilize), problems of corporate and political governance, and issues of credibility and expectations formation in international financial markets. Until recently the Fund had not even sought to develop such skills, for the Capital Markets division within its Research Department, had not been concerned with specifically 'emerging market' issues. The persistence of past modes, concentrating on macroeconomic adjustment by governments in countries where microeconomic business finance was the key, partly led to the Fund being criticized for a 'one size fits all' policy of unduly high interest rates and fiscal caution. The policies are defensible, and indeed were necessary, but highlighted the Fund's difficulty in finding a different identity.

However the real problem for the Fund's identity and coherence is that a focus on such countries has to coexist with a quite different Fund, the Fund that designs and monitors the macroeconomic dimensions of structural adjustment programmes in countries whose banks and firms do not register significantly in international investment portfolios. That is, in fact, the majority of developing countries. The World Bank calculates that while private capital flows to developing countries surged between 1992 and 1996, low income countries (excluding China and India) received only 3.4 per cent of that total and sub-saharan African countries received only 1.5 per cent. Eight countries, China, Mexico, Brazil, Korea, Malaysia, Argentina, Thailand and Indonesia, accounted for 70 per cent of net long-term private finance in the first half of the decade. Outside of those dynamic economies there are different types of developing countries under IMF supervised programmes. The IMF's engagement with, say, a typical sub-saharan country to which it loaned funds is one whose core is founded upon the financial programming, macro policies developed in the 1950s as the basis for conditionality. In principle that could be a consistent path, for such countries' finance continues to be dominated by the government's macroeconomic balance; they remain sufficiently outside 'global neoclassicism'. But such 'African-type' programmes themselves lack coherence because their world is different from the old one. Occurring in the midst of attempts to break out of Africa's relative economic decline, Fund programmes have become repeated with an appearance of permanence instead of being the short programmes to stabilize economies that they were originally designed to be. But neither has their design evolved to take account of that change, nor is it able to without the Fund becoming an institution with very different objectives from those in its Articles.

6

The IMF does, then, have a real identity crisis. It has to finance and supervise change in at least two very different types of developing country: the Asian countries with large corporate and financial sectors with strong private finance links to international financial markets, and poor countries in a growth trap without such developed structures. Additionally it oversees the economies and foreign exchanges of the G7 – historically and presently a major element of the Fund staff's work – and the construction of a market economy in Russia and other formerly planned economies.

In order to determine its future direction, the Fund has to identify properly the functions it has assumed over the years and that have been ascribed to it, and determine their relation to each other. They include: an international fund existing for and run by its members, national states; a short-term macroeconomic policy agency for middle income developing countries; a macroeconomic and long-term development agency for low-income developing countries; a surveillance agency providing a service to international financial markets; a lender of last resort to local financial institutions; and a supervisor of banking systems and financial structures.

But, in fact, determining its future roles is not a task that relates to the Fund alone, for several of its current roles have arisen from the absence of other institutions and a millennium version of Bretton Woods would have to consider the invention of other institutions. For example, the IMF is not well designed to be a lender of last resort partly because its structures are designed to relate to national governments rather than banking systems, and it is equally not suited to a role as supervisor of banking systems. That such roles have come to the fore for the IMF in 1997 reflects the absence of other institutions to undertake them. The Bank for International Settlements had, in the 1980s, been thought to be a candidate for such roles, but, despite its achievements in setting capital adequacy requirements, it has failed to fulfil those beliefs, and, in any case, is not currently structured in a way that is more appropriate to the task than is the IMF. There have been many calls for a new Bretton Woods, and they inevitably acquire a purely rhetorical character, but such an enterprise really is the only way forward for governance in international financial matters.

Notes

1 Banuri, T. and J.B. Schor (eds) *Financial Openness and National Autonomy*, Oxford: Clarendon Press, 1992.

2 Although the modern desirability of that provision is now the subject of intense debate.

3 World Bank, *Private Capital Flows to Developing Countries*, New York: Oxford University Press, 1997.

4 Sachs, J., 'The IMF and the Asian Flu' *The American Prospect*, March–April 1998, 16–21.

5 Wade, R. and F. Veneroso, 'The High Debt Model Versus the Wall Street–Treasury–IMF Complex', *New Left Review*, No. 228, 1998, 3–23.

6 Stiglitz, J. 'More Instruments and Broader Goals: Moving Toward the Post-Washington Consensus', WIDER Annual Lecture, Helsinki, January 1998, processed draft.

7 Wade and Veneroso *op. cit.*

8 Agenor, P.-R. and P. Montiel, *Development Macroeconomics*, Princeton, NJ: Princeton University Press, 1996, pp. 375–6.

9 Goldstein, M., 'Early Warning Indicators of Currency and Banking Crises in Emerging Economies' in *Financial Crises and Asia*, CEPR Conference Report 6, Centre for Economic Policy Research, March 1998.

10 Although the IMF's increased long term involvement in structural adjustment programmes has meant that, in addition to macroeconomic variables, it includes financial system reform and other reforms in qualitative conditions.

11 Ul Haq, N., M.S. Kumar, N. Mark, and D.I. Mathieson, 'The Economic Content of Indicators of Developing Country Creditworthiness', *IMF Staff Papers*, 43, 4 (1996) 688–724; ul Haq, N., M.S. Kumar, N. Mark, and D.I. Mathieson, 'The Relative Importance of Political and Economic Variables in Creditworthiness Ratings', *IMF Working Paper*, February 1998, processed.

12 Current work on models of leading indicators of financial crises offers a potentially valuable additional tool for improving information. But there is no reason for the IMF to have a special role in undertaking such work; as with other forecasting, it is desirable to have a multitude of competing forecasting teams without special status being given to institutional forecasts. Goldstein, M., 'Early Warning Indicators of Currency and Banking Crises in Emerging Economies', in *Financial Crises and Asia*, CEPR Conference Report 6, Centre for Economic Policy Research, March 1998.

13 Blanchard, O. and M. Watson, 'Bubbles, Rational Expectations and Financial Markets' in P. Wachtel (ed.) *Crises in the Economic and Financial Structure*, Lexington, MA: Lexington Books, 1982.

10   A world central bank?

John Smithin and Bernard M. Wolf

Introduction

When exchange rates first began floating in the early twentieth century, in the aftermath of World War I, Keynes (1924, 187) wrote that 'the academic dream of a hundred years, doffing its cap and gown, clad in paper rags, has crept into the world by means of the bad fairies'.[1] This particular 'dream' came true once more half-a-century later, when the major currencies began floating again after the break-up of the Bretton Woods system in the early 1970s.

However, to many, the results in the last quarter of the twentieth century have not been so much a dream as a nightmare. The flexibility, and hence potential volatility, of exchange rates, has been combined with other changes, such as the globalization of financial markets, de-regulation/financial liberalization, and technical change, all of which have acted to greatly increase both the volume and speed of international capital movements. The concern in such an environment is that, in balance of payments adjustment, it is the capital account, including speculative capital movements, which dominates or drives the current account via exchange rate changes. The results on current account, whether positive or negative, are no longer perceived as deriving from genuine economic effort, for example, a surplus arising if an economy becomes more 'productive' or 'competitive', but simply as a by-product of capital market activity. By the early 1990s, *The Economist* magazine had already dubbed this phenomenon 'The fear of finance'.[2] Indeed, at some level it hardly matters whether or not the capital transfers are pejoratively described as 'speculative' or are regarded as appropriate responses to genuine economic incentives. In either case, the impact on the current account is the same.

Very clearly, the actual course of events during the 1990s, including the crises in the exchange rate mechanism (ERM) in Europe in 1992/93, the Mexican peso crisis of 1994/95, and the Asian currency crises of late 1997, has only served to increase the sense of apprehension regarding the international monetary system (IMS). Even though, as a caveat, it should be noted that all of these episodes involved attempts to keep exchange rates fixed at inappropriate levels (rather than just being due to the potential flexibility of rates), it is nonetheless easy to understand why there is now increasing interest in proposals for a restructuring or revamping of existing international financial institutions (IFIs), and for thoroughgoing reform of the IMS itself. These include proposals to restore fixed exchange rates, to set up a world central bank (WCB) as in the title of this chapter, to regulate capital flows by taxation or some other means, to reform existing IFIs such as the International Monetary Fund (IMF), or to create a 'new Bretton Woods' (Grieve Smith, this volume).

Nevertheless, as in earlier work (Smithin and Wolf, 1993), we remain sceptical of both the feasibility and desirability of such a comprehensive institutional reform as the establishment of a WCB in the contemporary global economic environment. The purpose of this chapter is to set out some of the reasons for this scepticism. Many of these revolve around the likely deflationary bias of powerful international financial bureaucracies in the contemporary social and political environment, and mirror the concerns which have frequently been expressed about the regional Economic and Monetary Union (EMU) or 'single currency' initiative in Europe. However, there is also another strand to the argument. It is an implicit presumption of much of the literature on IMS reform that the alternative, the continued advocacy of appropriate nationally based public policy, is no longer viable in the emerging global economy, precisely because of the increased capital mobility referred to above. This is one aspect of what McQuaig (1998) has called the 'cult of impotence' or 'myth of powerlessness' in the context of globalization. However, recently, authors such as Eatwell (1996), Godley (1996), Paraskevopoulos, Paschakis and Smithin (1996), and Paschakis and Smithin (1998), have pointed to the existence of mechanisms whereby small and medium-sized open economies can influence their own economic destinies, even in a global environment characterized by virtually perfect capital mobility. These mechanisms, though, are critically dependent on the continued existence of independent national monetary systems, with exchange rates that are at least potentially free to change, even if in practice they remain fairly stable. In short, an independent monetary policy may be a necessary condition for an independent policy to be pursued in other fields, such as fiscal policy, labour-market regulation, social protection, etc. (Paraskevopoulos and Smithin, 1998; Smithin, 1998). This implies that there is a 'downside' to any kind of international solution which removes the possibility for an independent policy, unless we can be very sure of the *bona fides* of those who will actually be running the powerful international institutions.

The potential ability of individual political jurisdictions to pursue independent policies does not, of course, ensure a desirable economic outcome either for the economy concerned or the world economy as a whole. It is just as possible, and even likely, for independent national policy-makers to pursue perverse and deflationary policies as it is for international bureaucracies. In the best-case scenario, however, coordinated or like-minded expansionary policies in a number of jurisdictions would foster world growth, and allow for reasonable (real) exchange rate stability and approximate balance of the current and capital accounts across jurisdictions. In the worst-case scenario, in which the majority of countries were not taking such action, it would still be possible for one or two nations to escape from global pressures by taking a contrarian stance. The contrarian nations would have faster growth, lower unemployment, a real depreciation of the currency, and current account surpluses at the expense of their partners who would be in deficit. But, even in this case, there would be nothing, except perhaps the 'power of ideas' and/or 'vested interests' (Keynes, 1936), to prevent the deficit nations also reversing their stance and sharing in a general prosperity. In our view, the preservation of a certain room to manoeuvre for national economies would be a safer course at this juncture than anything resembling world government.

Such a position does not, however, rule out a wide variety of more limited suggestions for reform and restructuring for the existing IFIs, or even the introduction of new IFIs. For example, even in a managed float environment there is a case for increasing the role of an international reserve asset issued by an enhanced/reformed IMF. This would be primarily important from the point of view of the liquidity of the system, and dealing with crisis situations, rather than exchange rate management as such.

Alternative models of global central banking

There are clearly a number of different ideas of what an institution such as a WCB should look like, and several detailed individual reform proposals. It is not possible to do justice to all the different potential variants in a short chapter. However, the different models of global central banking can at least be grouped into three broad categories for the purposes of discussion. One which immediately comes to mind at the present time is something analogous to the European 'single currency', but on a global scale. That is, a world currency managed by a WCB similarly constituted to the proposed European Central Bank (ECB), and conducting monetary policy as if it were a national central bank, except that its jurisdiction would not be coterminous with a single territory under one government. However, given the controversy over the implementation of the European proposals even in the more restricted regional context, it seems unlikely that proposals for a world currency are a practical option at this stage.

Possibly more realistic are various proposals drawing their original inspiration from the plans which were on the table during World War II in the negotiations leading up to the establishment of the Bretton Woods system; for example the 'Keynes Plan' for an International Clearing Union (ICU), or the rival 'White Plan' on which the Bretton Woods settlement was actually based.[3] In other words, the second broad category of WCB models are those seeking to adapt something along the lines of the ICU concept to the circumstances and conditions of the present day. These would involve an ICU, possibly issuing an international currency for use as a numeraire in balance of payments settlement, fixed but adjustable exchange rates between the major players, and a set of rules, which could possibly include capital controls of some kind, designed to ensure the smooth operation of the system. There are obviously a number of possible variants on this outline and various strategic choices to be made in the design of such a system, to be discussed in more detail below. For example, it is possible in principle to separate or 'de-couple' a reserve creating or issuing function from the particular exchange rate regime. In other words, advocating an international currency for use as a numeraire in balance of payments settlement would be compatible with either a Bretton Woods-type system with a fixed but adjustable peg, a crawling peg, or a managed float system.

The final WCB model is not so much a plan, as a description of what has frequently occurred during the history of the IMS. This is the growth of a 'hegemonic' system of relationships between international financial networks (Eichengreen, 1989; Gray, 1992). The currency of one powerful nation in the world economy emerges as essentially a world money. The central bank of the hegemon effectively becomes the world central bank and its liabilities become the world standard of value and ultimate means of payment. The monetary policy of this central bank sets the tone for world monetary policy as well as domestic monetary policy. Obvious examples would be the role of the Bank of England and the pound sterling during the nineteenth and early twentieth centuries, and that of the Federal Reserve Board and the US dollar in the mid-twentieth century. In more recent years, the dominance of the German Bundesbank over the European Monetary System (EMS) during the 1980s and early 1990s provides an example of a hegemonic system at a more restricted (regional) level. Experience suggests that the emergence of world or regional 'monocentres', to use Hicks's (1982, 1989) expression, is based on fairly crude indicators of national economic success. Basically, a country seems to be able to claim a leading position for its central bank if over time it has built up a dominating net credit position. Whether or not the resulting system is successful clearly depends on the policies which the officials of the hegemonic central bank pursue. For example, it could be argued that the relative prosperity of the quarter-of-a-century after World War II was facilitated by the expansionary instincts of the US policy authorities during this period, particularly as exemplified by the European Recovery Plan, whereas in more recent times, the Bundesbank has spread deflationary pressure across Europe.

In the context of the present argument, it is an extremely important issue whether or not the relative economic prosperity of the Bretton Woods era was due to the detailed planning and successful implementation of the treaty, in terms of both the operating rules and the IFIs which were created, or rather due to historical circumstances which would include the particular set of policies pursued by the major player, the USA. Hicks (1986, 22–23) was in no doubt. In searching for the explanatory factors regarding economic performance down to the early 1970s, he remarks:

> The first step . . . is to recognise that Bretton Woods, the IMF, and all that, was largely a facade. The reality behind it was the US dollar. It was perfectly obvious, in the 1950s, much more than it had been in the 1920s, that America was the superpower, not only in the political, but also in the financial world . . . it came about without anyone having said that it should come about that the dollar became the international currency . . . the dollar became the centre of the world monetary system, the IMF being no more than one of the routes by which . . . [other] . . . currencies . . . were converted into dollars.

Hicks (1986, 23) then goes on to point out the main way in which the system differed from previous international financial regimes:

> [w]hat made a difference was a general feeling, which in former days had hardly existed, that the government of each nation had a responsibility, not only . . . for maintaining the value of its money but also for maintaining . . . the volume of employment. These . . . responsibilities could . . . clash; but . . . on the whole . . . in the Bretton Woods period . . . they balanced each other.

In the early postwar period, fiscal transfers to Europe and Japan from the USA became the chief means of keeping the system from going under. The USA, which had been reluctant to accept the obligations of chief creditor nation in Keynes's ICU plan, went well beyond its formal IMF obligations. It provided enormous liquidity for the IMS through the Marshall Plan for Europe and the Dodge Plan for Japan. One of the functions of the Marshall Plan was to underwrite the European Payments Union (EPU) that became the instrument for restored convertibility of the key European currencies. The salient point here is that it was the change in climate or economic philosophy, particularly in the USA, rather than the detailed rules and regulations set out in the international treaty, which proved decisive.

The majority of contemporary reform proposals nonetheless have focused on the question of institutional reform, frequently involving the creation of some form of clearing union as in Keynes, and also often stressing the importance of exchange rate stability. In summarizing a number of the proposals, Dow (1997) has argued that:

> the preferred Post Keynesian option is to design an international money, for which a global agency acts as a central bank; that money's attributes must be such as to make it the preferred money, relative to national currencies.

Davidson (1991, 1994, 1996) has put forward a detailed set of proposals, very much in the tradition of the ICU, which involves the creation of a unionized monetary system (UMS), in which national currencies are locked together via fixed exchange rates. There would also be an international clearing agency (ICA) to clear net balances between countries in terms of an international money clearing unit (IMCU), which would be 'money' only for these purposes. The exchange rates would be fixed in terms of the IMCU, but, as under Bretton Woods, they would be adjustable if unit costs in the different countries got too far out of line.

Grieve Smith (1997) put forward a 'ten-point plan', amongst the key features of which would be a new managed exchange rate regime, in which changes in parities should be 'relatively small and frequent' (1997, 221–22) rather than the traumatic political crises they have often been in the past, and also the establishment of a new international stabilization fund (IFS) with very large resources and a mandate to intervene automatically to support agreed-upon parities when necessary. Another important aspect would be strong measures to curb speculative capital movements involving both taxation; for example, variants of the famous 'Tobin tax' (Tobin, 1978), and the international regulation and supervision of financial institutions.

So the question of the correct institutional design remains very much on the agenda, with a crucial question being whether any or all of the suggested schemes would work out in practice as they would on paper.

Money and economic governance

The issue which ultimately lies behind disagreements over the appropriate financial architecture, whether on a national or international scale, is, of course, the relationship between money and power. In the case of a Maastricht-type treaty for the world as a whole, and certainly in the case of the hegemonic systems which arose in the past, the nature of the power relationships, and where power finally resides, would perhaps be fairly obvious. It must be stressed, however, that some issues must inevitably arise in the establishment of a new ICU, ICA, or ISF, or whatever acronym is finally applied to a new global agency. Perhaps, as Hicks has suggested, the IMF under Bretton Woods was a facade, concealing the reality of US domination. However, any new agency, assuming that it is to have the resources required to perform the job expected of it, that is, to maintain a regime of reasonably stable parities, achieve symmetry in balance of payments adjustment, and curb speculation, must inevitably dominate world monetary policy. As in historical cases of hegemonic systems, the WCB would be effectively setting the tone for global interest rates, and in the final analysis determining the pace of expansion of the system as a whole.

In the historic discussions about Bretton Woods, now more than half-a-century ago, it seems that the issue of responsibility for global monetary policy was not squarely addressed. It hovered on the edge of the discussions.[4] The emphasis was primarily on symmetry, the achievement of orderly balance of payments adjustment and so on, and not the overall direction of the system. Certainly a major part of the emphasis on symmetry was to avoid the deflationary bias of earlier systems such as the gold standard, in which all the burden of adjustment was placed on debtor rather than creditor nations. This found final expression in the famous 'scarce currency clause' of the Bretton Woods agreement.[5] Whether or not a deflationary bias should be replaced with an expansionary bias was left implicit. In fact, Keynes (1944; 1980, 16–19) explicitly defended the final Bretton Woods agreement precisely on the grounds that it preserved the ability of the various national authorities to pursue independent 'Keynesian' polices. In a speech to the House of Lords in 1944, he argued as follows:

> We are determined that, in future, the external value of sterling shall conform to its internal value as set by our own domestic policies and not the other way around. Secondly, we intend to retain control of our domestic rate of interest so that we can keep it as low as suits our own purposes . . . Thirdly, while

we intend to prevent inflation at home, we will not accept deflation at the dictate of influences from outside . . .

Have those responsible for the monetary proposals been sufficiently careful to preserve these principles from the possibility of interference? I hope your Lordships will trust me not to have turned my back on all I have fought for . . .

[I]t is above all as providing an international framework for the new ideas and techniques associated with the policy of full employment that these proposals are not least to be welcomed.

It should be remembered that at this time the continuation of extensive capital controls was taken for granted, but nonetheless there are grounds for questioning whether Keynes's defence was strictly accurate. It may be that Keynes expected more from the IMF than it was capable of delivering without additional support from the USA through the Marshall Plan. As mentioned, it turned out that under Bretton Woods there was indeed something approaching a global monetary policy, run not by the IMF but by the US Fed, and in a sense it was fortuitous that this did contribute to the relative prosperity of the post-World War II era.

It should be stressed that most of the newer proposals for reviving Bretton Woods, as discussed in the previous section, do not have these *lacunae* and do explicitly address the issue of the restoration of global full employment. However, there remains the issue of whether international bureaucracies, once created, will continue to play the part set out for them.

Interestingly enough, the question of the relationship between money and economic governance has been explicitly addressed in the recent revival of interest in the chartalist or 'state money' approach in the closed economy context.[6] For example, Wray (1997, 28) argues that:

[I]f a government can create at will the money that the public willingly offers goods and services to obtain, then . . . spending is never constrained by narrow 'financing' decisions.

The implication is that, with chartalist money, a wide variety of public policy initiatives can be undertaken. However, the corollary for international financial arrangements has not as yet been fully explored.

The power of the international bureaucracies

If we were to apply strictly 'utilitarian' concepts to questions of international finance and the global economy, then concepts such as monetary sovereignty or independence would presumably have no real status as such. They would be only useful or necessary if they contributed to achieving some generally desired result defined in other terms. What constitutes a desirable end differs also, according to political ideological, social and theoretical perspective of those making the judgements. For example, from a broadly 'Keynesian' point of view, desirable outcomes might consist of full employment, sustainable growth, a more equitable income distribution and so on, whereas neo-conservatives might regard price stability or balanced budgets as more-or-less desirable ends in themselves.

This difference in objectives does perhaps explain why the advocacy of alternative international financial arrangements, global institutions, and exchange rate regimes, frequently seems to cut across party lines. To take one example, advocacy of 'irrevocably fixed' exchange rate regimes in the context of the ERM (exchange rate mechanism) of the EMS (European monetary system) in the late 1980s and early 1990s was very clearly associated with a neo-conservative policy agenda. Similar remarks would also apply to the contemporary project of the single currency in Europe, or EMU. Clearly, the Maastricht Treaty took a Bundesbank-inspired stance with its criteria for admission to EMU. Price stability is the key consideration in terms of limits for debt and deficits as a percentage of GDP, interest rate convergence, and exchange rate stability, as opposed to goals for economic growth or employment.

On the other hand, as detailed above, many Keynesians or post-Keynesians also favour fixed exchange rate regimes, institutional reform such as the establishment of a WCB, and the detailed regulation of international financial markets, albeit with very different ultimate objectives in mind.[7] At one level, then, the point at issue is not so much the desirability of particular exchange rate regimes, particular institutional arrangements, and the drafting of formal regulations *per se*, but the actual conduct of policy by those who will eventually be responsible for making the decisions. This, in turn largely depends upon 'the theory of the economy' (Eatwell, 1996, 33) which those policy-makers hold.

It seems to us, therefore, that there are two general arguments for retaining as much scope as possible for independent national policy-making in the current global economic environment and contemporary political circumstances. The first is the issue of democratic accountability. From this point of view, there is clearly a case for aligning the responsibility for economic decision-making as closely as possible with existing political arrangements. The deficiencies of the proposed European EMU on this score have been so frequently discussed as to require little further comment. International institutions, generally, have a tendency to be lacking in this respect, as illustrated by many of the commentaries on the role of the IMF in the response to the currency crises in Asia at the end of 1997.

The second argument, which also seems to carry a good deal of weight in the contemporary social, economic, and political climate, is the potential deflationary bias of international bureaucracies in practice, regardless of the specifics of the charter or treaty by which they are set up. Keynes, after all, was one of the original architects of the IMF, but no-one would argue that the contemporary institution which bears that name is particularly imbued with the Keynesian spirit. The point is that contemporary economic and political orthodoxy is such that the international bureaucrats who would be appointed to administer any new global economic and financial institutions would almost certainly do so in a manner informed by neo-conservative economic theory, and possibly also by neo-conservative political ideology. In our view, this would be unlikely to produce desirable economic outcomes.

It cannot, of course, be claimed that independent national policy-making would *necessarily* be an improvement over the internationalist solution in this respect. This will depend on the biases, interests, and competencies of the national policy-makers themselves. For example, the inferior economic performance of Canada relative to the USA since the late 1980s, in spite of formal free trade arrangements such as CUFTA (the Canada–US Free Trade Agreement) and NAFTA (the North American Free Trade Area) is an obvious recent illustration. The Canadian difficulties were arguably directly related to the far more vigorous pursuit of 'zero inflation' by the Bank of Canada after 1988 than its American counterpart (Smithin, 1996).[8] Japanese macroeconomic policy at the time of writing provides another example. In spite of a strong possibility of a prolonged recession or even a deflationary period, the government is reluctant to see any significant increase in its deficit.

Nonetheless, in the long run we would argue that it is almost always in the national interest to possess a potential escape route from the strait-jacket that deflationary pressures applied at the national or regional level could become.[9] In the case of Canada, monetary (interest rate) policy was ultimately altered in the later 1990s, and most likely fiscal policy will be changed in Japan, especially since even the Governor of the Bank of Japan has begun to publicly chastise the government for its rigid stance, and some commentators have likened the present Japanese government to that of the Hoover Administration in the USA during the Great Depression.

It is significant that the original biographer of Keynes, Harrod (1951), made a very similar type of argument to the above in explaining Keynes's own changes of outlook on questions of international financial policy over the course of his lifetime. On the one hand, in his 1920s contributions Keynes certainly appeared to be an advocate of national monetary sovereignty (Smithin and Wolf, 1993). Similarly, when Britain was forced to leave the gold standard and float the pound in 1931, he was 'exuberant' (Meltzer, 1988, 229). However, by the late 1940s Keynes seemed to have moved toward a much more internationalist orientation. As mentioned, he was the principal author of the official British proposals for an ICU in 1943, and was one of the main negotiators on the British side in the discussions leading up to the Bretton Woods agreement of 1944. Harrod (1951, 525) explains the change of heart as follows:

> His instincts were for international co-operation. If these instincts had been dormant before the war, that was because such co-operation seemed impracticable; the internationalists tended to be those who had not accepted Keynesian economics, and to hand international arrangements over to them would be fatal . . . but was the world changing now?

As explained by Smithin and Wolf (1993), it is arguable that one of the main problems with an internationalist solution today is that the conventional wisdom on economic policy issues once again reflects similar attitudes to those prevailing in the 1920s and 1930s. From this point of view the world has changed back again.

Is monetary sovereignty an option in the contemporary global economy?

Whether or not an independent policy is desirable, it will clearly also be questioned in the contemporary global environment whether or not such a stance is even feasible. If not, then much of the preceding discussion would evidently be moot. An argument frequently aired in both the popular and financial press these days is that it is now almost completely anachronistic for the domestic monetary authorities to attempt to influence economic events in their own jurisdictions. The argument is that in the modern world they are more or less completely at the mercy of capricious worldwide economic forces, including the massive speculative movements of capital discussed above, leaving little choice but to conform to whatever international market forces dictate. In other words, the structural changes in the world economy at the end of the twentieth century have made the very idea of separate monetary systems and the nationally based conduct of macroeconomic policy somehow obsolete and unviable. The global capital market supposedly undermines any attempt by individual jurisdictions at an independent policy.

We argue, however, that this kind of argument is overly deterministic and misinterprets the real nature of the changes that have taken place. It is true, of course, that the globalization of financial markets, and that absence of any effective international regulation of capital flows, does move the world closer and closer to a situation of technically perfect capital mobility, as in the textbooks. However, as long as there are separate national monetary systems and exchange rates are potentially free to move, then the purely technical changes in themselves are unlikely to induce players in the financial markets, including speculators, to treat differently denominated financial assets as perfect substitutes. But it is the latter requirement, perfect asset substitutability, which would be required for the domestic authorities to legitimately claim that they have 'no choice' whenever interest rates are raised. Much more frequently such episodes are literally a matter of choice, the alternative being simply to let the exchange rate depreciate.

The real message of the increased capital mobility of recent years is simply to make dramatically clear, as highlighted earlier, the ultimate dominance of the capital account over the current account. This may certainly be regarded as an undesirable and uncomfortable development for all sorts of reasons. However, it does not follow logically from this that national policy-makers possess no leverage over domestic interest rates, relative to foreign rates, whereby they may attempt to influence or control the capital flows, or that they should give up whatever leverage that they still do possess. Indeed, the scenario outlined here may be interpreted as rather an argument for giving much more careful thought than hitherto about what a sensible monetary policy might be in each jurisdiction, and to devise a new set of principles for monetary policy in the new environment. This is a quite different response than abandoning control of the remaining monetary levers either to a WCB, some other form of international bureaucracy, or to the central bank of some other nation.

In work which is relevant to the argument, Paraskevopoulos, Paschakis, and Smithin (1996) and Paschakis and Smithin (1998) have shown that theoretically a mechanism does exist whereby the small and 'medium-sized' open economy can achieve monetary sovereignty even in modern conditions with free capital mobility. These results are also supported, in the context of a different theoretical model, in a recent simulation exercise by Godley (1996). The argument of the former authors rests on the important distinction between capital flight and capital outflow, and the potentially beneficial impact of an increase in a nation's foreign credit position on the risk premium demanded by foreign investors in order to hold assets denominated in the domestic currency. They show that if a small economy does succeed in (for example) depressing real interest rates to lower levels than those prevailing elsewhere then the end result, in addition to the beneficial impact of an increase in output and employment, is both a real depreciation of the currency and an increase in the real net foreign credit position, as standard economic reasoning might predict. However, the dynamic process involved is not necessarily unstable, as seems to be the implicit assumption of those who argue that any sustained cheap money policy will inevitably lead to a collapse of the currency. In other words, the relevant portfolio adjustments eventually come to an end, as the players in the financial markets adjust to the new situation. This conclusion is shown to hold even in modern conditions with essentially no barriers to capital mobility, except the basic condition that promises-to-pay denominated in different currencies are not perfect substitutes. The implied increase in the foreign credit position may actually have a beneficial impact on the risk premium, and it is this which enables the gap between foreign and domestic real interest rates to be maintained.

Although lower domestic real interest rates do lead to capital outflow and a real depreciation of the currency, the point is that this is not necessarily a bad thing from the point of view of the 'credit rating' of the economy. If the capital outflow does not actually become capital flight, in which both the capitalists and their funds decamp, the domestic economy experiencing capital outflow is actually building up a net credit position with the rest of the world which will eventually generate a future flow of interest and dividend payments to domestic residents. To the extent that the promises to pay of creditor nations are regarded as more trustworthy and reliable than those of debtors (which is usually assumed to be the case), this may improve the international status of the currency rather than damage it. If low real interest rates are also good for output and employment, there may therefore be a 'virtuous cycle' in nations with a low (but still positive) cost of capital.

The arguments naturally pre-suppose a jurisdiction with sufficient credit to be able to issue sovereign debt in its own currency, and also that it is possible to demonstrate at least saddlepoint stability in the dynamic processes for real exchange rates and debt/GDP ratios (Paschakis and Smithin, 1998). With these caveats, however, the suggested mechanism does potentially repair what has traditionally been regarded as a flaw in the typical Keynesian argument in favour of cheap money and expansionary policy generally. For example, Meltzer (1988, 202) criticized Keynes's (1936, 376) famous 'euthanasia of the rentier' because '. . . Keynes never mentions capital flight and does not explain how a single country can drive the rate of interest to zero'. One response to this is to suggest that the Keynesian analysis is meant to apply to the world economy as a whole (in which case, something like a WCB would be needed to enforce it). Another would be that Keynes was assuming that comprehensive capital controls would be in place. The above analysis, however, suggests that even a relatively small player may be able to implement 'Keynesian' policies, as long as the authorities retain control over their own currency, even in modern conditions with an extremely high degree of capital mobility. In effect, a judicious monetary policy is able to manipulate the risk premium on assets denominated in the domestic currency. The existence of a risk premium to be manipulated, however, does imply the continued existence of separate monetary systems, and also exchange rates which are potentially free to change, even if they are stable in practice and not actually *expected* to change. Participation as a member nation in an international monetary system with fixed exchange rates, and in which world monetary policy is effectively dictated by a WCB obviously eliminates this possibility, and therefore does imply a considerable sacrifice in terms of policy manoeuvrability. The advantages of a more structured system would need to be very great to offset this drawback.

The potential for limited international reserve creation by an enhanced IMF

It should perhaps be stressed, again, that the above analysis does not preclude advocacy of some reform and re-structuring of existing IFIs. For example, an enhanced and reformed IMF could play an important role in terms of the creation, from time to time, and as needed, of new international reserve assets. This is not really dependent on the nature of the exchange rate regime. Under a managed float, there can still be crisis situations, and/or periods when there is agreement that global liquidity is inadequate. There are several scenarios in which it might be agreed that it would be better for an IFI to create such reserves rather than relying on the balance of payments deficits of some of the players to create reserves. Whereas IMF-created Special Drawing Rights (SDRs), distributed in the 1970s and 1980s, constitute only about 2 per cent of the world's non-gold reserves, the potential certainly exists for them to play an increased role. However, they would not become the 'principal reserve asset' as originally envisaged by the IMF. Unlike the more powerful automatic reserve (Bancor) system under the Keynes plan for an ICU, which has both its upside and its downside in terms of the power structure of the global economy, a limited safety valve in terms of potential SDR creation (perhaps with a more suitable title) would provide benefits at relatively little political or economic cost.

Concluding remarks

The present monetary system is not hegemonic. Unlike the earlier gold standard or the Bretton Woods system, there is no overwhelmingly dominant player. Although the USA is clearly the leading economic power, it shares the stage with Germany/the EU and Japan. With three key players, and in combination with the other structural changes in the global economy discussed above, the chances for international monetary instability are increased. Certainly, the present system of managed floating rates among the major currencies has been anything but stable, and has been witness to large and frequent changes in both nominal and real exchange rates.

One potential solution, which suggests itself to many, is the establishment of a new IFI, by agreement among the major players, which would serve as something approaching a World Central Bank (WCB). Usually, the suggestion has been that the financial architecture should include a relatively fixed exchange rate regime, and also some measures to curb or limit the freedom of capital movements. While not rejecting the notion of reform and restructuring of the existing IFIs, in particular in the area of the provision of additional reserves (along the lines of SDRs and Bancor) when a consensus is reached that world liquidity needs to be boosted, this chapter has argued that fixed exchange rates are not the answer. Clearly, *no* exchange rate regime will have any chance of success if the appropriate macroeconomic policies are not followed. However, the chances for success in individual jurisdictions are strengthened when countries do not feel obligated to stick too long to either overvalued or undervalued rates.

We have argued that small and medium-sized open economies can achieve some degree of monetary sovereignty even in modern conditions with free capital mobility. However, the mechanisms which might enable them to do this do depend on the continued existence of independent national monetary systems and exchange rates which are potentially free to move. In our view the preservation of national monetary sovereignty is desirable, both from the point of view of democratic accountability and also concerns about the likely deflationary bias of international bureaucracies in today's political and social environment.

There are, of course, strong arguments for direct measures to limit the mobility of capital, but, in practice, at least for relations between the advanced industrial nations, we are somewhat sceptical of the potential for 'putting the genie back in the bottle' in contemporary conditions, either via a 'Tobin tax' or other methods. But note also that if the individual jurisdictions can indeed take steps to 'manage' the system and retain some degree of monetary sovereignty in the sense discussed above (e.g., by judicious interest rate policy), the costs of increased capital mobility *per se* may not be as great as is usually assumed; certainly not as compared with the deliberate pursuit of deflationary macroeconomic policies either by individual jurisdictions or internationally. The argument, however, might need to be modified in the case of developing economies, where the authorities, and particularly financial institutions, do have special problems in dealing with footloose capital. In these cases, regulation or taxation of capital flows, supported or orchestrated by the international community, may well be feasible and would perform a useful function.

Notes

We would like to thank the editors, John Grieve Smith and Jonathan Michie, for several comments and suggestions which have improved the paper.

1 That is 'the wicked Ministers of Finance' (1924, 187).
2 See 'A survey of the world economy', *The Economist*, September 19, 1992.
3 Keynes was the principal author of proposals put forward by the British government in Cmd 6437, *Proposals for an International Clearing Union*, London: HMSO, 1943. Harry Dexter White was the leading negotiator for the USA.
4 This phrase is due to John Grieve Smith in personal correspondence with the authors dated December 11, 1997.
5 As is well known, this clause was never invoked in practice.
6 Keynes, incidentally, fully subscribed to this view. See *A Treatise on Money*, vol. 1, (1930, 3–9).
7 Verengo (1998) has put forward a theoretical model which explains and defends this position.
8 The case could be made that the Canadian 'business cycle' since the late 1980s has actually been far more out of phase with that of the USA than at any time in previous history. This is in spite of ongoing globalization and moves towards continental free trade.
9 See, for example, Temin's (1989) discussion of the negative impact of attempts to restore the gold standard in the inter-war period.

References

Davidson, P. (1991), 'What international payments scheme would Keynes have suggested for the twenty-first century?'. In *Economic Problems of the 1990s: Europe, the Developing Countries, and the United States*, edited by P. Davidson and J. Kregel, Aldershot: Edward Elgar, 85–104.

Davidson, P. (1994), *Post Keynesian Macroeconomic Theory: A Foundation for Successful Economic Policies for the Twenty-First Century*, Aldershot: Edward Elgar.

Davidson, P. (1996), 'Reforming the international payments system'. In *US Trade Policy and Global Growth: New Directions in the International Economy*, edited by R.A. Blecker, Armonk, New York: M.E. Sharpe, 215–36.

Dow, S.C. (1997), 'International liquidity preference and endogenous credit creation'. In *Foundations of International Economics: A Post Keynesian Analysis*, edited by J.T. Harvey and J. Deprez, London: Routledge.

Eatwell, J. (1996), 'International capital liberalization: the record', CEPA Working Paper no. 1, New School for Social Research, August.

Eichengreen, B. (1989), 'Hegemonic stability theories of the international monetary system'. In *Can Nations Agree?*, edited by R.N. Cooper, Washington, DC: The Brookings Institution.

Godley, W. (1996), 'A simple model of the whole world with free trade, free capital movements, and floating exchange rates', mimeo, Jerome Levy Economics Institute.

Gray, H.P. (1992), 'Why a hegemonic system works better', mimeo, Rensselaer Polytechnic Institute.

Grieve Smith, J. (1997), *Full Employment: A Pledge Betrayed*, London: Macmillan.

Harrod, R. (1951), *The Life of John Maynard Keynes*. New York: W.W. Norton & Company.

HM Treasury (1943), *Proposals for an International Clearing Union*, Cmd 6437, London: HMSO.

Hicks, J.R. (1982), 'The credit economy'. In *Money, Interest and Wages: Collected Essays on Economic Theory*, vol. 2, Oxford: Basil Blackwell, 266–75.

Hicks, J.R. (1986), 'Managing without money?'. In *Chung-Hua Series of Lectures by Invited Eminent Economists*, no. 11, Tapei: Academia Sinica, 19–29.

Hicks, J.R. (1989), *A Market Theory of Money*, Oxford: Oxford University Press.

Keynes, J.M. (1924), *Monetary Reform*, New York: Harcourt, Brace & Company. (US edition of *A Tract on Monetary Reform*).

Keynes, J.M. (1930), *A Treatise on Money*, vol. 1, *The Pure Theory of Money*, London: Macmillan.

Keynes, J.M. (1936), *The General Theory of Employment, Interest and Money*, London: Macmillan.

Keynes, J.M. ([1944], 1980), *The Collected Writings of John Maynard Keynes*, vol. XXVI, *Activities 1941–46: Shaping the Post-War World: Reparations and Bretton Woods*, edited by D. Moggridge, London: Macmillan for the Royal Economic Society.

McQuaig, L. (1998), *The Cult of Impotence: Selling the Myth of Powerlessness in the Global Economy*, Toronto: Viking.

Meltzer, A.H. (1988), *Keynes's Monetary Theory: A Different Interpretation*, Cambridge: Cambridge University Press.

Paraskevopoulos, C.C. and J.N. Smithin (1998), 'Economic and financial integration: implications for nationally-based public policy'. In *Global Trading Arrangements in Transition*, edited by C.C. Paraskevopoulos, Aldershot: Edward Elgar, 3–10.

Paraskevopoulos, C.C., J. Paschakis and J.N. Smithin (1996), 'Is monetary sovereignty an option for the small open economy?', *North American Journal of Economics and Finance*, 7, 1, Spring, 5–18.

Paschakis, J. and J.N. Smithin (1998), 'Exchange risk and the supply side effect of real exchange rate changes', *Journal of Macroeconomics*, 20, forthcoming.

Smithin, J.N. (1996), 'Real interest rates, inflation and unemployment'. In *The Unemployment Crisis: All for Nought?*, edited by B. MacLean and L. Osberg, Montreal and Kingston: McGill-Queen's University Press, 39–55.

Smithin, J.N. (1998), 'Money and national sovereignty in the global economy', mimeo, York University.

Smithin, J.N. and B.M. Wolf (1993), 'What would be a "Keynesian" approach to currency and exchange rate issues?', *Review of Political Economy*, 5, 3, July, 365–83.

Temin, P. (1989), *Lessons from the Great Depression*, Cambridge, MA: MIT Press.

Tobin, J. (1978), 'A proposal for international monetary reform', *Eastern Economic Journal*, 4, 3–4, 153–59.

Verengo, M. (1998), 'A Post-Keynesian model of exchange rate determination', mimeo, New School for Social Research.

Wray, L.R. (1997), 'Government as employer of last resort: full employment without inflation', Working Paper no. 213, Jerome Levy Economics Institute, November.

11 A new Bretton Woods

Reforming the global financial system

John Grieve Smith

Introduction

The growing instability of the world financial system has been highlighted by the 1997 Asian crisis. It is now over fifty years since the last comprehensive attempt to draw up a blueprint for a stable international economic regime. The Bretton Woods Agreement, conceived in wartime but looking forward to the problems of the post-war world, provided a relatively successful framework for world trade and payments for a quarter of a century. But the break-up of the post-war fixed exchange rate system and financial globalisation mean that a new international system is well overdue. The two main Bretton Woods institutions (the IMF and the World Bank) have survived and partially adapted to new circumstances; and a series of piecemeal agreements on trade and investment have established a new liberal trade and payments regime. But there has been no comprehensive attempt to establish a structure of international economic institutions and rules appropriate to current conditions. As a consequence the world economy is threatened by dangerous disruption with untold potential for damaging individual lives and democratic institutions. This is a danger not just for vulnerable developing countries, but also for the advanced industrial economies in Europe and North America whose industrial strength has gone hand in hand with the growth of complex and delicate financial inter-relationships.

There is an urgent need to identify the main problems that the international payments system faces as it enters the new millennium, and consider the changes needed in the policies and structure of international institutions to cope with them. In doing so, it is important to ask what lessons should be drawn from the Asian crisis, while not falling into the trap of assuming that future crises will necessarily follow the same pattern. Financial crises generally have multiple causes; and whilst most of these factors continually reappear, their relative importance varies from case to case. For example, hitherto post-war exchange rate crises in the industrialised economies have not (at any rate, not to such a significant extent) involved the solvency problems which have been a major feature of the Asian crisis. The current crisis has given a new perspective to people's perception of global payments problems, because it involves the re-emergence of many of the features of pre-war crises relating to the solvency of banks and firms.

In looking at the problems and possible solutions to which any new agreement should be directed, the best starting point is still Bretton Woods. Its fixed exchange rate regime, combined with the facility for countries to borrow from the IMF, was an attempt to restore the stability of the gold standard without its deflationary bias. What was fortuitous was that wartime conditions had led to the general imposition of exchange controls on both current and capital transactions, so that in advocating the continuance of controls over *capital* movements Keynes did not have to argue for the imposition of new restrictions which would have been strongly resisted by financial interests: he could start from the *status quo*. What Bretton Woods did not solve, or the ERM after it, was the problem of changing rates when necessary. Finance ministers were effectively committing political suicide if they devalued after having been forced to assert that there would be no change in parity. In addition, larger countries, or groupings like the ERM, face the difficulty that changes in their rates are effectively a matter of *mutual* adjustment, which can only be achieved by multilateral agreement.

That is an eternal problem. The new problem to emerge (or rather re-emerge) in recent years has stemmed from the liberalisation of capital movements combined with the globalisation of financial markets, which have made possible enormous waves of speculation to support or attack individual currencies. As Keynes put it, inter-war experience suggested that without controls on capital movements 'Loose funds may sweep round the world disorganising all steady business' (Keynes, 1941). This is a more fundamental weakness of the international economy than the prudential weaknesses of firms and banks in developing countries. Without capital liberalisation, they would not be borrowing so heavily abroad, and when confidence weakened foreign lenders would not be able to withdraw their support so speedily. This again is closely linked to the problem of the exchange rate regime: both currencies with fixed rates and those which were floating have been in difficulties or have depreciated drastically. Falling exchange rates can cause critical problems for institutions or firms in developing countries which have borrowed through instruments denominated in foreign currencies, such as the dollar, in order to make such loans more attractive to lenders. When their currencies depreciate the additional interest burden can threaten their solvency. But any attempt by individual banks or firms to reduce this risk by borrowing short-term leads to the additional danger of not being able to renew the loans when they fall due. In many cases this is now a more important consequence of devaluation than the effects on the trade balance.

The Asian crisis

Short-term borrowing in foreign currencies was clearly a major factor in the 1997 Asian crisis. Previous chapters show that the main factors behind the crisis are recurring ones, which unless tackled soon are likely to lead to further, and possibly greater, upsets. At one extreme it can be seen as a distinctively 1990s phenomenon due to the recent liberalisation of private capital movements and the globalisation of capital markets. At the other, it can be seen as a reversion to a long series of international financial crises going back to the nineteenth century and beyond. Certainly, in so far as the crisis was associated with a speculative boom and collapse in asset prices, there are many historical parallels, from the South Sea Bubble to the 1929 Wall Street Crash. The crisis led to familiar scenarios of meetings of major creditors, agreements to roll-over debt and governments or central banks acting as lenders of last resort. There was also something depressingly familiar in the pressure on governments concerned to take deflationary action 'to restore confidence' irrespective of the needs of their internal economies. What is different from the pre-World War II era is the fact that some of the structural changes leading to crisis, in particular financial liberalisation, had been newly imposed on the countries concerned by international agreements; and an international organisation, the IMF, is providing assistance on terms involving far-reaching conditions, both as regards economic policy and the structure of the economy (e.g. privatisation).

The foreign exchange crisis in Asia may be said to have formally started on 15 May 1997 when Thailand introduced capital and exchange controls in an effort to maintain its exchange rate peg to the dollar. The baht had been subject to speculative attacks during 1996 and in January and early February 1997. Thailand was suffering from a large current account deficit, high short-term foreign debt, the collapse of a property price bubble, and a loss of competitiveness resulting in part from the rise in the dollar against the yen.[1] Equity prices had been falling. On 2 July 1997 Thailand abandoned its exchange rate peg and allowed the baht to float, which raised doubts about exchange rates elsewhere in the region. The Philippines had also been maintaining a *de facto* peg to the dollar, and after seeking briefly to defend it, the authorities floated the peso on 11 July 1997. Malaysia came under pressure and the ringgit was allowed to depreciate. In Indonesia the rupiah fell sharply within the intervention band on 21 July and was floated on 14 August. The Singapore dollar and the new Taiwan dollar weakened moderately in July and the Hong Kong dollar came under temporary attack in early August. By mid-October, the baht and rupiah had depreciated by over 30 per cent against the dollar, and the ringgit and peso by over 20 per cent. The Korean won also came under pressure.

In each case the currency had become vulnerable to any interruption or reversal of the inflow of capital. In 1996, Indonesia, Malaysia, the Philippines and Thailand all had sizeable balance of payments deficits, which were more than covered by corresponding large inflows of private capital (see Table 11.1). Korea had a deficit of a similar order just matched by the inflow of private capital: but unlike the others it had a net *outflow* of *direct* investment reflecting large Korean companies' investment in plant abroad. The major component of this inflow was in all cases international bank lending to local banks and firms. 'Large amounts of foreign currency credit were taken on, directly or indirectly by Korean financial institutions to provide finance for Korean enterprises at home and abroad, and many Korean firms took on increasing amounts of short-term foreign currency debt, little of which is thought to have been hedged' (IMF 1997b).

Table 11.1 Deficits and capital inflows in 1996 (% of GDP)

Current account deficit		Net inflow of private investment		
		Direct	*Portfolio*	*Other*[a]
Indonesia	6.3	2.8	0.8	2.7
Korea	4.9	−0.4	2.3	3.0
Malaysia	9.6	5.1	—	4.5
Philippines	9.8	1.6	−0.2	8.5
Thailand	9.3	0.9	0.6	7.7

By mid-1997 foreign bank loans had reached the following figures:

	$ Billion	
	Non-banks	*Total*
Indonesia	37.2	60.3
Korea	26.2	116.8
Malaysia	7.4	32.8
Thailand	13.3	98.9

Sources: IMF, *World Economic Outlook: Interim Assessment*, December 1997; BIS (1997).

Note
a   Including bank loans.

As the crisis developed in the second half of 1997, equity prices throughout the region fell sharply. By December the fall for Asian developing countries as a whole was over 40 per cent. The combined effect of falling stock market prices and currency depreciation led to falls from highs to lows in dollar terms of 89 per cent in Indonesia, 82 per cent in Malaysia and 85 per cent in Thailand. Financial developments in the stock markets and currency markets were linked to a series of solvency crises in financial institutions and industrial companies across the region. In May 1997, Thailand's largest finance company, Finance One, closed along with 15 other cash-strapped finance firms. By December, 56 of the 58 finance companies were permanently shut. In Indonesia 16 banks in difficulties closed at the beginning of November.

Bankruptcies seem to have been a particularly important catalyst in Korea. Whereas the economies of the developing countries in South East Asia could be said to be intrinsically vulnerable to attack, the Korean economy was much more advanced and in industrial terms a major player on the world stage. But the Korean *chaebols* (or conglomerates) had financed their expansion by excessive reliance on short-term foreign loans which left them vulnerable. In January 1997, Hannbo Steel collapsed under $6 billion in foreign debt – the first bankruptcy of a leading conglomerate in a decade. In March another steel company, Sammi, failed. In July, Korea's third largest car maker, Kia, asked for emergency loans and was eventually nationalised after the banks refused additional credit.

One feature of the collapse was an insupportable boom in real estate. Real estate loans accounted for about 25 per cent of outstanding bank loans in Malaysia and the Philippines and 20 per cent in Thailand (World Bank, 1998). In Thailand the stock market index for building and furnishing companies fell from a peak of just below 8,200 in late 1994 to 1,100 in late 1997. Such asset price bubbles made the banking system vulnerable to any downturn in demand.

Lessons of the crisis

The preceding brief account of the crisis up to mid-1998 suggests that the main factor behind it was the volume and nature of the flow of foreign capital to the countries involved. This reflects in turn the liberalisation of capital movements and financial structures generally. The growing volume of foreign borrowing fed on and contributed to asset price bubbles, whose collapse contributed to solvency problems. Short-term capital movements and changes in sentiment led to exchange rate crises and depreciation which in turn accentuated the difficulties of borrowing firms and financial institutions. The structural problems of financial liberalisation and prudential regulation in the various developing countries concerned have much in common and require tackling at both an international and national level. After all, the international pressure on these countries to liberalise their financial systems has been a major element in the crises. The issue now is twofold: how to strengthen prudential regulation and the structure of financial institutions in developing countries; and how to establish an international regime for the flow of private capital which will do more good than harm.

In addition there is the closely related question of devising a more stable exchange rate system, or systems. Both the developing countries and the advanced economies need to find a middle way between (1) the rigidities of fixed or pegged rates, where adjustments become synonymous with crises, and (2) the excessive volatility of freely floating rates. The Asian crisis highlighted the difficulties which arise when smaller countries peg or stabilise their currencies against a major national currency, such as the dollar. Such a tie may involve an unwanted and inappropriate appreciation when the major currency itself appreciates as the dollar did against the yen from mid-1995. The Asian countries involved then lost competitive position *vis-à-vis* Japan, which in certain fields such as electronics was a close industrial rival and their export growth slowed down.

The natural evolution of the yen, rather than the dollar, as an anchor currency for other Asian countries has been held back by its relatively limited international role. About two-thirds of official foreign exchange reserve are still held in dollars and less than 10 per cent in yen. Although the proportion of international securities denominated in dollars has fallen from around two-thirds to one-third in recent years, the rise has been mainly in European currencies with the yen still accounting for less than 15 per cent.[2] In time, however, it could seem natural for European countries to anchor round the euro, Western hemisphere countries around the dollar and Asian countries around the yen.

IMF policy

IMF policies towards countries in difficulties have been heavily criticised both as inappropriate and as going beyond the remit of an international lending agency. In a sense their policy prescriptions merely reflect the predominant ideology of most Western governments with their emphasis on liberalisation, privatisation and deflationary fiscal policies. But apart from the merits of the policies *per se*, there is the more fundamental question as to whether, or how far, an unelected international agency has the right to dictate to a democratic member country the very nature of its economic institutions, such as public or private ownership. Agreement to such a neo-liberal structure is not a condition of membership. Indeed membership of the Bretton Woods organisation originally implied a commitment to achieving full employment. While it would seem reasonable for the Fund to agree with the country concerned a programme of measures to enable it to repay its borrowings, the IMF's prescriptions go very much further than this alone would require.

In the case of the 1997 crisis, the IMF is open to the criticism that it actually helped precipitate the crisis. Jeffrey Sachs alleges that instead of discreetly trying to slow down the flight of creditors and encouraging the major banks to mount a rescue operation, the Fund 'arrived in Thailand in July . . . and deepened the sense of panic not only because of its dire public pronouncements but also because its proposed medicine – high interest rates, budget cuts and immediate bank closures – convinced the markets that Asia indeed was about to enter a severe contraction' (Sachs, 1998). Or, in Joseph Stiglitz's words, 'irrational exuberance' gave way to 'irrational pessimism' (Stiglitz, 1998). The IMF's insistence on closing 'weak' banks encouraged banks to call in their loans. If we are moving into an era where crises are more about confidence and solvency than actual balance of payments deficits, more attention needs to be paid to the potential role of the Fund as a *facilitator* of rescue measures by creditors, if not an actual lender of last resort. (The Fund's extension of credit to central banks does not in itself put them in a position to expand the domestic credit base, but it can provide them with the wherewithal to enable domestic banks to obtain the foreign currency needed to pay off maturing loans.)

Financial regulation

The former head of the IMF Capital Markets and Financial Studies Division has said that one reason why the Fund was caught out by the South East Asian crisis was that while the Fund was monitoring macro-economic developments in the countries concerned it was not paying equal attention to banking developments – although they had previously commented on the precarious nature of the banking situation in some countries.[3]

Although there had been numerous banking crises, particularly in developing countries, in recent years, they had hitherto been more or less successfully contained without major international consequences. At least a dozen severe banking crises (involving losses amounting to 10 per cent or more of GDP) had occurred during the previous 15 years. Indeed, adopting a less demanding definition of a crisis as an exhaustion of all or most of the banking system's capital, there had been as many as 67 such crises since 1980, involving 52 developing countries.[4]

The origins of these crises lay partly in general economic developments and partly in the banking system. Any unforeseen economic developments can affect the borrower's ability to meet the interest costs or repay the loan and the lender's willingness to renew it. In addition to cyclical changes in domestic business conditions, developing countries may be very susceptible to changes in external circumstances, such as commodity prices, exchange rates and international interest rates, all of which may adversely affect both the profitability of the borrowers and the cost of borrowing – loans at variable interest rates denominated in foreign currencies being an outstanding example. Exchange rate-based stabilisation plans in the 1970s and 1980s may have reduced the rate of inflation, but also led exchange rates to appreciate to unrealistic levels, culminating in financial crises and devaluation. Either pegged rates followed by dramatic depreciation, or volatile floating rates, can lead to drastic increases in loan costs denominated in foreign currencies, and also if domestic interest rates are raised drastically, a sharp rise in the cost of loans in the domestic currency. The way in which the present unstable exchange rate regime contributes to banking crises (which then in turn accentuate exchange rate problems) is yet another powerful argument for seeking a new regime offering greater stability whilst leaving scope for undramatic adjustments in rates where needed.

Asset prices

A further major contributor to banking and financial crises is the volatility of asset prices. Unsustainable booms in stock market and property prices lead to drastic falls when the bubble is pricked. The boom phase encourages borrowing, and the subsequent reaction makes repayment difficult. This is partly a domestic problem but also an international one. Rises in asset prices are traditionally fuelled by domestic borrowing, but nowadays an inflow of private capital from abroad frequently accentuates it. This was clearly a factor in Korea, for example. Leveraged speculation in a variety of forms has become a major feature of the recent international bull market. How far it will survive any reversal remains to be seen. These developments pose questions for both national and international policy. Possible conflicts between employment objectives and price stability are a commonly discussed aspect of monetary policy. But attempts to achieve greater asset price stability may also give rise to a further conflict. For example, in the US, Alan Greenspan tried to talk down the boom on Wall Street, but the Fed did not tighten its credit policy to stave off a further rise in asset prices for fear of unnecessarily throttling the continued expansion of output when the current rate of inflation (of current goods and services) was acceptable. Whether or not monetary policy may have been too lax in particular developing countries, there is an endemic problem of trying to avoid asset price inflation whilst maintaining the supply of credit for industry and commerce. Similarly there is a need to find ways of maintaining and stabilising the flow of foreign capital for industrial development, whilst restricting the inflow of speculative capital. This, of course, raises difficult problems of differentiation.

Bank regulation

The third aspect of banking crises concerns the behaviour and regulation of the banks themselves, either in the developing countries themselves or elsewhere. The issues here are: the credit-worthiness of the borrowers and the amount and terms of the loans. These in turn raise questions about the factors affecting banking management: lending to 'connected' borrowers; government influence over the direction of lending; the nature of the incentives under which they operate; the framework of prudential regulation; and disclosure and accounting standards. These have hitherto been regarded as matters for national regulation, subject to some attempt to achieve comparable standards. The key questions now are: (1) the feasibility and nature of possible international standards for banking and other financial regulation; and (2) how to establish effective international co-ordination, including the possibility of a new international regulatory authority or authorities.

A Group of 10 Working Party Report on *Financial Stability in Emerging Market Economics* issued just before the crisis emphasised the need for tighter regulation but saw this as a national responsibility and made no recommendations for any new international authority – apart from urging the Fund and Bank to assume greater roles in this field. The Basle Committee on Banking Supervision published a set of *Core Principles for Effective Banking Supervision* in September 1997. But again it is not clear how national regulators can be made to enforce its 25 Commandments in practice, or whether national regulation on its own is sufficient. The Committee calls on banking supervisors to:

> practise global consolidated supervision over their internationally-active banking organisations, adequately monitoring and applying appropriate prudential norms to all aspects of the business conducted by these banking organisations worldwide, primarily at their foreign branches, joint ventures and subsidiaries. A key component of consolidated supervision is establishing contact and information exchange with the various other supervisors involved, primarily host country supervisory authorities.

Morris Goldstein has argued persuasively for an International Banking Standard (Goldstein, 1997) aimed at reducing the incidence of serious banking crises in developing countries. This would involve both changes in banking structure and regulatory regimes. An international standard would not imply full harmonisation because it would effectively be a *minimum*, with some (particularly developed) countries having more stringent requirements. Indeed Goldstein, himself, argues for a two-level standard. The upper level would probably attract banks and countries more heavily involved in international capital markets, and the basic (transitional) standard would apply to all participants. The signatories would be countries as a whole, although individual banks might be able to claim acknowledgement that they were operating in accord with the higher standard. As Goldstein says:

> To be truly comprehensive an IBS would need to specify guidelines for all the important aspects of banking supervision, including, inter alia: deposit insurance; lender of last resort operations; bank licensing and permissible banking activities; external audits; internal controls and internal audits; information requirements of bank supervisors; public disclosure; limits on large exposures and connected lending; capital adequacy; asset valuation and provisioning; foreign-exchange exposures; on-site banking inspections; legal powers and political independence of bank supervisors; the mix between rules and discretion in the implementation of corrective actions; globally consolidated supervision; cooperation (including exchange of information) between home- and host-country supervisors; and measures to combat money laundering. In addition, one would want to offer some guidance on the relevant infrastructure for good banking, including: interbank and government securities markets; payments, delivery, and settlement systems; and the legal and judicial framework.

The Basle Committee would need to play a leading role in drawing up such a standard, but others would also need to be involved: in particular, international financial institutions, regulatory authorities and banking representatives.

How should compliance with any new international standard be monitored? Goldstein argues that home-country control on its own would be insufficient and domestic controls should be monitored by an international organisation or organisations, such as the IMF and World Bank. This would mean that satisfactory performance in this field would become part of the Fund and Bank's stabilisation and conditionality agreements. Whilst the Fund's ability to prescribe (often inappropriate) economic policies for members which seek its assistance is open to criticism, bank regulation could be a field in which their approach might be appropriate, provided they acquired the necessary expertise. But bank regulation is just one of the tasks which needs to be fitted into a new international governmental structure.

A lender of last resort

In his study of financial crises Kindleberger concluded that there always has to be a lender of last resort, but for prudential reasons it is best if no-one can rely on that in advance (Kindleberger, 1996). This is a neat historical judgement, but no help in planning for the future! There are at least two roles. The first is to *coordinate* the actions of creditors, as the US Treasury appears to have done in the case of Korea.[5] This may lead to repackaging debt, as for example with the issuance of 'Brady bonds'. The second role is actually to provide funds to keep banks and their clients afloat. Do national central banks need the backing of some international facility of last resort, or indeed should there be such a facility for lending directly to major financial institutions in difficulties?

In times of crisis, the original concept of the IMF lending to meet balance of payments deficits *per se* has had to be broadened to include the need to restore confidence by lending enough to offset or reverse any run on the currency. In the case of the Asian crisis, however, there was the additional somewhat cloudy area as to how far it was also providing funds which are in effect assisting the borrowing central bank to deal with the closely related solvency aspect of the crisis. Certainly it was helping to establish the conditions in which other creditors were prepared to help. Should it go further and have some special facility akin to the SDR's for this purpose?

This function is closely allied to that of prudential regulation, rather than currency management, *per se,* although the necessity for it is likely to arise at the same time as the need for intervention to preserve exchange rate stability. The role of international lender of last resort cannot, however, be regarded as that of a world central bank in the purest sense (i.e. analogous to that of a national central bank or a European Central Bank), as long as there are separate currencies and the ability to change the rates between them. Indeed the creation of the ECB underlines the point, because its function is to run a common currency and interest rate policy. Certainly we do not want any greater pressure towards global uniformity of interest rates, when different parts of the world are experiencing different macro-economic conditions. What we do need, however, is to remove any upward bias in world interest rates if we are to try to re-establish a regime based on full employment. Reducing speculative capital movements and thus the need to raise interest rates to meet crises is one way of doing this.

Reforming the exchange rate system

Financial crises apart, the degree of exchange rate instability now resulting from short-term capital movements creates serious problems for industry and employment, and makes nonsense of any idea of the exchange rate as a rational price mechanism for organising foreign trade. The experience of the pound since leaving the ERM in 1992 is a recent example. The effective rate fell by 16 per cent between the third quarter of 1992 and the fourth quarter of 1995 and then rose by 23 per cent between the first quarter of 1996 and the third quarter of 1997. But this was nothing exceptional. The dollar appreciated by 50 per cent in the first half of the 1980s and then fell back to below its original level at the end of the decade, while the yen moved in reverse.[6] Movements of this magnitude have profound effects for the viability of industrial capacity, apart from any effects they may have on countries' balance of payments.

How can we devise a more stable system? Clearly one solution is currency union, as in the EMU. But whilst a single currency obviates exchange rate crises, it is only practical where there is a high degree of integration and convergence of the economies concerned. Monetary union without the creation of a federal government also raises major issues of political principle. It represents an extreme case of regional integration. But while monetary union solves the exchange rate problem between members, there still remains a need to find means of stabilising its relation with other currencies. In addition, in the case of EMU, there is a particular problem of stabilising rates between the euro and those members of the EU who are not in EMU.

Managing rates

In searching for a solution to the problem of exchange rate instability, the objective must be to devise a system which facilitates adjustments in rates in response to fundamental factors such as changes in relative costs or shifts in a country's desirable payments surplus or deficit, but to prevent fluctuations in rates due to variations in short-term capital movements and currency speculation. This points inevitably to some form of managed, as opposed to floating, rates. But managing rates successfully depends on solving two basic problems: securing agreement between the countries concerned on changes in rates; and preventing currencies being driven off their agreed parities or bands by speculative forces.

The problem of agreeing changes in parities in any form of managed system stems from the conflict of interest which arises because such changes will affect countries' relative competitive position and hence their trade. For example, it is not in Germany's interest to agree to a devaluation of the franc relative to the deutschmark for fear of increased competition from French industry. This problem is most acute when large changes are made which substantially alter existing relativities. But reluctance to change rates is, of course, equally a problem in countries which need to devalue. The problem is partly political. Finance ministers and officials, who have been forced to deny that there is any question of devaluation up to the very last moment, inevitably find their reputations damaged when devaluation does eventually take place. In economic terms, although the stimulus to trade is beneficial, there are always fears that devaluation will have an inflationary effect in prices. The resultant tendency to delay devaluation until it is overdue accentuates the role of speculation by creating a situation where selling the currency short becomes virtually a one-way bet.

The problems of securing mutual agreement and minimising speculation both suggest that small and relatively frequent changes in parities should be easier to manage than large and infrequent ones. This view is reinforced by considering the practicalities of changing parities in a target zone system with agreed bands of $\pm x$ per cent around parities, as in the ERM (i.e. a system in which a change in parity involves a corresponding movement in the band). If changes in parity are sufficiently small to allow the new parity to lie within the old band, the spot rate will not necessarily go down (or up) the morning after the change. For example, with a band of ± 2.5 per cent and a 1 per cent change in parity, the new parity would be well within the old band (and even a rate 1 per cent off the new parity would still be within the old band). If rates were reviewed monthly, and changes limited to say, 1 per cent, there would still be enough scope to adjust rates to allow for differing inflation rates etc. in all but exceptional circumstances. Such an approach to changing rates would be similar to that now adopted by many central banks in changing key interest rates – monthly meetings and small changes. That does not stop the commentators having a lot to say before each meeting, but it does limit the magnitude of the effects on financial markets.

Automatic stabilisation

For such a system to be successful, there need to be effective means of keeping rates within their specified bands. This depends on some system of *automatic* (rather than discretionary) intervention. In principle this could be achieved by an obligation on the key central banks to intervene as required. But in practice it is difficult to make central bank intervention automatic when any concrete action requires a number of banks to discuss and agree what should be done. Certainly if there is no automatic obligation to intervene, as in the ERM, everything depends on the willingness of the key central bank to do so – in that case the Bundesbank. When that support was not forthcoming, devaluation was inevitable. Moreover central bank resources nowadays are limited in relation to turnover in currency markets. The need for new thinking about how to stabilise currency markets reflects the fact that official foreign exchange reserves and gold holdings are now equal to approximately one day's global turnover. There is therefore a strong case for establishing a special stabilisation fund with power to borrow from central banks in order to intervene as required. The mere existence of such a fund should in practice obviate the need for it to take action. (The danger then is the nuclear power station control room syndrome: when things are going smoothly, the job is not challenging enough to justify the sort of staff you need in an emergency! The solution here would be to put the fund in an existing organisation with plenty of other things to do, like the IMF.)

   Although arrangements for automatic stabilisation might seem a further complication in setting up a formally managed system, in practice the existence of a central organisation with this obligation might facilitate agreement on realistic rates – certainly it should reduce the prevailing bias towards maintaining excessively high rates. For if the central institution, such as the IMF, has the obligation to intervene when rates are threatened, they will have a clear incentive to use their influence to see that rates remain realistic.

A two-tier system

The general formula proposed for an effective managed rate system is then first that changes in parities should be small and relatively frequent – with an agreed limit on changes in parity of less than half the width of the bands (i.e. a limit of less than x per cent on changes in parity where the band is $\pm x$ per cent). The second essential is that there should be automatic intervention by an international fund to keep rates within their bands. How far would such a formula be appropriate for arrangements (1) *within* regional groups such as the EU or NAFTA, or (2) *between* regional groups, based on say the euro, the dollar and the yen? A relatively close-knit regional group such as the EU would seem perfectly capable of setting up and operating a formal system of this nature, and I have proposed[7] that such a system should be introduced to manage the link between the euro and the pound, together with the currencies of other EU countries which are not members of the EMU.

It would also seem feasible for a limited number of major currencies, such as the dollar, yen and euro (*cum* sterling), or regional groupings based on these currencies to start up a major currency stabilisation club. In this case, however, the establishment of an intervention fund would require amendments to the IMF constitution and would have to be part of a new Bretton Woods agreement. Regional differences and the difficulties of making such a system universal from the start (e.g. including Africa) would suggest that any new constitution for the IMF should provide for the formation of regional groupings over a period of years and thus a gradual increase in the number of such groups participating in a new global management system. The width of bands, the limit on parity changes and the frequency of meetings of the managing board would all need to be capable of change and not written in stone in any new international agreement.

Arrangements within regional groups might differ from case to case. Where there is a leading currency such as the dollar or yen, and a potentially dominant partner, such as the US or Japan, the other currencies would tend to be linked to that currency, but linked flexibly, rather than pegged. The regional arrangements would then be concerned with provisions for changing rates *vis-à-vis* the leading currency. This flexibility is important to ensure that changes in rates between the yen and dollar for instance, do not result in an inappropriate rate for, say, the Korean won. Automatic intervention in the case of the dollar or yen zones would in practice be largely the responsibility of the US or Japan. In other cases the arrangements might be more genuinely multilateral. Regional stability funds might be developed in parallel with regional development banks. The initial question is whether such a two-tier, regional *cum* global system, is a useful approach.

A purely global approach as at Bretton Woods seems impractical for a flexibly managed, rather than fixed rate system. There are just too many currencies involved. But to operate a two-tier system with three or more regional groups, there has to be either an anchor currency in each group, or a numeraire in the form of a basket of currencies in the region (such as the ECU) with a global authority responsible for securing agreement on the rates between them. Such a dual system might initially be constituted on an informal basis; but eventually a new Bretton Woods type of agreement would probably be desirable, provided it was elastic enough to allow for the evolution of varying arrangements in different regions, albeit with certain common guiding principles.

Under such a dual system, the rate between sterling and the dollar, for instance, would depend on decisions (1) within a new ERM about the rate between the pound and the euro; and (2) in the new major currency stability system about the relative rates between the dollar and the euro. But that, of course, is analogous to the situation in the market at present where the rates between the pound and the deutschmark are inter-related with their relations with the dollar.

Guiding principles

To sum up, the guiding principles for both global and regional arrangements would be as follows:

1   Exchange rate management should be compatible with economic stability and the maintenance of full employment and low inflation.
2   Exchange rates should be as stable as possible, subject to adjustment to meet changes in relative costs or other factors affecting the desired flow of foreign trade and productive investment.
3   The pattern of rates should be based on an agreed strategy for the broad magnitude of trade surpluses or deficits and the flow of long-term capital between or within regions.
4   Changes in rates should be small, and if necessary, relatively frequent, rather than large and infrequent.
5   To achieve this, the general pattern of management would be to establish target zones of suitable widths and change parities in steps of less than half the width of the zone, so that the new parity would be in the old zone.
6   Automatic stabilisation arrangements should be established to ensure that currencies, or groups of currencies, remain within their agreed zones.
7   The design of automatic stabilisation arrangements might differ globally and regionally, but the objective should be to establish an international fund or funds rather than rely on agreements between central banks.

The supply of reserve currencies

The existence of international stabilisation agreements would tend to reduce the calls on national foreign exchange reserves, but any comprehensive new system needs to take into account the need to ensure an adequate supply of reserves. In the run-up to Bretton Woods the supply of reserve currencies and the function of lender of last resort were regarded as virtually the same. This reflected the fact that under the gold standard, central banks' stocks of gold represented both their foreign exchange reserves and their credit base. Bretton Woods was directed primarily at financial crises arising from balance of payments deficits and made the IMF the lender of last resort as far as countries' foreign exchange reserves were concerned. But it was not given the function of lender of last resort in the sense of a supplier of credit to individual banks or institutions threatened with bankruptcy. Nor (as argued above) would the role envisaged above for an international stability fund – to operate in the markets to offset the effect of speculative capital movements on exchange rates – include lending money to banks or firms in financial difficulties.

The problem of ensuring an adequate supply of reserve currency has been fortuitously solved during most of the post-war period by the emergence of the

United States' substantial payments deficit. Two factors have preserved the role of the dollar as the world's primary reserve currency despite this deficit. The first is the size and industrial strength of the US economy. The second, closely allied, factor is the attraction of the US to foreign investors and the consequent inflow of capital to finance the current deficit. This situation cannot necessarily be assumed to continue indefinitely. A reduction in the US deficit could reduce the supply of dollars as a reserve currency; or loss of confidence in the dollar or US financial assets could reduce the attraction of dollar holdings. If any new arrangements are to last as long as Bretton Woods, they should provide means of augmenting the world supply of reserve currency. If and when it becomes necessary – for example, if the yen became a popular reserve currency and Japan continued to run a major surplus – the most obvious means is to increase Special Drawing Rights (SDRs). This raises the question of how any such increase should be distributed. One approach is to base the increase on existing quotas, thus giving the bulk of it to the richest countries. Another is to regard the increase, or at least part of it, as additional capital for developing countries. The latter approach seems to confuse two problems. Extra *reserves* should be regarded as a stand-by for emergencies, not as something to be spent willy-nilly. Additional official *capital for development* should be openly channelled through the World Bank, not disguised in this way.

In both connections, however, there is a case for resurrecting Keynes's idea that persistent creditors should be subject to some sort of compulsory levy – in present circumstances perhaps to supply development grants or loans. But if (as at the present time) there is only one major persistent creditor of any significance, Japan, the politics of securing such an agreement would be invidious.

Curbing capital movements

The creation of a more stable exchange rate mechanism and finding means of curbing speculative capital movements and currency transactions need to go hand in hand. It is encouraging that there seems to be an emerging consensus that 'something must be done' to reduce the instability of short-term capital movements. As George Soros has said 'To argue that financial markets in general, and international lending in particular, need to be regulated is likely to outrage the financial community. Yet the evidence for just that is overwhelming' (Soros, 1997). There is, however, little agreement on how this should be achieved – apart perhaps from greater prudential regulation in some form. There are two related problems: first the general one of the growth of speculative short-term capital movements between countries whether industrialised or developing; second (and a major feature of the Asian crisis) the particular vulnerability of developing countries who have liberalised their capital markets.

The first problem is familiar. Only a small percentage of the turnover in currency markets is now accounted for by trade or other current payments; the remainder represents capital movements in one form or another. In so far as these movements do not directly affect the solvency of banks or companies (as they have in the Asian crisis), the main problem is the resulting instability of exchange rates. The two feed on each other. Measures to stabilise exchange rates, as proposed below, will reduce short-term capital movements, and limiting short-term capital movements would help stabilise exchange rates. What are the possible means of limiting short-term capital movements?

The first question is: how far is it possible, or desirable, to restore direct controls on capital movements either generally, or in developing countries? The capital controls originally inherited from World War II in the early Bretton Woods era depended on a general system of exchange control which (after a transition period) permitted freedom of current payments, but restricted capital payments. As these controls were dismantled in industrialised countries, the remaining restrictions (e.g. in the EU) depended on more specific restrictions which were gradually eliminated by negotiation as part of a general process of liberalisation. The problem in trying to isolate or curb essentially 'speculative' movements is that foreign exchange transactions can involve any type of asset, as well as currency itself. Very careful examination is therefore required to determine whether any universal restrictions on particular types of transactions on capital assets would be feasible or effective. A more promising line would be to consider restrictions on 'leveraged' or 'margin' transactions (e.g. in derivatives) which clearly multiply the possible magnitude of speculative activities. In so far as asset price and exchange rate speculation go together, curbing leveraged transactions would also help to tackle the problem of asset price bubbles.

In the case of developing countries, the problem is essentially to control the *inflow* of capital to avoid a sudden reversal at a later date. Here there seems a more straightforward case for controlling the access of banks and companies in these countries to foreign loans, and for prudential oversight of their maturities and the currency in which these are denominated. Where these developing countries are in the process of developing their capital markets, there is a need to keep a close watch on the relationship between foreign holdings of securities and exchange reserves which may be hit by a sudden outflow.

Credit insurance

George Soros has proposed:

> setting up an International Credit Insurance Corporation as a sister institution to the IMF. This new authority would guarantee international loans for a modest fee. The borrowing countries would be obliged to provide data on all borrowings, public or private, insured or not. This would enable the authority to set a ceiling on the amounts it is willing to insure. Up to those amounts the countries concerned would be able to access international capital markets at prime rates. Beyond these, the creditors would have to beware.
>
> (Soros, 1997)

Although this would at first sight appear to be a market mechanism rather than a system of direct controls, the insurable limit could in practice prove an effective ceiling on foreign borrowing for that country involved. In the aftermath of the crisis, borrowing might remain below the ceilings and the introduction of insurance would help to *maintain* lending and mitigate the crisis, as Soros suggests. But in the longer run, when borrowing might once again tend to be too high rather than too low, it is not clear what would determine which borrowers or lenders would qualify to get into a country's quota – or would it be merely a case of first come first served? Such a system would need to be accompanied by regulation within the countries concerned. A pre-condition of the Soros proposal or any other international surveillance mechanism would be to establish the transparency required to determine reasonable limits. But experience suggests that knowledge that excessive risks are being taken is seldom enough on its own to prevent them being incurred, only to ensure that at some point confidence may suddenly crumble.

The Tobin tax[8]

A market-based approach to reducing currency speculation is the proposal to impose a tax on currency transactions – the so-called 'Tobin tax' discussed in Chapter 7. Professor James Tobin first suggested imposing a small tax on foreign exchange transactions in his Janeway Lectures at Princeton in 1972, but in his own words 'It did not make much of a ripple' (Tobin, 1996). Today, however, the harsh experience of exchange rate crises and the chronic instability of international currency markets have led to increasing interest in the Tobin tax as a possible means of dampening down exchange rate volatility. This interest has been enhanced by the growing potential of such a tax as a source of revenue for international institutions and national governments. The effects of the tax on the volume of transactions is necessarily conjectural, but a 0.1 per cent tax has been estimated to raise $150 billion a year or more (at 1995 levels) (Felix and Sau, 1996).

Since Tobin first proposed such a tax the volume of foreign exchange transactions has expanded explosively. Global *daily* turnover rose from $18 billion in 1977 to $230 billion in 1995, or $1,300 billion if futures and options are included (in addition to spots, outright forwards and swaps) (Felix and Sau, 1996). In 1995 30 per cent of turnover is estimated to have taken place in London, with New York (16 per cent) and Tokyo (10 per cent) the runners up. Of these transactions 85 per cent were between dealers or other financial customers and only 15 per cent with non-financial customers. The two basic questions are whether it would be feasible to levy such a tax (and if so, at what level), and how effective it would be in reducing exchange rate instability.

Feasibility

The first key issue is how to ensure comprehensive geographical coverage (the so-called 'off-shore' problem'). Kenen defines the two alternative ways to collect the tax as on a 'national' or a 'market' basis (Kenen, 1996). In the first case banks would pay the tax to the governments of the countries in which their head offices were located. In the second case the tax would be paid to the country in which the deal took place. If the tax were levied on a national basis, banks would have no incentive to move dealing off-shore to tax-free locations. But the main disadvantage of this approach would be to favour banks whose home countries refused to impose the tax. Those banks would enjoy a competitive advantage in all foreign exchange markets, not only in their home markets. (The national approach would be particularly disadvantageous to the UK, which has the largest foreign exchange market, but where total transactions by foreign banks appear larger than total transactions by British banks at all other dealing sites.)

If, on the other hand, the tax were levied on a market basis, and national governments kept part of the proceeds, they would have no incentive to set up tax-free zones to encourage off-shore dealing in their territory. On the contrary they would have a strong incentive to levy the tax in the same way as others concerned. So although banks would have an incentive to find suitable tax-free zones for off-shore dealing, governments would be unlikely to welcome them. For this reason the market approach seems the better option and with the tax being levied at dealing sites. A further measure to discourage the development of tax havens would be to impose a punitive tax on transactions between those in the tax net and those outside.

Kenen suggests that banks would be required to collect the tax on all their foreign exchange transactions. When the bank's transaction was with a retail customer, the bank would be liable for the full rate of tax, which could either be explicitly charged to the customers or added to the bank's spread. In the case of wholesale transactions between two banks, each would be responsible for half the tax (and if a transaction involved two dealing sites in different countries, both governments would presumably receive half the tax).

The question then arises as to what transactions should be taxed. Kenen makes a clear case for taxing both spot and forward transactions. A short-term forward (e.g. three days) is a close substitute for a spot and could be used to evade a tax levied only on spot transactions. If forwards are taxed, it would be logical to extend this to futures; but taxing futures contracts raises the question of whether the contract itself should be taxed or only any ultimate settlement involving a currency transaction. Again options can serve the same purpose as futures and invite parallel treatment. If the main objective is to raise revenue, it would be sufficient to limit the tax to transactions involving the actual delivery of currency. But if the objective is to curb speculation, then the instruments which are most used for this purpose must be taxed as well.

While the implementation of the tax may appear complex, it is not any more complicated, probably much less so, than the detailed provisions of many existing taxes. Relatively few institutions are involved and the tax calculation could be built into their computerised systems. Indeed if the standards of what is feasible employed here had been used before imposing income tax or VAT they would never have been introduced! The dominant feature in the introduction of new taxation has always been the political will rather than administrative feasibility. The initiation of a global tax system for financing international activities and development would be a revolutionary move in the development of global institutions.

Governments would naturally be hesitant to impose such a tax purely as a punitive measure in the face of the strong pressures to be expected from the financial institutions concerned. But then when have governments ever gone to the trouble of imposing new taxes unless they appeared to be a worthwhile source of revenue? In the end the Tobin tax's political appeal may be its attraction in raising revenue both for national governments and international development by taxing an activity which, where taken to excess, is increasingly seen as anti-social. The main problem is that of reaching international agreement on the basic proposal to levy such a tax and the broad outlines of a scheme for doing so. Kenen suggests that to be effective it would need to include the European Union, the United States, Japan, Singapore, Switzerland, Hong Kong, Canada and Australia. Ideally the tax should be universal.

If proceeds were split 50:50 between national and international uses they would be of appreciable benefit to countries with significant foreign exchange markets, such as the UK, which could benefit to the extent of around £15 billion a year from a 0.1 per cent tax. As a revenue raiser at a time of generally high unemployment the new tax would have the benefit of reducing government debt without having the same downward effect on the demand for goods and services as income or sales taxes.

Effects on exchange rate volatility

The likely impact of such a tax on exchange rate volatility is difficult to assess (see Chapter 7). Even a very low tax would have a major impact on short-term transactions – and 80 per cent of foreign transactions involve round trips of seven days or less. The key point is its effect in reducing the probability of short-term switching between currencies to exploit differences in interest rates or small movements in exchange rates. With a 0.1 per cent tax rate, a movement in and out of a currency for a week would incur a tax equivalent to a 10 per cent (annual) rate of interest. Such a tax would, however, have little effect on speculation in crisis conditions, where a devaluation of say 10 per cent is expected in a matter of days or weeks. The tax should be regarded as a means of reducing run of the mill speculative transactions rather than as a means of avoiding crises.

A world payments strategy

Any system of managed exchange rates is only sustainable if it is based on a measure of agreement about the desired pattern of payments between the countries involved, i.e. their current surpluses or deficits together with long-term capital movements. On a global scale, there is a need to consider the pattern of trade and payments and long-term investment flows between major groups or players. (Some major capital flows will be between regions and some within regions.) On a regional scale there are two dimensions to the problem. The first is the need to agree an acceptable pattern of trade and payments between the countries in the region as a basis for agreeing on *relative* rates; the second is a view about the position of the bloc as a whole and the level of rates *vis-à-vis* the rest of the world.

The fundamental economic and political problem is to devise a rational and acceptable economic basis for proposing and agreeing changes in rates – something which has been largely lacking in international discussions in the 1970s and 1980s. The discussions leading to the Smithsonian Agreement in 1971 were an interesting exception to this, in that the US indicated that they were looking for an improvement of $13 billion in their newly emergent balance of payments deficit and asked their main trading partners who would accept a corresponding deterioration (Volcker and Gyohten, 1992). The Americans sought an 11 per cent trade-weighted devaluation of the dollar and eventually achieved a little under 8 per cent overall, with the yen up 17 per cent and the deutschmark up 14 per cent.

The most obvious omission today is the lack of any coherent view of the desirable resolution of the problems of the Japanese and US balance of payments and hence whether the yen should be stronger relative to the dollar or vice versa – or even in some quarters recognition that such a problem exists. For the US to continue indefinitely running deficits of the magnitude in recent years seems problematical. There is always a danger that a major loss of foreign confidence in US securities or the dollar could lead to a potentially disastrous outflow of funds from New York and the present system could collapse virtually overnight. But apart from the financial dangers, it does not make sense for a major industrial power like the US to be absorbing resources in exchange for financial claims on its assets, rather than running a balance of payments surplus combined with a substantial flow of aid and productive investment to the rest of the world, particularly developing countries. It would, however, be disastrous at the present time for the US to try to remove its balance of payments deficit by deflationary measures which reduced demand and activity in the US economy – for example, by taking measures to speed up the reduction of the budget deficit without any reduction in the exchange rate or other measures to improve the balance of trade. On the contrary the immediate need is for the prosperous industrial countries to be prepared to run deficits to keep up demand in the Asian economies and help them restore their exchange reserves. In the longer term, any reduction in the US balance of payments deficit needs to be aimed at reducing corresponding surpluses elsewhere, not driving countries already in deficit further into the red. This means that such a reduction must for the most part be matched by a corresponding reduction in the Japanese surplus.

Mutually consistent objectives are needed for both the US and Japanese balance of payments to provide a rational basis for any agreement on the desired relativity between the dollar and the yen. These objectives need in turn to be part of a world payments strategy setting out a consistent and desirable pattern of trade, aid and productive investment between key areas, which would in turn provide a rationale for a pattern of agreed target zones. This is not, of course, to imply either that there is one ideal world payments scenario, or that anyone can calculate precisely what set of exchange rates would achieve it. Rather that, without a broad concept of the direction in which we are aiming to go, there is little rational basis for any agreement on exchange rates. In practical terms any such exercise would, initially at any rate, concentrate particularly on the interplay between the three major players: the US, EU and Japan or the corresponding regional groupings.

Formulating a world economic strategy may seem a formidable undertaking, but the difficulties are political rather than technical. The problems arise in reaching agreement on the objectives proposed and the exchange rate targets designed to achieve them. Obviously, in practice, any agreed pattern of exchange rates will depend heavily on the *status quo*, and *ad hoc* haggling. But to put them in the context of a world payments strategy would serve both to help focus on wider issues and establish formally the *mutual* nature of exchange rates between major players. Bretton Woods tacitly assumed that each country (apart from the US) was sufficiently small in relation to the total for a change in its exchange rate to be regarded as a matter of restoring equilibrium between that country and the rest of the world taken as a whole. The ERM experience, on the other hand, highlighted the mutual nature of any adjustments between members, and in this sense was a microcosm of the relations between the major players on a global scale.

When we come to the regional level, the picture varies considerably. For example, within the EU, the prime concern would be the relation between the non-EMU currencies and the euro: the general level of rates *vis-à-vis* the rest of the world would inevitably be dominated by the level of the euro. Once the initial rates against the euro had been set, decisions on subsequent variations would be tactical rather than strategic. But in any Asian bloc the magnitude of the flows of capital from Japan and other regions to the developing countries could be a major strategic consideration.

Summary and conclusions

The manner in which the world financial system at present operates is dangerously unstable and represents a potentially serious threat to industrial prosperity and employment in both the developing and industrialised world. The fact that the major industrial economies have not suffered any major crises in recent years should not obscure the fact that they too are vulnerable to destabilising movements in world financial markets, as might for example occur if there were a sharp fall on Wall Street or a sudden outflow of capital from the US. There are welcome signs that the Asian crisis may have made the major powers, whose backing is needed to give any reform the necessary impetus, more willing to take a new initiative.

Any agenda for a new Bretton Woods needs to be based on a twin-pronged attack on exchange rate instability and speculative capital movements. A framework is needed for a combined global and regional approach to managing exchange rates, which would avoid the difficulties of both fixed and floating rates. The general principle should be to establish parities and bands by mutual agreement, and to adjust them in small steps relatively frequently, rather than make large and infrequent adjustments. To reduce the incentive for speculation there should be an agreed limit on say, monthly changes in parities and bands. If such changes were limited to less than half the width of the permitted band, any new parity would lie within the old band; thus minimising overnight changes in spot rates when parities were changed.

Regional arrangements would differ from area to area. In the EU, there would need to be arrangements linking the pound and other currencies not in the EMU to the euro, although these would have to pay heed to movements between the euro and the dollar. In the Western hemisphere there might be a grouping based on the dollar, and in Asia one based on the yen, with other currencies flexibly linked, but not pegged to, the leading currency. Such regional groupings could be members of an exchange rate stability system operating on the principles set out above.

To ensure that currencies remained within their agreed bands, there should be arrangements for *automatic* intervention when required. This would be the function of global and regional stabilisation funds rather than central banks. Central banks' resources are now limited in relation to the turnover of foreign exchange and even an automatic stabilisation obligation could lead to difficulties and delays in agreeing on the necessary operation. The existence of such international funds should in practice largely obviate the need for actual intervention.

Any new exchange rate system must go hand in hand with measures to reduce speculative capital movements. These might include the introduction of a small ('Tobin') tax on foreign exchange transactions to help finance international development activities. There is an urgent need for a new international agreement on banking regulation monitored and supervised by an international institution, which might also be given responsibility for the prudential oversight of foreign exchange markets including the use of derivatives and other instruments. There is also a need to examine other means of stabilising the volume of capital flows, particularly to developing countries, by such methods as the Soros credit insurance scheme.

Any rational system of exchange rate management or regulation of capital flows depends on having an agreed view on the general pattern of payments surpluses and deficits that is desirable – this is most obvious in the case of the dollar and the yen and the US/Japanese imbalance. An integrated world economic strategy is needed in which the net flow of productive capital (private or official) and aid will be directed towards the most pressing needs of the developing and transition economies, and exchange rates will reflect the need to establish a pattern of trade surpluses and deficits consistent with these movements.

To fulfil these new functions the present structure of international and economic institutions needs to be radically reviewed. Some have outlived their original purpose (such as the OECD), others such as the IMF and the World Bank need to have their remits and constitutions reviewed. In particular there is a case for re-establishing the Bank's primacy over development lending, leaving the Fund to concentrate on establishing the new exchange rate regime. In both instances there is a need to reconsider the voting systems involved in order to strike a better balance between the democratic yardstick of numbers of people involved and the weight of industrial strength. The use of conditional lending to dictate the political and economic structure of borrowing countries needs to be re-examined. Consideration should be given to setting up a more effective body to oversee these institutions and the emerging regulatory bodies under the auspices of the UN: for example, an Economic and Social Security Council (Stewart and Daws, 1996).

Discussion of more effective international structures cannot be separated from the question of what objectives and general approach to economic policy those in charge of any strengthened organisations will adopt. To put it starkly: if we wish to establish a more stable global economy in order to pursue or safeguard full employment and reduce poverty, it would be perverse to increase the power of the IMF to dictate deflationary policies and heavy doses of unemployment to countries in difficulty. Improving the machinery of international economic governance must go hand in hand with a revolution in the approach to economic policy guiding international organisations. This may sound a tall order, but in fact the two go together. The adherence to extreme liberal market philosophy in recent years has been a major reason why there has been no attempt to strengthen international economic governance. If national governments should abandon macro-economic policy and leave it to independent central banks, *a fortiori* there is no need for international governmental involvement. Restoring world economic governance to the political agenda depends on a rejection of the monetarist-inspired orthodoxy of the 1980s. Tackling these economic problems must also be seen as part of a wider need to make international organisations more effective in dealing with contemporary global problems, such as peace-keeping and environmental regulation.

The policy areas to be covered by any new international economic agreement are potentially vast. But at their heart lie the related problems of devising a more stable exchange rate regime, and controlling the flow of international capital in such a way as to encourage productive investment and discourage short-term speculation. The prize for success is a world in which economic integration can help in the fight to conquer poverty and unemployment. The price of failure is the misery and suffering of millions and a threat to democracy and peace.

Notes

1 This account is based largely on the IMF, *World Economic Outlook, Interim of Assessment* (December 1997b) and earlier reports, the World Bank, *Global Development Finance 1998*, the BIS 67th *Annual Report* (June 1997) and the extensive coverage in the *Financial Times*.
2 BIS (1997), Graph V.II.
3 David Folkerts-Landau, interview in *The Times*, 16 January 1998.
4 G. Capiro and D. Klingiebel (1996) *Bank Insolvencies: Cross Country Experience*, Washington, DC, World Bank quoted in Goldstein (1997).
5 *Financial Times*, 7 January 1998.

6 IMF effective exchange rates.
7 *The Times*, 3 March 1998, 'Unstable Exchange Rates Pose Threat to Industry World-wide'.
8 This section draws on Grieve Smith (1997), a review of *The Tobin Tax: Coping with Financial Volatility* (eds ul Haq *et al.*, 1996).

References

BIS (1997), *67th Annual Report*, Basle (June).

Felix, D. and Sau, R. (1996), 'On the Revenue Potential and Phasing in of the Tobin Tax', in ul Haq *et al.* (1996).

Goldstein, M. (1997), *The Case for an International Banking Standard*, Washington, DC, Institute for International Economics.

Grieve Smith, J. (1997), 'Exchange Rate Instability and the Tobin Tax', *Cambridge Journal of Economics*, vol. 21, November.

Group of 10 (1997), *Financial Stability in Emerging Market Economies*, Basle.

IMF (1997a), *International Capital Markets: Developments, Prospects and Key Policy Issues*, Washington, DC (November).

IMF (1997b), *World Economic Outlook, Interim Assessment*, December, Washington, DC.

Kenen, P.B. (1996), 'The Feasibility of Taxing Foreign Exchange Transactions' in ul Haq *et al.* (1996).

Keynes, J.M. (1941), 'The Post-War Currency Policy' (8 September 1941), Keynes papers Vol. XXV, Basingstoke, Macmillan.

Kindleberger, C.P. (1996), *Manias, Panics and Crashes: A History of Financial Crises* (3rd edition), Basingstoke, Macmillan.

Sachs, J. (1998), 'The IMF and the Asian Flu', *The American Prospect*, March–April.

Soros, G. (1997) 'Avoiding a Breakdown: Asia's Crisis Demands a Rethink of International Regulation', *Financial Times*, 31 December.

Stewart, F. and Daws, D. (1996), 'Global Challenges: The Case for a UN Economic and Social Security Council', in *Viewpoint*, no. 10, Christian Aid.

Stiglitz, J. (1998), *Sound Finance and Sustainable Development in Asia*, keynote address to the Asia Development Forum.

Tobin, J. (1996), 'Prologue' in ul Haq *et al.* (1996).

ul Haq, M., Kane, I. and Grunberg, I. (eds) (1996), *The Tobin Tax: Coping with Financial Volatility*, New York, Oxford University Press.

Volcker, P.A. and Gyohten, T. (1992), *Changing Fortunes: The World's Money and the Threat of American Leadership*, New York, Times Books.

World Bank (1998), *Global Development Finance*, Washington, DC.

Index